PERFORMANCE MANAGEMENT AND APPRAISAL

A How-To-Do-It Manual for Librarians

G. Edward Evans

HOW-TO-DO-IT MANUALS FOR LIBRARIANS

NUMBER 132

NEAL–SCHUMAN PUBLISHERS, INC.
New York, London

Published by Neal-Schuman Publishers, Inc.
100 William Street, Suite 2004
New York, NY 10038

Library of Congress Cataloging-in-Publication Data

Evans, G. Edward, 1937–
    Performance management and appraisal: a how-to-do-it
manual for librarians / G. Edward Evans.
    p. cm.—(How-to-do-it manuals for libraries; 132.)
    Includes bibliographical references and index.
    ISBN 1-55570-498-0 (alk. paper)
    1. Librarians—Rating of—Handbooks, manuals, etc. 2. Library
personnel management—Handbooks, manuals, etc. 3. Librarians—
Rating of—Forms. I. Title. II. Series.

Z682.28.E93 2004
023.9--dc22

                                                    2004046006

DEDICATION

To all the people who have shared the stress of
"That Time of Year"

and

To two wonderful grandsons, Travis and Trenton,
may they experience something better in their working lives.

CONTENTS

LIST OF FIGURES AND TABLES

PREFACE

Performance appraisal (PA) is a fixture in management and a fact of life in the majority of libraries in the United States. Unfortunately, it's a part of library life that most people dread, no matter on what side of the appraisal they find themselves. Performance appraisal isn't just a yearly challenge for those being appraised—it is a daily challenge to the institution, the raters, and the ratees involved in the performance appraisal process. What if PA became less of what people dreaded and more of what they wanted—a way of improving their work, their relationships, and their workplace? Appraisal is a key element in salary, but it is also a major factor in promotion decisions, personnel development, and institutional expansion and improvement. *Performance Management and Appraisal: A How-To-Do-It Manual for Librarians* is for all of us who have been raters and ratees; it is designed to make the process less stressful and more beneficial for all concerned.

The PA process could become a more successful part of each librarian's job and every library's year. By focusing on behavioral aspects of performance, appraisal can become a tool of improvement for the rater, the ratee, the library, and maybe even our profession as a whole. Though this book respects the PA systems that are currently in place in libraries across the country, it presents information that will inspire institutions to reassess, redesign, and restructure their current evaluation process. It is intended for all libraries—school, academic, public, and even special—and the instruction, tips, and advice demonstrate that. The sample forms and CD-ROM contents encourage libraries to pick from the best that is available and adapt it to their own needs. Every library has their own unique characteristics, but there is always something that can be learned from the work of our colleagues.

This book begins by examining the process itself before anything else. Part I, "Before You Begin," explains why we appraise and manage performance, how to choose a development and appraisal system, and the process of conducting the appraisal. Chapter 1, "Why Do We Appraise and Manage Performance?" outlines the goals and purposes of PA and how they affect salary, promotion, behavioral, and a wide variety of other issues that are sometimes incompatible with one another. Chapter 2, "Choosing a Development and Appraisal System," helps administrators to go beyond the traditional systems of appraisal to develop new performance standards and develop the behavioral side of PA. Chapter 3, "Conducting the Appraisal," offers advice for making the most of PA review time. Walking you through an evaluation meeting step-by-step, this chapter helps create a plan for maximizing the effectiveness of your PA, including performance, behavioral, developmental issues, and even a suggestion for how to handle the dreaded negative performance appraisal meeting. This beginning will help you get your bearings whether you are an experienced supervisor or a newly promoted manager facing their first year of delivering appraisals.

Part II, "Appraisal Methods You Can Use," builds on the information from Part I with new methods and approaches to PA that will work in your library. With the practical essentials you'll need to conduct your employee performance appraisals, this is content you will refer to again and again as the appraisal needs and demands change in your library. Chapter 4, "Outcome Oriented," explains essay/narrative forms, critical incidents forms, standards of performance forms, and management by objectives forms of evaluation. Chapter 5, "Scaling," describes weighted checklists, Graphic Rating Scales, and Behaviorally Anchored Rating Scales (BARS). Chapter 6, "Ranking," looks at the general ranking format, paired comparisons, and forced distribution formats. Each of the chapters uses pros and cons lists to help determine the best method for use in your library and provides valuable sample forms for public, academic, and school libraries. Chapter 7, "Team," gives practical advice for this new and emerging phenomenon among small and large libraries alike. Evaluating the performance of teams can be difficult, but this practical advice will help you organize your appraisals so that they are effective for the team as a whole and the individual members alike. Chapter 8, "Manager/Executive," takes on what may be the most difficult types of appraisals—those of your senior and middle managers. Though advocating the 360° method, this chapter discusses the issues of subordinate appraisal, the scope and coverage of manager appraisals, self-directed appraisals, CEO appraisal methods, leadership competencies, and tips for coaching managers. The last chapter of Part II, "Tying Them Together," places an emphasis on pay increases, training, rater performance, and fairness.

Part III, "Performance Appraisal Forms You Can Adapt," gives you the basic tools to begin the appraisal process. Sample evaluation forms—covering everything from Faculty Evaluations to Page Performance Evaluations—are ready to be adapted to your library's personal needs. The forms come from community college libraries, major academic libraries, small and large public libraries, school libraries, and even library associations. In addition to the appraisal forms, there are examples of an evaluation criteria form, behaviors associated with success forms, employee input sheets, performance pay dispute resolution forms, supervisor's preparation forms, and employee work profiles. Part III and its forty forms are really meant to be used with the CD-ROM. Each of the forms is reproduced and ready to be changed, modified, or improved for your library and your employees. In short, these forms, like the performance appraisal process itself, are meant to improve the overall working environment of your library.

Performance appraisal is just one part of a library's administrative process, but it is a part interwoven in the lives of all library workers. It should not be thought of as a stand-alone process, but rather as a way of bringing your library together, improving it, and improving the careers of your employees. PA can be, when properly done, an essential ingredient in creating a humane, effective, and efficient library operation. I hope *Performance Management and Appraisal: A How-To-Do-It Manual for Librarians* brings your library closer to the library you want it to be.

ACKNOWLEDGMENTS

I owe a lot to a great many people. There are the many colleagues who shared "war stories" about performance appraisal (PA) over the years. My friend, Bendict Rugaas, who introduced me to the fact that libraries can be productive, efficient, and effective as well as customer oriented *without* using a PA system—Nordic Country libraries.

Certainly, I acknowledge all the libraries that contributed their appraisal forms and in several cases the "instructional" materials that raters receive when it is "that time of year." There are two academic libraries represented: Colorado State University (a large research library) and Loyola Marymount University (a medium-sized academic library). Two forms represent community colleges: Cerritos Community College and the Commonwealth of Virginia. Rand and the Huntington Libraries represent the special research library environment. Hayward and Mountain View are the public library representatives, and Maine and North Carolina provide coverage of the school media library environment. Finally, there is a "generic" form that provides a format for corporate libraries.

Special thanks are due Mr. Frank Montalvo, Assistant Vice President for Human Resources, Loyola Marymount University (LMU), who kindly read the manuscript and provided many valuable comments as did Dr. Charles Vance, professor of Human Resources Management at LMU's Hilton College of Business Administration. I am especially grateful to Margaret Zarnosky Saponaro, Manager of Staff Learning and Development, University of Maryland Libraries, who provided invaluable comments and suggestions. Brianne Gillen was an exceptional research assistant and performed incredible work throughout the project, especially with the process of securing appraisal forms from libraries, getting the permissions to use the forms, and most importantly converting them to a useful electronic format. Finally, heartfelt thanks to my Neal-Schuman co-author, Patricia Layzell-Ward, for her insightful comments on the 360° appraisal process.

Those are the people who made possible whatever is good about this book. The errors and omissions are mine.

G. Edward Evans
Flagstaff, Arizona

I. BEFORE YOU BEGIN

1 WHY DO WE APPRAISE AND MANAGE PERFORMANCE?

Performance appraisal (PA) probably ranks near the top of the "least favorite" work activity for most people. There is often a sense of dread—"it's that time of year"—atmosphere in the workplace. This sense is shared by those receiving a review as well as those conducting the process. It is the very rare, medium or large U.S. library that does not have an annual performance review system in place. The sense of anxiety about the review is common even in organizations where there is excellent communication about work activities on a daily basis. Herbert Meyer (1991) noted that PA is one of the most frequent sources of dissatisfaction in the entire human resources (HR) system and, further, that few supervisors or staff are satisfied with their current PA system. What is it then that causes this sense of apprehension? There are a number of answers to that question, and in the following chapters, I will address the most common causes.

PERFORMANCE APPRAISALS BACKGROUND

The practice of appraising performance probably goes back to the time humans became bipedal. However, making it a formalized process in the workplace is relatively recent. There are sporadic references to assessing work performance, going back to the third century A.D. in China and occasional use of the same type of "merit" assessment in nineteenth-century industries.

Before 1940, not many U.S. companies had a formal process in place. Perhaps the fact that the U.S. military did employ such a system during World War II may account for the rapid spread of the process during the first two decades after the end of the war. By the early 1960s, more than 60% of the organizations surveyed had a system (Spriegel, 1962). Today, it is the exception rather than the rule to find an organization that does not have an appraisal system in place. In addition, many organizations now have performance appraisal programs for top managers as well as staff. There is a pattern of large- and medium-size organizations having a system whereas small organizations (fifty people or less) are less likely to have a formal process.

Two other factors, beside the military role, played a role in the spread of the concept. Peter Drusker's concept of management by objectives (MBO) certainly was significant as was Douglas McGregor's work in the area of worker motivation and his Theory X and Y. To some degree, the passage of the Civil Rights Act of 1964 caused many organizations to put in place formal appraisal systems. Perhaps organizations were more motivated by the need to have "paper trails" to demonstrate their lack of discrimination than they were in improving performance.

Administrative purposes were, and still are, a major driving force in having a PA system. By the late 1950s and early 1960s, the counseling/development component became attached to the administrative aspect. It was in the late 1960s and early 1970s that PA was employed in the personnel planning process. Finally, in the 1970s, legal concerns became an issue in the PA process.

BELIEFS ABOUT PERFORMANCE APPRAISAL

One key cause of why PA is not well liked is the host of beliefs about what the process is supposed to address, at least in theory. Some years ago, I published an article on performance appraisal (Evans and Rugaas, 1982) that was, in part, a review of the literature on the topic. The following are the sixteen beliefs that we identified.

1. The process is essential to good management.
2. The process is natural or normal.
3. The process is the only reasonable method available for assuring at least minimal performance.
4. The process is the only valid basis for granting or withdrawing employee economic benefits.
5. The process is the primary means of maintaining control of staff productivity.
6. The process is essential for the growth and well-being of the individual employee.
7. The process is an important element in an effective system of motivation.

8. The process is essential in work orientation programs.

9. The process is or can be an objective assessment of an individual's strengths and weaknesses.

10. The process is primarily directed toward the subordinate.

11. The process is continuous and reflects a careful analysis of the individual's daily performance.

12. The process is equally effective whether carried out by a supervisor or the employee's peers.

13. The process is concerned with all aspects of an individual's work, not just the performance of assigned duties.

14. The process is useful in assessing an employee's future and potential progress in the organization.

15. The process is essential in planning organizational personnel needs for the present and the immediate future.

16. The process is important in counseling and suggesting areas of improvement that the individual should achieve if the individual hopes to gain more responsible positions either in the organization or outside it (p. 62–63).

With any long list, regardless of purpose, some items receive greater or lesser attention depending on individual and, in this case, organizational emphasis/preferences. It is also true that such lists often contain somewhat conflicting activities. The performance list really has two basic components: administrative (organizational operations) and behavioral (individual issues). Administrative and behavioral goals are often in conflict in the PA process.

The primary administrative purpose of the performance appraisal process is compensation management (determining salary increases). (Surveys such as C. A. Peck's *Pay and Performance: The Interaction of Compensation and Performance Appraisal* [Peck, 1984], A. Locher and K. Teel's "Performance Appraisal—A Survey of Current Practices" [Locher and Teel, 1977], and Robert Cordy's "Performance Appraisal in a Quality Context" [Cordy, 1998: 140] indicate salary adjustment purposes dominate the process with feedback about how to improve performance a distant second.

Some years ago, Saul Gellerman (1976) outlined the basic challenges that exist in the dual process; unfortunately, those challenges remain to this day. He outlined the issues associated with the activity of both sides (see Table 1.1). For the administrative side to be successful, the decisions must be confidential with the salary decision for each person known to a limited number of people—essentially, those who handle the payroll. This is for ethical and legal reasons. Most organizations have a large number of employees, and there is a need to maintain some degree of salary equity (equal pay for equal work). This usually translated into some form of structured salary/compensation plan. For this to work requires a structured process that often becomes bureaucratic.

Administrative Purposes	Behavioral Purposes
Secretive	Candid
Fixed	Flexible
Bureaucratic	Individualized
Table 1.1 Gellerman Challenges	

Behavioral purposes are almost the complete opposite in character. To provide useful feedback to people about their work performance, the procedure must be open and honest. It must also allow for a wide range of approaches depending on the specific circumstances. Each employee is different even if they are performing the same task. That means that how they do the work and respond to feedback is also individualized.

One can imagine, if not already experienced, the stress and conflict the two sets of purposes generate. John Lubans (1999) summarized the situation as follows:

> At best, PA (performance appraisal) is an important approach. Its application probably does encourage communication "for the record" and can benefit staff unclear about job expectations. But the process can become superficial and a ready source for feeding corporate cynicism....Sometimes we want PA to do too much. For example, coupling PA to salary decisions may seem efficient. But invariably, the two processes work against each other (p. 87–88).

To say, "you are a little below (or a little above) average, but not enough to warrant disciplinary action or to receive an award," will generate anger, arguments, tension, and frustration. The individuals assessed as slightly below average are *not* likely to change their performance because they *know* the rater is wrong. For those assessed as slightly above but not rewarded, the most likely outcome is a *drop* in performance.

When one says to a person, "you did an average job this year," it usually results in the ratee thinking the rater cannot recognize excellence when it is sitting right in front of them. It generates anger, arguments, tension, and frustration and will not reinforce the subordinate's good work habits.

The end result is a steady escalation of ratings until it appears as if all employees "walk on water" all year. That, in turn, leads to the organization imposing quotas that force supervisors to have a bell-curve result. I worked for one university that required every department to have one employee in the unacceptable category every year. Needless to say, this was difficult, unpleasant, and, in reality, inappropriate. One year when I dismissed a staff member and thought that would count for that year's "unacceptable" requirement, I was unpleasantly surprised when told that did *not* count because the person was gone! The way we circumvented the system was to get everyone on the staff to agree that each person, including the supervisor (myself), would each take a turn at being "unacceptable." A drawing of numbers set up the order in which we would become "unacceptable." The result was an improvement in morale because everyone had agreed it made the best of a bad situation.

Earlier, I mentioned several surveys that researchers conducted about how organizations use performance appraisal. Most of the surveys identify seven broad categories of use. Table 1.2 lists the usages in rank order, and one will note that development is in third place. This is

1. Compensation
2. Counseling
3. Training and development
4. Promotion
5. Staffing requirement planning
6. Retention/discharge
7. Validation of selection techniques
Table 1.2 How an Organization Uses PA

because the training and development component usually refers to long-term development and training. The "counseling" category refers to the performance of existing activities and usually in areas where improvement is needed.

A little more than 10 years ago, Tom Philp published a book on PA (Philp, 1990) that was based on interviews of more than 500 individuals. From the interview data, he identified several general "problem areas" for supervisors as well as some widely held attitudes of people being appraised. Table 1.3 lists paraphrased and shortened statements of Philp's data. Note that his data covered a wide range of issues. The ones I selected are those that are also addressed in this book.

Supervisors	Job Holder
• Lack of skill/knowledge in setting clear performance standards	• Suspicion of why they are being appraised
• Lack of skill in determining areas of performance within job holder's control and those that are not	• Doubt it will be "fair"
	• Believe it to be totally subjective
• Failure to recognize/accept the idea that manager's actions influence job holders	• Believe it is personality and relationship to "boss" not results that are appraised
• Fear of discussing performance	• Has no value beyond salary adjustment

Table 1.3 Problem Areas of PA: Philp's Results

A great many of the forms accompanying this book (on the CD-ROM) employ descriptive terms such as dependability, initiative, loyalty, attendance, judgment, and leadership. Though such terms can be related to work results, they are personal characteristics of a person as well and make it clear why there is widespread belief that it is "personality" not work results that are being appraised.

There are several disadvantages to using such terms. They are ambiguous, and, even with special directions about use and meaning, it is most unlikely that a group of managers will fully share a single definition of a term. Linking a personal term such as dependability to actual productivity is often difficult to communicate, and many supervisors do not have or receive training in how to accomplish the linkage(s). Such terms provide no guidance about how to improve performance. Using what are essentially personality characteristics shifts the emphasis to "fitting in" rather than "being productive."

Another drawback is, given that PA's primary usage is for salary adjustments and retention purposes, those giving the appraisal tend to avoid any confrontation and over-rate staff.

No matter what the flaws are in the system, the fact remains most U.S. libraries have an annual performance appraisal cycle. One example, from the academic library area, is the data collected by the Association of College and Research Libraries in 1989–1990. The group sent 250 questionnaires out and had 208 returned. Of that number, 88% engaged in formal performance appraisal activities, and only 17 libraries indicated their institution did not have or plan to have such a program (Association of College and Research Libraries, 1990. 2). As is true of surveys of a wide variety of organizations, the survey data showed the top two purposes of the process were salary increments and retention followed by staff development and promotion.

A 1996 *Wall Street Journal* article reported "in almost every major survey, most employees who get...evaluations and most supervisors who give them rate the process a resounding failure" (Schellhardt, 1996: A1). Regardless of what people think about the process, it is a fixture in U.S. management practice. Thus, we must try to make it more useful, less "painful," and more meaningful. The remainder of this book will provide some methods and ideas that may help us all improve the way we carry out PA.

SUMMARY

The following are some general thoughts about what we might consider doing to improve PA, keeping in mind we often have little choice in the formal document we must prepare. However, we can select how and what to focus on. Each of us, those giving the appraisal, can strive, with input from the appraised, to be as precise as possible in defining and measuring the performance issues. Whenever possible, focus on "valued" outcomes and relative frequencies of behavior when appropriate. Link PA, as much as possible, to meeting internal and external customer/user needs. We should also incorporate consideration of situational constraints when doing PAs and find a way to convey this information, even if the formal form does not take such factors into account.

For PA to be effective, it is essential for the organization to assist managers/supervisors in developing a skill set for engaging in the appraisal process. One element in the skill set is the ability to set performance standards that actually contribute to the achievement of specific outcome objectives. Another element is how to monitor performance year-round in a cost-effective manner rather than a once-à-year dreaded obligation. Being able to analyze differences between actual and desired/required performance in order to differentiate between personal performance issues and issues beyond the job holder's control is yet another important skill. And finally, it is necessary to develop the communication skills needed for effectively discussing with the individual the true causes of a shortfall and to develop a plan of action for overcoming the cause(s) identified.

In many ways, this volume supplements two other Neal-Schuman titles related to performance appraisal: Stueart and Sullivan's *Performance Analysis and Appraisal* (1991) and Goodson's *Complete Guide to Performance Standards for Library Personnel* (1997). Stueart and Sullivan's work contains good sections on defining a job (category of work to be performed) as well as the position (a person holds a position; a single job may consist of a number of positions). They also cover job requirements and standards. All of these issues are crucial in the selection and hiring process and, ultimately, in assessing performance after the fact. Their discussion of results-orientated versus duties-orientated job descriptions is particularly important in terms of PA. The chapters on legal issues focus on the selection and hiring process more than PA; however, there is some overlap. I cover legal issues related to PA in Chapter 3. The other topics noted above are not duplicated in this volume.

Goodson's book provides excellent material on setting performance standards. Given that fact, I devote only a limited amount of space to standards in the next chapter. Because standards are so important to the PA process, I strongly recommend using Goodson's book in conjunction with this one.

REFERENCES

College Libraries Section. Association of College and Research Libraries. 1990. *Performance Appraisal in Academic Libraries,* CLIP Note no. 12, edited by Barbara W. Jenkins and Mary L. Smalls. Chicago: American Library Association.

Cordy, Robert L. 1998. "Performance Appraisal in a Quality Context: A New Look at an Old Problem," in *Performance Appraisal: State of the Art in Practice,* edited by James W. Smither, 132–162. San Francisco: Josey-Bass.

Evans, G. Edward, and Bendik Rugaas. 1982. "Another Look at Performance Appraisal in Libraries," *Journal of Library Management* 3 (Summer): 61–69.

Gellerman, Saul. 1976. *The Management of Human Resources*. New York: Holt Rinehart.

Goodson, Carol. 1997. *Complete Guide to Performance Standards for Library Personnel*. New York: Neal–Schuman.

Locher, Alan H., and Kenneth S. Teel. 1977. "Performance Appraisal—A Survey of Current Practices," *Personnel Journal* 56(5): 245–247, 261.

Lubans, John. 1999. "I've Closed My Eyes to the Cold Hard Truth I'm Seeing: Making Performance Appraisal Work," *Library Administration and Management* 13 (Summer): 87–89.

Meyer, Herbert H. 1991. "A Solution to the Performers Appraisal Feedback Enigma," *Academy of Management Executive* 5(1): 68–75.

Peck, Charles A. 1984. *Pay and Performance: The Interaction of Compensation and Performance Appraisal*. Research Bulletin no. 155. New York: Conference Board.

Philp, Tom. 1990. *Appraising Performance for Results*, 2nd ed. New York: McGraw-Hill.

Schellhardt, T. 1996. "Annual Agony: It's Time to Evaluate Your Work and All Involved Are Groaning," *Wall Street Journal* November 19: A1.

Spriegel, William R. 1962. "Company Practices in Appraisal of Managerial Performance," *Personal* 39: 77.

Stueart, Robert D. and Maureen Sullivan. 1991. *Performance Analysis and Appraisal*. New York: Neal–Schuman.

2 CHOOSING A DEVELOPMENT AND APPRAISAL SYSTEM

In this chapter, I will briefly explore who appraises whose performance, the need for establishing performance standards, differences in career paths (support and professional staff), mentoring/coaching, models for assessing performance, staff development, and the consequences of failing to handle the process effectively. Essentially, there are two broad issues in this chapter: evaluating performance and developing staff to improve performance. This separates the two functions identified in Chapter 1 that are commingled in the traditional approach to performance appraisal (PA)—administrative and behavioral.

WHO APPRAISES WHOM

When most people think about PA, they think in terms of one-on-one assessment conducted by a supervisor of a subordinate; furthermore, that it occurs for individuals in the middle and bottom levels of an organization. Though that is a reflection of much of the real-world workplace, there are two areas of growing importance. First, more and more organizations are employing team-based or matrix workgroups that create special issues for PA (see Chapter 7). Second, there is recognition that executive/senior management personnel also should undergo the process (see Chapter 8). Recent events in the corporate world of chief executive officers (CEOs), chief financial officers (CFOs), and so forth, will probably increase pressure for upper-management appraisals.

Clearly, the who is being appraised has implications for who does the appraisal. The "who does it" list is longer than most people consider; possibilities are the following:

- Immediate supervisors (typical)
- Supervisor's supervisor (common at least in review capacity)
- Peers/coworker (team/matrix settings)
- Self-appraisal (seldom the sole method)

- Subordinates (somewhat rare)
- Internal and external "customers" (not very common except for promotions)
- Independent trained observers (rarely used except for senior managers)

TIP: Even if the system in place does not call for using multiple sources, doing so will produce a more complete and accurate picture of performance.

As noted above, organizational structure is a major factor in the who appraises question. Even though libraries are almost always part of a larger organization (city, university, school district, corporation), they may use a different staffing structure than does the "parent" organization. An increasing number of libraries use team or matrix workgroups, regardless of the typical pattern of the parent organization. (The parent overall structure will set the pattern for the formal PA process and its format.) Three of the most common structures are functional, team, and matrix. Functional structure in the library are the familiar departments—acquisitions, circulation, reference, and so forth. Linking different functional activities by creating a workgroup with various functional area skills with one person functioning a leader is the typical team structure. A matrix structure is a combination of functional and team approaches. An example would be a public library branch system that uses a young adult team to handle all the branches' young adult (YA) activities. In such a case, both functional and team issues would come into play. Depending on the combination, the workgroup will have two or more "supervisors," one for each functional area involved in the matrix.

An additional factor in the decision of who does the appraisal is the overall managerial style of the parent organization. With controlling styles, the most likely person to do the appraisal is the immediate supervisor with perhaps the supervisor's supervisor providing a review that only focuses on the "how" of the process rather than the content. Styles that emphasize involvement are likely to have PA systems that involve a number of people in the assessment process.

ADVANTAGES OF DIFFERENT APPRAISERS

Returning to the list of possible appraisers, what are the particular advantages of each type? Clearly, the *immediate supervisor* has the most direct knowledge of a subordinate's performance, unless there is no supervisor (team environment). Another reason is that one of the functions of PA is to improve performance, and, obviously, the immediate supervisor is in the best position to know what would improve a subordinate's performance. Furthermore, unit supervisors have a unit-wide perspective that no one else has. It is equally obvious that in team and matrix settings, a single immediate supervisor doesn't exist.

A *supervisor's supervisor* should play a role in the appraisal process. There is the need to assure that the proper PA procedures were followed, and there should be at least a minimum degree of content review as well. Everyone recognizes there is an element of subjectivity in the process, and the higher level supervisor can serve as a check on bias, either positive or negative in character. In addition, the next-level supervisor will have a broader perspective than immediate supervisors and may have knowledge of performance issues beyond the immediate unit. Thus, the supervisor's supervisor can and should function as a check on the PA process in reporting units.

Peer assessment is essential in team settings if the appraisal is to reflect accurately individual performance. Team members, including the leader, are in the best position to know who does what and how well within the team. Even in a functional structure environment, evaluations by peers can bring a useful perspective to the PA process. One aspect of peer evaluation that is a plus for the PA process is the fact that peers tend to evaluate and compare the performance of coworkers with their own. Furthermore, peers often have significant, occasionally unique knowledge about the behavior of coworkers. On the down side, in highly controlled environments, peers may not be as willing to engage in peer review or may see the process as a means of undermining one another.

Self-appraisal is, or should be, based on the most complete knowledge of performance; however, the person may not have an accurate picture about the outcome(s) of that performance. There is a tendency to focus on skills, competencies, and intentions. A carefully constructed self-appraisal system can overcome such tendencies (behaviorally based system). Team and matrix workgroups require self-assessment as part of the process if it is to be accurate. In almost every instance, self-appraisal is one element used in combination with other forms.

Subordinates' assessment of supervisors/managers is a growing area of PA. Such appraisals are valid as the number of people making an assessment; that is the greater the number of people doing the rating the greater the validity. One example of this process that most readers have had an experience with is teacher/course evaluations that are common in academic institutions. Certainly, subordinates have a clear sense of how well the supervisor/manager handles work with those reporting to them. Peer, subordinate, and "customer" assessments have a fairly long history of use in terms of use in terms of developmental purposes. Again, in a team/matrix setting, such evaluations help create an accurate/valid understanding of performance.

An interesting fact about library staff appraisals is that in spite of their customer-service orientation, few libraries make use of *"customer" appraisals*. Not that it is not used when data is available, but rather the point is few of us seek out such information except in rare instances. If the process is not formalized, the most likely "causal" data on file will probably be from an unhappy customer. In the absence of formal process, it would be the exceptional customer that took time to put into writing a compliment for a staff member. Many businesses with face-to-face service staff have form holders on the service desk inviting customer comments.

Another fact to keep in mind is there are both external and internal customers. Though gathering useful assessment data from external users is somewhat complicated, at least at the outset, there are internal customers that can provide very important information about the outcome of performances. That is how performance affects work in another unit. A library example is the acquisitions department, whose "internal customers" are the cataloging department in terms of workflow; selectors of materials in terms of when and how orders are placed; institutional budget offices in terms of invoice payments; and senior library administrators in terms of overall fiscal management.

Use of *trained observers* has limited but nonetheless valuable contributions to make to the appraisal process. The two most useful inputs relate to current performance and basic capabilities. Note: Not all jobs lend themselves effectively to this approach; for example, a paraprofessional handling serials check-in routines. However, public service or any position that involves end-user contact with all the variations that can arise in such transactions are likely candidates for this approach. Clearly, the observer's time for making an assessment is short, thus restricting the range of behavior observed. Another consideration to keep in mind is the so-called Hawthorne effect. This is labeled for the impact that a known observer has on the behavior of the individual being observed. (The performance may be better or worse than "normal" depending on a number of factors (see Evans, Layzell-Ward, and Rugaas, 2000).

In spite of the influence the observer may have on performance, the technique is very useful for assessing basic skills as well as a ratee's potential. This is especially true when the ratees understand there will be an observer, and the person should make every effort to perform at the maximum possible level. The trained observer will assess the fundamental skills the person uses in the transaction as well as the potential for further training/development.

Further Thought

Think about the various assessment techniques you have experienced. Which one(s), if any, do you think were useful experiences? Why were they useful? How often have you experienced the use of multiple methods for a single appraisal process? If you have had such experience(s), do you think the multiple inputs were a more accurate/"fair" assessment?

Table 2.1 provides an overview of the possible assessment techniques in terms of a hypothetical support staff position in an acquisition unit.

ESTABLISHING PERFORMANCE STANDARDS

Clearly one of the most important steps in the PA is developing a standard of performance for a particular job. (Note: one must keep in mind that "job" and "position" are two separate concepts. A job is a category of work activities and several individuals do that job while each person holds a position within the job category.) There also needs to be a common understanding on the part of the supervisor and those performing the job of just what the standard is. Goodson's *Complete Guide to Performance Standards for Library Personnel* (1997) is an excellent starting point for anyone establishing or revising performance standards.

Though most agree that a performance standard is essential to reducing the subjectivity in the PA process, there is also widespread concern that a standard imposes restrictions, causes conflict, and can actually limit productivity ("I don't need to do more than meet the standard"). However, lacking such standards means that *any* performance level must be acceptable! One only needs to look at the literature relating to performance litigation to see quickly how much emphasis the courts place on clearly stated *and* communicated performance standards.

When establishing useful standards, it is important that four crucial components are taken into consideration: validity, agreement, realism, and clear definition. These may seem self-evident components, but one or more of them is frequently overlooked in a rush to establish "something." Make certain the standard relates to actual performance requirements and not just managerial perceptions of what is necessary.

Getting agreement on a standard is easier if all concerned see that it is a valid standard. One of the most effective methods for assuring validity and agreement is to involve the job holder in the process of standards setting. Imposed standards invite criticism, conflict, and, not infrequently, the job holder becoming certain the manager/supervisor "hasn't a clue" what the work is really about. One effective starting point for a discussion of, say, a copy cataloger job is to look at it from three points of view: past, present, and future. Look at past productivity data and note what were issues that limited productivity. Then turn to the present; what, if anything, has changed? And, finally, are there potential

> **What Is a Performance Standard?**
>
> It is an evaluation "yardstick" that identifies acceptable and unacceptable ranges of behavior, activity, events, beliefs, and so forth, that are of concern to a work unit/organization.

Rater	Advantages	Data Volume	Purpose(s)	Limitation(s)
Head of acquisitions	• Daily observations • Comparative • Daily interaction	Large	• Overall unit effectiveness • Staff development • Rewards	• Personal bias • Internal focus
Head of technical servers	• Broader perspective • Comparative • Less personal bias	Small	• Proper process • Planning • Unit coordination	• Based on exception(s) rather than average • Limited interaction
Self	• Knowledge of work • Barriers to performance • Skills	Large	• Involvement • Training development • Feedback	• Too positive or negative depending on personality • Limited knowledge of overall outcomes of performance
Peers	• Comparative • Relations oriented • Feedback	Medium	• Problem solving • Rewards • Planning	• Too personal • Narrow perspective
Part-time staff (subordinate)	• Relations oriented • Supervising skills assessment • Communication skills	Medium	• Planning • Training/ development • Feedback	• Highly personal • Narrow perspective
Customer(s)	• Service quality • Interpersonal relations skills • Communication skills • Small	Small	• Feedback • Training/ development • Rewards	• Rare interactions (end users) • Personal bias (internal customers) • Narrow perspective
Trained observer	• Basic skills • Potential for advancement • No personal bias toward ratee • Small	Small	• Planning • Training/ development • Placement	• Few observations • No long-term perspective • Little unit perspective

Table 2.1 Assessment Techniques for Acquisitions Staff

changes in the foreseeable future that might affect the work; for example, the library moving to some use of OCLC's PromptCat services. In the case of a copy cataloger position, it is reasonable and possible to have a standard related to the number of units processed during a given period of time.

Some supervisors have difficulty with the idea of allowing the job holder to state a "reasonable" level. This is usually due to the belief that individuals are essentially lazy and will thus pick a level that is easy to achieve. Setting an easily achieved level is the likely outcome *when* the work relationship between the individuals is strained. (Perhaps one reason for the strained relationship is the supervisor's belief that people are lazy. This is an example of where the supervisor's behavior/belief can and does have an impact on others' work performance.) Where the relationship is positive, the typical response is to set a very realistic goal that the job holder will be required to have to "reach for" rather than achieve a certain outcome. In the case of a new job or one that is redesigned, the past and present data do not exist, but it is still worthwhile to involve the job holder in the process. One essential in such circumstances is for both parties and the supervisor's supervisor all to understand that the standard is only an educated guess and that no one will be faulted if the estimate is inaccurate (Philp, 1990: 27).

Realism is something that can be misunderstood by supervisors. Sometimes supervisors forget that *no one*, including themselves, is always perfect in every or even most of their work activities. Thus, setting a "zero" tolerance for anything is unrealistic—"no user complaints" for circulation department personnel is not only unrealistic, it is unfair. There is no way that staff can be held fully accountable for actions taken by end users. A better approach is to set some percentage

---

WHAT ARE SOME POSSIBLE "REALISTIC GOALS?"

Acquisition units

- No budget overage and less than 1.5% underspent
- Orders placed within 48 hours of receipt
- Invoices processed within 2 working days
- No more than 2% duplication rate

Serial units

- Incoming serials checked-in within 24 hours of receipt
- Missing issues claimed within 7 working days of due date
- 90% of completed volumes sent to the bindery within 20 working days, if budget allows.

Cataloging units

- Copy cataloging materials, shelf ready within 45 days of receipt
- 97% of all U.S. imprints catalogs and shelf ready within 90 days of receipt
- 99% of withdrawals processed within 24 hours of receipt

Circulation units

- Returned items are processed and re-shelved within 72 hours
- Shelves are "read" at least once every 6 months
- Users receive a status report on a "missing" item within 72 hours of receipt

Reference units

- Telephone questions have a response within 4 hours of receipt
- E-mail questions have at least an acknowledgement of receipt within 1 hour during service periods
- Updated versions of electronic resources will be installed within 24 hours of receipt

Other units

- Written complaints will have a response within 24 hours of receipt
- Reserve materials will be processed within 18 hours of receipt of request/material
- Document delivery status report will go to the requester within 72 hours

* Returned/lost is the situation in which the user claims to have returned the item but the library has no evidence it was returned. The circulation system still shows the item is checked out and the item is not on the shelf.

reduction of some average. A standard such as reduce user complaints about "returned/lost"* materials by 3% from the 5-year average of x per month/year could be a reasonable and realistic goal. The goal should require some effort to achieve but not be beyond reach. Again, to be effective, there needs to be agreement that the goal is realistic.

Clearly, standards are most effective when there are objective measures that one can use in establishing the standards. The rather widespread, strong belief that PA is a subjective exercise undertaken for the sole purpose of justifying salary adjustments makes it very important to use the maximum number of objective measures. Such measures assume there are clear definitions. Though it is unlikely that one will completely avoid subjectivity, one can think about some questions that will help both parties feel more comfortable with the subjective side of the process. (A review of the PA forms in Part III shows where subjective boxes require completion.) Some questions to think about are as follows: What does initiative mean in the context of the position being

---

SOME STANDARD-SETTING QUESTIONS TO PONDER

- What are the productivity goals for the position?
- What effect do I want the position to achieve?
- Are there effects that should be avoided?
- What does it mean to perform properly?
- What are the consequences of poor performance—individual, unit, library-wide?
- What are the outside factors that are beyond the control of the job holder that can impact performance?
- What aspects of the position are quantifiable?
- What is an effective (fill in the blank) service?
- Are there predictable development issues to address?
- What are the realistic standards for this position?

---

appraised? In what way(s) does "judgment" apply to the work? In terms of "attendance," how does one decide if it is acceptable or not? What is it that differentiates between a poor, fair, good, excellent, and outstanding working relationship? Thinking about the answers and discussing the answers with staff and reaching agreement on them will improve at least the attitude about the process and usually its value/impact as well.

Establishing performance standards should be considered an ongoing process—not a one-time task—even for the same job. Also, an annual performance appraisal can serve as a regular occasion in which job descriptions and performance standards can be reviewed to ensure that standards and expectations are accurate and work performance needs are addressed. Thus, establishing performance standards relates to developing, reviewing, and revising job descriptions as needed.

Figures 2.1 and 2.2 are two examples of library staff performance standards: one for support staff and one for professional staff. They are reprinted from Carol F. Goodson's *Complete Guide to Performance Standards for Library Personnel* (Goodson, 1997). Her book provides detailed information on performance standards as well as twenty-six example standards. It is a must read for anyone thinking about reworking their appraisal process. The examples illustrate how one might implement the above material into standards.

A. CATALOGING

Includes but is not limited to:

1. Is a competent user of all modules of the library's automated system needed in this position
   - correctly edits item records and connects to MARC record
   - correctly creates copies, volumes, item records
   - runs reports daily and prints labels
2. Creates new records/workforms with less than 5% error rate
3. Requires little assistance in completing copy cataloging of assigned materials using national cataloging system (e.g., OCLC) bibliographic records (less than 5% error rate)
   - selects correct cataloging system record and edits CIP record to match item in hand
   - uses correct ISBD punctuation, AACR2, MARC formats, local authority file, holding codes, etc.
   - exports records correctly
   - processes books correctly (labels neat, accurate, and legible)
4. Takes responsibility for keeping up to date on changes in cataloging codes and formats
5. Works efficiently, is able to complete assigned work on an average of x items per month
6. Works cooperatively with departmental colleagues, acquisitions, and public service areas so that materials flow smoothly and rapidly through the system to the shelves
7. Keeps accurate statistics as required by supervisor

B. DATABASE MAINTENANCE

Includes, but is not limited to:

1. Deals with error reports within one business day
2. Edits records for subject heading changes as directed by supervisor within 2 business days
3. Files/checks and corrects filing in shelflist, applying knowledge of correct ALA filing rules
4. Notices and corrects holdings and other errors in bibliographic databases

5. Adds copies/volumes promptly and correctly
6. Promptly and correctly processes withdrawals
   - correctly deletes holdings in shared databases (e.g., OCLC, other regional cooperative systems, etc.)
   - correctly edits or removes record in library's outline system
   - pulls shelflist cards

Assessment: peer, user feedback; supervisor observations and sample checking of work; portfolio items; self evaluation

C. MATERIALS PROCESSING

Includes, but is not limited to:

1. Places labels on new or rebound materials neatly and accurately, according to library's established specifications (straight, clean)
2. Covers labels with label protectors (straight, no wrinkles)
3. Secures date due slips in books (or other materials) according to established specifications (straight)
4. Stamps material with appropriate ownership stamps in locations specified (stamped information clearly readable)
5. Correctly inserts magnetic detection strips into materials that are to be stripped
6. When processing is completed, arranges new books on New Books shelves according to class number (or other established procedure)
7. Files shelflist cards correctly (less than 1% error rate)
8. Processes reclassified material
   - carefully removes old label so as not to damage material
   - places new labels on materials neatly and accurately
9. Processes withdrawals
   - stamps DISCARDED in all specified places on the item
   - disposes of items correctly, according to library policies and procedures

D. OTHER DEPARTMENT DUTIES

Includes, but is not limited to:

1. Maintains accurate annual leave/sick leave records for department; has weekly report ready for supervisor's signature by noon on Friday

2. Answers phones courteously and promptly by 4th ring

3. Responds to requests from public services desk immediately

4. Assists with training of new workers, resulting in competent new employees

5. Assists with scheduling of subordinates and keeping them on task

6. Assists in performing essential duties of absent staff members without prompting from supervisor

7. Assists in evaluation process by documenting job performance of subordinates for the Head of Cataloging

8. Models good work habits for others (i.e., avoids personal phone calls while on duty, stays on task, etc.)

9. Corrects subordinates courteously but firmly when required

Assessment: peer feedback, supervisor observations

Figure 2.1 Cataloging Assistant Performance Standards

Note: The task of Reference Librarians is to assist library users in locating information, either from resources available within the library or from some other source. The behaviors identified below, representing standard performance, are not meant to be inclusive: they are merely examples of conduct expected of those who are assigned to Reference duty.

REFERENCE LIBRARIAN
A. RESPONSIBILITIES TO LIBRARY USERS

1. Conveys a warm, yet professional attitude

   Includes, but is not limited to:

   • Listens carefully, asks questions as necessary in order to be sure s/he understands what is needed

   • Treats all users with equal courtesy and consideration, is tactful and nonjudgmental

   • Avoids behaviors, casual remarks, or jokes that could be construed as sexist

   • Invites approach by acknowledging the presence of library patrons as they enter the Reference area (makes eye contact, smiles, etc.)

   • Appears to be truly concerned with the user's request

   • Tries to instill confidence in users who project or express feelings of inadequacy, etc.

   • Encourages user to return to the desk for further help if his/her information need is still not satisfied after s/he has followed the suggestion first provided

- Readily asks colleagues for help when needed

2. Gives full attention to primary task

   Includes, but is not limited to:

   - While on duty at the desk, avoids personal conversation (including phone calls)
   - Keeps consultations with other staff members as brief as possible
   - If engaged in other work while at the desk, does not become so absorbed as to ignore patrons
   - Notices and approaches individuals who look like they may need help

3. Embodies the qualities expected of a good teacher

   Includes, but is not limited to:

   - Chooses sources appropriate to the question asked and the questioner's objectives and level of expertise
   - Accompanies user information source whenever possible, and shows him/her how to search effectively
   - Makes certain that the user understands how to operate equipment or use the recommended source before leaving him/her to work alone.
   - Provides correct information in response to brief queries
   - Uses all available resources (as appropriate), including Internet, print, online, telephone, etc.
   - Follows up with information seeker to be sure that needs have been adequately met
   - Prepares guides to information resources and keeps them current
   - Takes responsibility for self-training in areas identified as personal weaknesses
   - Stays up-to-date on new resources as they are added to the collection or to which access has been provided
   - Suggests other support services (such as ILL, scheduled information literacy classes, regional cooperative borrowing arrangements, etc.) when appropriate
   - Provides clear directions to users trying to locate materials
   - Effectively uses and teaches functions of the library's online system and other computer databases

B. RESPONSIBILITIES TO THE LIBRARY COWORKERS

1. Treats colleagues with consideration and respect

   Includes, but is not limited to:

   - Punctually arrives at desk for scheduled hours

- Gives sufficient advance notice when unable to be present for scheduled hours, or arranges for a substitute
- Remains available near desk during duty periods, except when s/he must leave in order to accommodate the needs of a patron request
- When briefly leaving the desk during duty hours, lets colleagues know (why, where, and for how long)
- Does not speak negatively about the library, the profession, or colleagues
- Records scheduled vacation, sick leave, etc., on departmental calendar
- Arrives for meetings on time, and constructively participates in discussion
- Keeps colleagues informed of own work status and/or developments that might affect work
- Interacts effectively with colleagues; cooperates and collaborates to achieve departmental goals
- Accepts and acts on constructive criticism from supervisor and coworkers
- Does not ignore problems or leave them for others to take care of (e.g., copier out of paper, microfilm reader/printer needing toner), but deals with them promptly whenever necessary

2. Satisfactory performs tasks needed in order for the library to function efficiently and meet its institutional goals

   Includes, but is not limited to:
   - Collects and maintains statistical records necessary to evaluate accomplishments of service goals and objectives
   - Creates/maintains attractive and useful departmental WWW pages
   - Knows library policies and procedures; accurately interprets them, and clearly and courteously communicates policies to patrons and staff as necessary
   - On the infrequent occasions when exceptions to library policy are made, uses good judgment in making these decisions
   - Identifies and recommends for purchase materials appropriate to the reference/general collection
   - Identifies items which should be weeded and initiates orders for newer editions, etc.
   - Checks ILL request forms received at the Reference Desk for completeness and accuracy
   - Encourages patrons to utilize fully the resources available or accessible locally before choosing Interlibrary Loan
   - Uses time, supplies, and equipment effectively and efficiently

- Completes projects within agreed-upon standards of accuracy and timeliness
- Sees to it that any Reference Department assistants (such as students or part-time workers) are engaged in productive work while they are on duty
- Shelves reference books whenever necessary

Assessment: peer and patron feedback; supervisor observations; portfolio items; self-evaluation

©1997. Reprinted from *Complete Guide to Performance Standards for Library Personnel* with permission of Neal-Schuman Publishers, Inc. All rights reserved.

Figure 2.2 Reference Librarian Performance Standards

CAREER PATH DIFFERENCES

Within libraries, there are usually a minimum of three categories of employees (full-time professional and support staff and part-time staff), and in larger libraries there can be a surprising number. For PA to be effective, there need to be different formats. For example, the career path and expectations for a librarian (professional staff) is very different from that of a computer system specialist (professional staff). Another example of the differences, from the support staff, is the secretarial staff and paraprofessional staff in cataloging. Part-time staff may or may not aspire to a full-time position doing what they now do. In many cases, the part-time person has no long-term interest in the work; it is simply a source of income. Each of the above, and there are many other distinctions, call for a slightly different PA process as well as a different format.

One category of library worker is generally ignored in the PA literature: volunteers. In periods of tight economic conditions and/or cost-reduction efforts by parent institutions, libraries make ever increasing use of volunteers to perform essential activities. There are times when a volunteer may be performing the same work as a paid staff member. When that occurs, managers must address the question, do I/we do a performance review of the volunteer? A second question often follows: what will the impact be on the paid staff who do the work if I/we don't appraise the volunteer? The best approach is to engage in some type of "review" process with the volunteer in such cases. Clearly, the administrative aspects of the usual PA process generally are not relevant, so the focus is on the behavioral.

Even if the official HR system does not call for different formats/processes for the various categories of library workers, one can and should develop internal systems to reflect the variations, if one wants to have an affective PA process. For an internal system, devote some serious thinking time to what variations exist at the professional, paraprofessional, clerical, full-time, part-time, and volunteer levels. After thinking about the variation, draft some forms for each variation you think is significant. (A draft form shared with the staff is sure to generate input—rather like lightning rods attract lightning.) What one wants to include in such forms are the vision and values of the unit (customer service in the case of libraries), the core competencies required to achieve the vision, and performance standards.

The discussion/debate generated by the form should assist in communicating organizational and unit goals and objectives. It should, in a participative management environment, lead to open discussions of what is needed to achieve the goals as well as what barriers exist. That in turn can lead into the development of performance standards for classes of jobs (copy cataloger, circulation clerk, reference librarian, etc.)

MONITORING, MENTORING, AND COACHING

> **Monitoring, Mentoring, and Coaching**
>
> - Monitoring is observing performance and assessing that performance against performance standards.
> - Mentoring is advising; though it generally focuses on performance, it can and should also concern career development beyond the immediate position of the mentee.
> - Coaching is teaching, correcting, and showing how to achieve performance standards.

It takes time and effort to develop standards and agree on appropriate processes. However, to have a truly effective work unit performing at its best requires supervisors to devote substantial amounts of time to monitoring, mentoring, and coaching. Too often, the emphasis is on monitoring and "recording the pluses and minuses of performance." Though monitoring—assessing how well the standards are being met—is an important activity, it will not lead to a top-functioning unit if that is all the supervisor does.

What leads to successful performance is noting the problem areas through monitoring and then spending time in mentoring and coaching the staff who are experiencing difficulty. Less effective supervisors act on the belief that coaching and mentoring only needs to take place at the time of the annual/semiannual formal PA process. To be effective, mentoring/coaching should begin as soon as a supervisor observes a nonsatisfactory performance issue (immediate feedback).

Supervisors provide feedback constantly, and many are not aware of that fact. Daily behavior on the supervisor's part sends messages, intended or not, to the staff. A supervisor who stays in their office and is not often seen in the work area sends the message that staff performance is unimportant. Even if the supervisor has, in fact, good staff performance and believes the staff is competent to work independently, there is a positive value to "making the rounds" of staff to give some praise or encouragement. Failure to do so, over time, sends a message that the supervisor does not care. On the other hand, constant "hovering" in the area sends the message that the supervisor does not trust the staff to work independently ("when the cat is away the mice will play" concept). Too much of either approach will create problems for performance.

Reinforcing good performance is a crucial step in the coaching/mentoring process. New employees need daily reinforcement during the start-up/probation period, even those with prior experience in the same type of job, but with another library. D. M. Brethower (1982) identified five important reinforcement methods.

- Regular feedback on job performances
- Regular feedback on performance improvement
- Regular feedback on progress toward goals
- Positive supervisor comments on good performance
- Positive supervisor comments on performance improvement

Coaching is a two-way communication process based on the assumption the employee desires to perform well. Like a sports coach, the supervisor's role is to develop the necessary skills-set as well as share their knowledge and experience in performing the work in question. On the employee's part, there is the need to put forth the best effort to develop the skills, to give feedback on problem areas, provide ideas on how it might be possible to perform the activity more efficiently/ effectively, and information on their overall progress.

An important aspect in the coaching process is the need to identify properly causes of poor performance. Jumping to the conclusion that it is the employee's fault can create barriers to good performance that will last for a long time if the facts show the cause was outside the employee's control. The number of common causes outside the employee's control often come as a surprise to supervisors; these go far beyond work-flow/material/equipment issues. A few of the causes are:

- Poor policies and procedures
- Inadequate job design
- Faulty performance standards
- Ineffective communication about performance standards
- Inadequate equipment and/or material
- Ineffective training methods
- Ineffective hiring/selection process (person does not have knowledge or skills needed)

As one can see from the list, most of these are the supervisor's responsibilities. It requires good supervisors to look at themselves as a potential cause of poor performance; effective supervisors look at such issues before assuming it is the employee that is at fault.

Needless to say, many of the poor-performance issues are the employee's. Some of the common causes are:

- Lack of acceptance of one or more performance standards
- Poor relationships with other members of the work-group
- Dissatisfaction with the supervisor
- Unwilling to put an effort into improving performance
- Allowing personal (home) issues to interfere with work performance
- Knowingly accepting a position of low interest
- Knowingly accepting a position in the belief it is just temporary

Some of these causes will be difficult for the supervisor to identify.

One method of assessing performance issues is to employ a "problem-solving" technique. Start by carefully describing the problem. What is it about the performance that is unsatisfactory? Is there more than one aspect to the performance issue? For each issue, clearly state why it is important/significant. If performance was satisfactory in the past, look for/at changes that have taken place in the unit/library. Often, a "minor change" elsewhere has unexpected consequences in other units, especially if there was little or no communication about the changes.

Is it a lack of skills problem? If the answer is "yes," consider the following questions:

- Is there a simple way to achieve the desired results?
- Does the person have the necessary potential to develop the skill?
- Does the original training still meet the needs of today's circumstances?
- Is the skill used often enough for the person to develop proficiency?
- Was there sufficient feedback on performance?

If the answer is "no," consider the following questions:

- Is there a perception that "good" performance will have negative consequences in relationships with the employee's peers?
- Does poor performance provide a perceived reward?
- Does good performance provide tangible rewards?
- Is it possible that nonwork issues are impacting performance?
- Do appropriate consequences exist for poor performance?

Whichever the answer(s) is, the next step is to consider possible actions and the consequences of each. Review the resources available to carry out each action, and finally select the one that appears to be the most appropriate.

EVALUATING PERFORMANCE AND RATING ERRORS

Each of the possible rater categories has some limitations in terms of evaluating performance; these are in addition to those mentioned on pages 19–23. Some of the sources of error lie in differential access to performance information.

Supervisors know about work behaviors and outcomes. Employees tend to focus on behaviors at the expense of outcomes because they may not fully understand the relationship of their outcomes to the workflow of other units. Peers tend to see behaviors, and only a few have a knowledge of outcomes. Supervisors' supervisors are very aware of outcomes and frequently know little about behaviors. A customer experiences behaviors and outcomes but of course has only limited exposure to both. Outside assessors observe only limited behavior outcomes. Certainly, they will attempt to have a sample of the full range of performance areas/standards, nevertheless, it is a sampling. Therefore, the observer has no way of knowing how typical the observed behavior is beyond comparing observed outcomes against data about unobserved outcomes.

Perhaps one of the best-known limitations/issues for the direct supervisor is the "halo effect." Often, past high-level performance or exceptional performance in one task area becomes *the* focus of the assessment rather than assessing all aspects of current performance.

TIP: Providing the ratee with a draft of what the appraisal will say can reduce stress and make for a more open feedback process during the formal appraisal session. This assumes that the organization's process allows for such a practice.

TIP: The presence of the observer creates what is called the Hawthorne effect. This means that the pressure of the observer will affect the behavior of the person(s) being observed. Some individuals become nervous and perform below their normal level, others will perform well above normal, and a few do not change their performance.

There is also the opposite issue ("horns effect"), in which past poor performance, poor performance on one current task, or for a few supervisors, is failure to have "perfect" performance. Occasionally, nonconformity in some aspect of the work but which is still done well can create a "horns effect" in the mind of a supervisor. For supervisors, it is a good practice to be wary of letting trivia, oversimplification, rigidity, or stereotyping becoming factors in assessment.

There are two other areas where supervisor assessment/ratings may become flawed: overrating everyone or making everyone average. Probably, overrating is the most common of the two problems. Most people don't like conflict, and PA is a place where conflict is common. One way to avoid conflict in the PA cycle is to give only high ratings.

Supervisor
- Halo
- Horns
- Conflict avoidance
- No one is perfect
- Longevity
- Personal bias
- Reflecting own appraisal

Self
- Overrating
- Underrating
- Leniency
- Misplaced value/priority

Subordinates
- Get even
- Lack of experience and training in assessment
- Relationship
- Fear
- Lack of knowledge of all aspects of job

Outside trained observers
- Limited time frame
- Unknown priorities of worker(s)
- Hawthorne effect
- Lack of information about linkages

Supervisor's supervisor
- Frequency of contact (halo/horns)
- Personal bias
- Longevity
- Priorities

Peers
- Popularity contest
- Friendship
- Get even
- Self-enhancement

User/customer
- Sporadic contact
- Personal relationship
- Lack of knowledge of technical issues
- Lack of knowledge of assessing
- Quality of service

Table 2.2 Potential Assessment Errors

To some degree, the supervisor's supervisor can reflect either halo or horns effect when doing an assessment. Likewise, personal bias, either positive or negative, can come into play. (Note: If the ratings of the supervisor and the supervisor's supervisor are very different, there is a strong possibility that one or the other ratings is a reflection, to some extent, of personal bias.) Longevity, years of working together, is also a potential source of error. The tendency is the longer the association, the less likely the rating will be an accurate reflection of current performances; historical patterns often carry forward and override the existing situation—either better or worse than in the past. One area where the ratings of the supervisor and the supervisor's supervisor may well differ is in terms of priorities. A supervisor's first priority is in terms of their unit's functionality. On the other hand, the supervisor's supervisor has a broader scope to consider and thus places a different emphasis on some or all of the performance issues.

Two common self-rating errors are over- and underrating. To a great degree, these errors are the result of deeply held beliefs about oneself and what is "proper" behavior. This can be summed up in two popular sayings: "Don't toot your own horn" and "If you don't toot your own horn no one will." Users of self-rating systems have to beware of at least two pairs of factors that can interact to create ratings with errors. The pairs are individuals who have confidence and those that don't about their activities and the confidence is appropriate or misplaced; and those who believe it is appropriate to "toot their own horn" and those that do not. Clearly, individuals reviewing self-appraisals need to have some understanding of how these pairs relate to each person doing an appraisal.

Another possible error in self-appraisal is leniency. This error tends to arise from three sources: attribution, self enhancement, and social comparison. For many people, it is difficult to admit to any shortcomings in performance, much less accept responsibility for failures. Such people attribute problems to others, to processes, resources, and so forth, but never to themselves. They are, however, very quick to take credit for successes. One very human characteristic is thinking of ourselves as competent people and that in the workplace we are high performers. This generally results in a somewhat biased self-assessment. When there are no clear performance standards that relate to the library work being performed (very often the forms are "generic" to the parent institution rather than to units within it), people compare their work to what they observe/think others are doing. The common tendency is to compare to a low performer, which is self-enhancing.

One other error in self-rating is misplaced priorities. This can cause a problem that goes beyond the PA process. Researchers, including myself, have from time to time asked supervisors and their subordinates to rank the tasks the subordinates perform in terms of importance and, occasionally, the barriers to performing the tasks. More often than not there is a surprising degree of divergence between the priority lists, even with those who have long-term working relationships. Thus, it is not at all surprising that a self-rater may place greater or lesser emphasis on a performance behavior/activity than does his or her supervisor.

Though peers probably have the most complete knowledge of the factors affecting work performance behaviors and outcomes, the process is not well accepted outside of format team settings. Peer appraisals also have four common sources of error. Perhaps the most common is the perception that it is nothing more than a popularity contest. That is, who is best "liked" among the peers doing the rating rather than reflecting job performance. The second error is closely related to the first; there is a perception that friendship plays a big role—I rate my friends highly because they are friends and expect they will do the same for me. "Getting even" with someone is the third source of error. Peer evaluations do give people opportunity to get back at an individual for something that is unrelated to work performance and in a manner that the rater is fairly certain the ratee will not be able to determine the source of the poor rating. Finally, there is the opportunity to rate others poorly in order to/in the hope that this will make the rater's performance look better—self-enhancement.

Although a group of subordinates' ratings can/should be a more accurate assessment than a single supervisor's rating, very few organizations use this method on a regular basis. Subordinate (or even "360° ratings") rating errors arise from a number of sources: getting even with the ratee, lack of experience in doing PAs, lack of training in assessment, relationship between rater and ratee, fear of retaliation by ratee, and lack of knowledge of all aspects of ratee's position.

As I was preparing this chapter, my institution's PA cycle came around. Its pattern is the fairly typical supervisor rating those they supervise. In thinking about subordinate ratings, I talked with my administrative assistant about the idea of having the library staff do an appraisal for me. Having taught for many years in graduate library schools and recently in upper division undergraduate courses in anthropology, I was used to having students evaluate my courses. We set up the process so the staff could do this anonymously. My assistant sent copies of the LMU appraisal form to each staff member (37 people) along with a cover memo. The cover memo indicated the process was voluntary, that the forms would go to the assistant who would compile the results, the compiled results would be shared with me and my supervisor, and that individual responses would not be seen by either of us.

The results of the endeavor confirmed what the literature has to say about subordinate evaluations and potential sources of error. First of all, the exercise was not viewed favorably; in fact, only three individuals turned in forms. Essentially, it supported the idea that unless the process is a regular ongoing activity, people will wonder why this is taking place and not take part. According to my assistant, some staff members who did not give appraisals made statements suggesting they do not understand the purpose of assessment: "I think he is doing fine, there is no reason to do this." Some felt a lack of knowledge about the job, and one person asked for a copy of the job description; we do not know if that person was one of the three people that did turn in a form. We received no feedback suggesting fear was a factor but it is possible it was. One comment, "I forgot all about it," may have reflected an unwillingness to do it or the form may have gotten stuck in a pile of things "to do later" as we did give the staff more than a 3-week time frame for submitting the forms.

Sources of user/customer error are types one would expect: limited contact, lack of knowledge of technical performance issues as well as a basis for judging quality, and relationship. Most of the library customers one would attempt to get evaluations from are the end users. (Other customers might be vendors, branch libraries, or business offices in the case of library bookkeepers or budget office.) Clearly, the evaluation is, in most instances, a "snapshot" of service or at best a small sample of the total performance. Generally, end users have very little knowledge of technical aspects of performance or a basis for judging the quality of service they receive. The evaluation tends to fall into one of two categories: satisfactory or very unsatisfactory. (Think about how often you have taken time to fill out the "how are we doing" card one finds in most hotel rooms. Usually, only exceptionally good or bad experiences motivate one to fill out the card.) Table 2.3 is a sample of what one might put in a library customer form and Table 2.4 is a sample for internal customers.

The assessments of outside trained observers can contain some of the same errors as end users. Most important is the limited time frame for the observations. That means it is highly unlikely the observer will have the opportunity to assess the full range of performance behaviors/activities. Though the Hawthorne effect is known, there may not be hard data available that will allow a comparison of observed behavior/productivity with a typical unobserved performance. Where such data does exist, it is possible to assess how much impact the observer presence had on the performance.

There are two other sources of observed error. One is a lack, or limited, knowledge of the priorities of the observed person and those of the person's supervisor. As noted above, there can be significant differences between them. The second is there may be a lack of knowledge about the linkages between the work being observed and other activities that may affect the work. An example would be the observation of a receiving clerk in an acquisitions department where some activity(ies) in the mail room require some extra steps not usually required in the receiving process. Another example might be that the cataloging department may have some requirement(s) that call for "nontraditional" receiving steps.

Knowing sources of possible error allows one to take steps to keep them from happening or at least to take them into account when using assessment forms. Performance assessment does have a long-term impact on people; some of it good and some of it not so good. An ideal PA system would incorporate many, if not all, of the elements of all the rater systems. However ideal that might be, the reality is that using all of them would take too much time and effort. Nevertheless, there may be ways to pick up/incorporate some of the best elements of each given a little careful thought.

Further Thought
Here are some questions to ponder:

- Thinking back to your student days and evaluating instructors: Did you rate the "tough" instructors highly? Did you really rate the instructor or how much you had to do?
- How did you think you would feel (emotion) and react to peer or to subordinate assessment of your performance? Do the error sources seem worrisome to you?
- How could you gain customer input/assessment about your job performance?

HOW IS OUR SERVICE?
HELP US IMPROVE _____ SERVICE POINT

Please take a minute or two to give us your assessment of your most recent service experience. Your response will be confidential and combined with data from other responses. For us to improve, we do need to know the date and time of the service interaction.

Date: _____   Time: _____

Please circle one of the numbers or the question mark to indicate the degree you agree with each statement.

1 = Strongly disagree   4 = Agree
2 = Disagree   5 = Strongly agree
3 = Neither agree or disagree   ? = Unsure

Service Attitude

I was listened to carefully.	1 2 3 4 5 ?
My question/need was understood.	1 2 3 4 5 ?
I was treated with courtesy and respect.	1 2 3 4 5 ?
I am confident that I can locate needed information in the future based on the assistance given.	1 2 3 4 5 ?
I was comfortable in asking for additional assistance.	1 2 3 4 5 ?

Service Quality

I had to wait a long time or return for later assistance.	1 2 3 4 5 ?
My need/question was met.	1 2 3 4 5 ?
I was shown how to use the computer system.	1 2 3 4 5 ?
I was asked if I needed any follow-up assistance.	1 2 3 4 5 ?
I am confident in the information received.	1 2 3 4 5 ?

Overall Service Satisfaction

How would you rate the service received?	1 2 3 4 5 ?

What might we do to provide more satisfactory service?

_____

_____

_____

_____

If you would like to follow-up on this survey, please call ext. XXXX.
Thank you for your time in assisting us to improve our service.

Table 2.3 User Evaluation Form

INTERNAL CUSTOMER FORM

As an ongoing effort to improve our processes and activities, from time to time we ask staff members to assess the effectiveness of internal workflow. Please fill out a form for each unit with which you have regular (once a week or more) work-related interaction.

Rating scale: 1 = Strongly disagree 2 = Disagree 3 = Neutral 4 = Agree 5 = Strongly agree

Your department: _____   Other department: _____

1. Cooperation/coordination is good.   1 2 3 4 5
2. Interaction is professional.   1 2 3 4 5
3. Effort is made to understand needs of both units.   1 2 3 4 5
4. Effort is made to explain technical issues.   1 2 3 4 5
5. Information about changes is given in a timely
    manner.   1 2 3 4 5
6   Adequate time is provided for changes to allow
    adjustments to be implemented.   1 2 3 4 5
7. There is a willingness to be flexible/make
    compromises.   1 2 3 4 5
8. There is a willingness to explore a variety of options.   1 2 3 4 5
9. Quality of work is satisfactory.   1 2 3 4 5
10. There is a teamwork approach to problem solving.   1 2 3 4 5
11. Overall, the interdepartmental work relationship
    is good.   1 2 3 4 5

Table 2.4 Internal Customer Form

REFERENCES

Brethower, D. M. 1982. "Total Performance System," in *Industrial Behavior Modification: A Management Handbook*, edited by R. M. O'Brien, A. M. Dickinson, and M. P. Roscow, 350–369. New York: Pergamon Press.

Evans, G. Edward, Patricia Layzell-Ward, and Bendik Rugaas. 2000. *Management Basics for Information Professionals*. New York: Neal-Schuman, 14–15.

Goodson, Carol F. 1997. *Complete Guide to Performance Standards for Library Personnel*. New York: Neal-Schuman.

Philp, Tom. 1990. *Appraising Performance for Results*, 2nd ed. London: McGraw-Hill.

3 CONDUCTING THE APPRAISAL

Effective performance feedback should obviously occur as close to the time of the performance as possible. Good supervisors and managers do that as a matter of course. Nevertheless, the meeting to go over/review the performance appraisal (PA) form often causes stress, at least in the day or two prior to the meeting. What makes this meeting more stressful than other sessions that address performance feedback is that the annual review meeting may be, and often is, the first time that the content of a session gets recorded on a form that goes beyond the unit. In addition, no matter what is said, people believe that what is recorded *will* have an impact on future salary increases and perhaps even promotions. Because of those factors, the rater should give some careful thought to what to "do" in the session.

PLANNING REVIEW SESSIONS

Raters should carefully plan the evaluation meeting, keeping several points in mind. The session should have limited objectives; it should be controlled by the rater rather than the ratee; it should be a two-way process with equal listening time for both parties; it should include a planned strategy for attaining the objectives; and finally, it should be part of an ongoing process. The last point, relating to the ongoing nature of the process, does not mean the session is just another in perhaps a long series of annual PA meetings. It means this is one aspect of a year-round assessment and feedback process. It means there should be no surprises for the ratee in terms of the content of the appraisal; nevertheless, this is the time when the total assessment of the past 12 months, or occasionally just 6 months, takes place. There is often a worry on the part of the ratee that they may have forgotten something "bad" that occurred during the rating period and which may resurface. The worry/concern is high during the formal review phase because this is normally when performance information is put on paper and goes beyond the unit. It is also generally believed, as mentioned earlier, that "The Form" *is* the basis for salary increases. With thoughtful planning using the above points, it is possible to have a review session that is productive and useful to both parties.

Keep in mind that although the meeting covers the past 6 or 12 months of performance, it is a good idea to focus on accomplishing one or two objectives during the actual meeting. There are two broad categories of PA reviews: those dealing with satisfactory performance and those addressing unsatisfactory outcomes. However, in reality, the workplace is more complex. There are a multitude of variations within each category. I will just touch on a few of the more common variations in both of these general categories.

SESSIONS DEALING WITH UNSATISFACTORY PERFORMANCE

We will start by reviewing four of the more difficult/unpleasant variations in the unsatisfactory category: minor correctable issues, major but correctable performance concerns, disciplinary action sessions, and dismissals. The first two variations share several characteristics. Though it is easy to say a problem/issue is correctable, especially when there are only one or two requiring attention, one needs to keep in mind the factors listed in Table 3.1.

- If there are two or more areas of concern, how many do you address now?
- Which of the areas do you select, if not all can/should be addressed at once?
- How willing will the ratee be to try to correct the performance issues?
- What should you do if the ratee does not see the issues as issues?
- Is there a clear standard for assessing what is an improvement?
- Do you, the rater, have time to adequately monitor the ratee's progress and still do your other tasks?
- If additional training is needed, is it available and affordable within the required time frame?

Table 3.1 Potential Concerns for Correctable Performance Issues

Typically, when there are only one or two issues requiring attention, the individual is capable of working on them and can make progress before the end of the next PA cycle; assuming of course they are willing to make the effort. Giving a person more than two areas to improve upon at one time can be counterproductive; obviously, that depends on the nature of the areas identified as below par as well as the amount of improvement that is required. Identifying too many areas to work on during a single PA cycle can and often does lead to discouragement on the employee's part; it can cause good performance in other areas to decline as the person's focus shifts to the problem areas. Those types of issues can even lead to the loss of a staff member who could be a productive employee.

If a number of areas of concern emerge regarding the ratee's performance, the rater should spend some time thinking about each one and the level of improvement that would be acceptable. Which of the deficiencies are critical? Is one more important than another? Which one(s) have issues that are outside the employee's complete control? And, are there any training issues associated with one or more of the areas that would lengthen the time for achieving the necessary improvement(s)? Considering these questions can assist the rater in deciding how many or which one(s) to address.

Another consideration is whether or not the improvement areas could be dealt with in a sequential manner, thus making it easier for the person to maintain good performance in satisfactory areas. Dealing with one improvement area at a time is easier, although it is not always possible. However, it is a good technique to at least consider when faced with multiple "problem" areas.

A final factor in deciding how, or if, to limit the improvement objectives is to think about the employee. Do they have the confidence, skill, knowledge, background, and so forth, to actually make the necessary adjustments to improve the performance deficiencies? If there is some doubt about that, perhaps one can structure a sequence of activities in such a way that allows the person to build confidence, skill, and so forth, and still meet the unit's performance needs. Though the ratee's lack of confidence, skill, knowledge, and so forth, are important concerns, they ought to be dealt with during rather than at the end of a PA cycle.

There is another more common and significant employee factor to think about when planning a review session. That is, how accepting will the person be to seeing that there are performance issues that require improvement? It is not uncommon for raters to assume that because they see a problem, so will the ratees. The assumption partially rests upon the fact that in well-run units, there has been regular feedback and discussion of performance throughout the PA cycle. What tends to be forgotten is that discussing an issue does not always translate into a person accepting that there is a problem to address. Spending some time thinking about how to handle a potential lack of acceptance can pay dividends during the review session.

Finally, one should decide *before* the session how much improvement is acceptable. Setting a goal at the "perfection" level is a recipe for failure in almost every instance. When the amount of improvement required is significant, it is generally best to plan to have a series of improvement steps rather than making it an "all or nothing" situation. This allows the ratee to see progress taking place rather than what may seem to be an impossible Mt. Everest–sized goal. With major areas of improvement, it is also helpful for the improvements to be observable and objective—even for "attitudinal" issues, difficult as they may be to establish. (This is yet another reason why planning the sessions is so crucial to having successful outcomes.) Examples of objective improvements include increase output by x% over the next z months, reduce errors of x type by z% by the end of the next PA cycle, or reduce arguments with other staff by 50% (this of course assumes one has a baseline). By establishing goal(s) beforehand, especially if you think having room to "negotiate" would be helpful in gaining agreement, you are able to present a set of circumstances that will meet both the organizational and developmental goals.

Turning to the session itself, "people skills" are crucial to having worthwhile reviews; that is, reaching agreement and acceptance of what needs to improve and what will constitute successful completion. Though the rater should control the session, this does *not* mean the person dominates the process, as doing so is very likely to make the ratee less willing to actually put forth the effort to improve. About the only accomplishment of such sessions will be completing required paperwork.

PA review sessions are best thought of as interviews, and good interviews require sound people skills. Sometimes the rater is almost as uneasy about the session as is the ratee, especially when it is time to concentrate on areas of perceived shortcomings on the ratee's part. This can result in the rater falling into an "I'm the boss and in control" mode of behavior rather than calling upon people skills. The "I'm the boss" mode results in trying to use authority, power, implied threats, or turning to a lecture in which the rater "lays down the law," none of which produces anything more than an occasional success. (Anyone who has had long-term experience as a supervisor has had the very occasional employee with whom only the "authoritarian" approach seems to work. However, the vast majority of staff respond positively to a more open process.)

A successful session is normally one in which the ratee does most of the talking. In fact, based on research done of tape-recorded PA review sessions, Robert Johnson (1979: 72) suggested that the most successful sessions were those in which the rater spoke 10% or less of all the words spoken.

No matter what type of review session is anticipated (satisfactory or unsatisfactory), most ratees are nervous, worried, anxious, concerned, or even fearful at the beginning of a session. As a result, getting the person to talk can be a challenge. Treating the session like an interview and using well-developed people skills is the most effective way to get ratees to start talking.

Skillful use of preplanned questions is a proven technique for getting the process started. Obviously, simple/short answer questions (such as, "Do you think you have had a good year?") normally do not achieve the desired results, especially with a person who is nervous. Open-ended questions (such as, "Tell me what you thought was your biggest challenge this year?") are very effective but have the disadvantage that there is no way to tell where the ratee may go with their thoughts—the person may not address the work areas of concern. Planning some questions that lie somewhere in-between yes/no and completely open-ended queries will probably be the most effective approach to getting the person to talk about specific work issues. For example, asking, "What do you see as barriers to doing your work as well as possible?" limits the respondent's choices in a way that asking, "Tell me what you think about your performance during the past year" would not. In the case where the session has a possible promotion component, formulating several "problem" questions can provide some insight into how the person might react to a future situation.

Naturally, if one gets the ratee talking, the person expects some response in return. Though silence can encourage some people to continue talking, too much silence on the rater's part can be counterproductive. Rephrasing what the person has said indicates you have been listening, that you are trying to understand, encourages the person to continue, and allows the person to clarify points made.

Learning to "hear" the message stated and making an appropriate response takes practice. How would you respond to the ratee who says, "I'm sick and tired of working hard for the library for such rotten pay?" or "Everyone *knows* the library doesn't care about its employees?" An even more difficult situation occurs when the ratee says something like, "We all know you are lazy and palm off all your work on us and then take all the credit for what we do!" Experienced supervisors have probably encountered some form of these statements at some point in their careers. They are most often heard during PA review sessions that focus on a ratee's unsatisfactory performance.

A personal attack is difficult to handle in a detached manner, but that is what is called for in all of the above situations. This is where having spent time planning the session can pay big dividends. Though everyone can be caught off-guard at times, the rater should have some understanding of how the ratee is likely to respond to the content of the session and be able to more or less anticipate potential problem areas. One can reply with any number of appropriate responses given a set of circumstances. For example, for the first two statements given above, some response that indicates having heard and understood the statement but not agreeing or disagreeing with the content would be reasonable.

There are some categories of response that one should avoid; most of them, outside the tension/heat of a PA review session, seem so elementary that no supervisor would ever make such a statement. The unfortunate truth is that as tensions rise, it is easy to slip into making one, especially if one is responding to a personal attack. Some of the responses listed in Table 3.2 should always be avoided in the workplace, not just during a PA review session. Throughout the review session, both judgment and advice are required, but in carefully phrased statements rather than in "off the cuff" remarks or responses.

• Judgmental	• Free advice
• Sarcasm	• Criticizing
• Threats	• Bluffing
• Humiliation	• Name calling
• Diversionary	• Profanity/strong language

Table 3.2 Responses to Avoid

When handling a session in which there are serious (disciplinary) issues, all of the above advice applies with some very significant additions/differences. First, and foremost, careful planning is absolutely essential. One should prepare a mental, if not a paper, "script" covering the entire session, at least in terms of what one can reasonably anticipate. In the case of a dismissal, there will very likely be a tightly scripted plan with the text prepared by a labor attorney to insure that what must be covered is and nothing more. It is not uncommon for such sessions to be handled by someone from the human resources unit, often in the presence of the organization's labor counsel, rather than by the direct supervisor.

Second, with disciplinary sessions, there is seldom much room for negotiation. The rater's position should be firm but fair. One can reasonably expect the ratee to be unhappy, even angry, and not all that accepting of the supervisor's assessment. In anticipating such an event, it is worthwhile to recall the public service six-step technique for handling an upset customer:

1. Listen carefully while observing nonverbal behaviors that may provide clues as to the person's emotional state.
2. Rephrase the person's statement(s) to ensure full understanding.
3. Maintain a nonemotional state, if possible.
4. Acknowledge the person's emotions but do not agree with them.
5. Avoid being defensive about the situation.

6. Clearly state the situation with its options and the consequences of each; if possible, allow the person to select the option to follow.

PROGRESSIVE DISCIPLINE

A proper disciplinary PA session should occur after there have been several counseling sessions in which the supervisor has employed the "5Rs" of performance counseling, because such sessions are part of what is commonly referred to as "progressive discipline." The 5Rs of counseling are considered the right purpose at the right time in the right place using the right approach and right techniques.

Progressive discipline involves a series of steps of increasingly severe consequence for failure to improve performance and that can end in, in extreme situations, the employee's dismissal. Early steps in the process involve verbal counseling followed by one or more combined verbal and written counseling efforts (this could include a PA review session). A rather typical progressive discipline program contains five stages: oral warnings, written warning(s)/counseling, written reprimand, suspension, and dismissal/release. Table 3.3 lists *some* of the behaviors that can lead to disciplinary action.

1. Insubordination, including improper conduct toward a supervisor or refusal to perform tasks assigned by a supervisor in the appropriate manner.
2. Possession, distribution, sale, use, or being under the influence of alcoholic beverages or illegal drugs while on library property, while on duty, or while operating a vehicle or potentially dangerous equipment leased or owned by the library.
3. Release of confidential information about the library.
4. Theft or unauthorized removal or possession of property from the library, fellow employees, students, visitors, or anyone on library property.
5. Altering or falsifying any timekeeping record, intentionally punching another employee's time card, allowing someone else to punch one's own time card, or removing any timekeeping record from the designated area without proper authorization or destroying such a record.
6. Absence for one or more consecutive workdays without notice to one's own supervisor or department head.
7. Falsifying or making a material omission on an employment application or any other library record.

8. Misusing, defacing, destroying, or damaging property of the library, a fellow employee, a student, or a visitor.

9. Fighting on library property.

10. Bringing on library property dangerous or unauthorized materials, such as explosives, firearms, or other similar items.

11. Use of force or threat of force.

12. Misconduct.

13. Sexual harassment of coworkers or supervisors.

14. Unsatisfactory performance.

Table 3.3 Possible Behaviors Leading to Disciplinary Action

No one wants to be involved in disciplinary actions much less have to handle a dismissal case. However, the longer one is a manager, the more likely it is you will have to do so. By keeping in mind the above points and working very closely with the human resources department (this is an *absolutely essential* point), the experience can be less difficult.

What is progressive discipline?

1) It is a way of supervision that emphasizes prevention of serious personnel problems, not punishment of employees for misconduct.

   a) It helps to determine the causes of unsatisfactory work or conduct.

   b) It helps to improve employee performance.

   c) It ensures that employees have a fair chance to succeed on the job.

2) It is a procedure for taking thorough, corrective steps when it appears that an employee has failed to perform their work or to conduct themself in accordance with requirements.

How does it work?

1) There are two main aspects of progressive discipline: being thorough and following a step-by-step procedure when a discipline problem arises.

   a) Being thorough means doing the following things when the employee appears to be at fault:

      i) Assess the situation—get the facts.

      ii) Weigh and decide the action to be taken, taking into consideration special circumstances, if any.

      iii) Act, being sure the action taken is appropriate to the offense.

      iv) Evaluate the action taken—did it work?

b) Following a step-by-step procedure entails: i) Oral warning   ii) Counseling   iii) Reprimand   iv) Suspension   v) Release

Table 3.4 Progressive Discipline

SATISFACTORY PA SESSIONS

Two of the three typical satisfactory PA reviews are relatively easy to do: good performance with the prospect of a nice salary increase and those that involve possible promotions. Unfortunately, those are not nearly as common an occurrence as are sessions dealing with satisfactory performance, even at the excellent level, that have little or no prospect of a salary increase. The past few years have, more often than not, been ones of "tight budgets" and situations for libraries where salary increases are nominal or nonexistent.

Without question such review sessions present the biggest ongoing challenge for supervisors in terms of maintaining unit productivity and staff morale. How does one go about encouraging people to continue their good performance when one lacks whatever motivating power salary increases may have? About all one can do is to fall back on some of the traditional work-motivation techniques. Even when using those techniques, one must exercise care.

In Chapter 2, I mentioned the possibility that poor performance might be rewarded. Tom Philp (1990: 60–63) raised two interesting and unfortunately all too common PA situations in the form of questions: does good performance result in punishment and does poor performance result in a reward?

The answer to the first question may well be yes, especially where budgetary considerations constrain, if not eliminate, the prospect of positive salary changes. Where salary freezes are the order of the day or, worse yet, reductions in hours worked with a reduction in salary, the answer is a definite yes. When trying to come up with a way to motivate a good performer in such environments, a supervisor may think of some traditional work-motivation methods such as job enhancement—which is in reality a punishment for doing well. "I can't reward your good performance with more money but I can give you some other 'interesting' work to do." Put that baldly, it is clear the person is likely to have to do more as a result of performing well. However, the usual approach is more indirect or hints at some future rewards for continuing good performance. (Such hinting/implying something in the future is a dangerous practice—even when the rater has the best of intentions. It can lead to serious consequences, as I will discuss later in this chapter.) The poor performer is unlikely to get such suggestions/hints and, in the tight budget situations, is in a sense rewarded by not having to make a decision to accept or reject additional/different activities.

So, what can one do to motivate and yet not make unfair requests or imply things that are often outside the control of the rater? One good technique is to make greater use of coaching and mentoring. Mercer Human Resources Consulting (www.mercer.com) conducted a study of 2600 respondents about their experiences, attitudes, and feelings with and about PA in 2002. One of the findings was a link between PA, job satisfaction, and satisfaction with the employer (Mercer, 2002: 9). For example, 80% of the workers who said they had received regular coaching or mentoring had a strong sense of commitment to the organization, and 81% of those who had received a positive PA review expressed overall satisfaction with their employment situation.

Another idea for handling motivation in the "tight budget" environment is to use something called "feedforward," which is a variation of mentoring/coaching. Marshall Goldsmith (2003) is a proponent of the concept based on his work with thousands of employees. He suggests that performance feedback is limiting by nature:

> But there is a fundamental problem with feedback: it focuses on the past, on what has already occurred—not on the infinite variety of things that can be in the future. As such, feedback can be limited, static, as opposed to expansive and dynamic (p. 35).

His feedforward concept can, in many situations, provide positive motivation by involving the rater and ratee in a process of changing a behavior that can/should make a major positive difference in the ratee's work life. Note: This is *not* related to a negative performance issue. Rather, it is something the ratee identifies as a behavior/skill that they think would improve their work situation—in some cases, this may be a behavior/skill that could lead to a promotion or a different type of job within the organization. Working together, the employee and supervisor identify something the employee wants to develop, improve, change, and one that the supervisor can assist with in some manner.

According to Goldsmith, one of the reasons people appear to accept feedforward so easily is they do see it as valuable to their future work goals, whereas feedback can have a negative influence or connotation. Though in theory, work-related feedback should focus on the performance/behavior *not* the person, the reality is rather far removed from theory. Few of us are capable of viewing feedback on our work performance/behavior that suggests it needs to "improve" in some manner as anything but personal. *I* did not accomplish something, made too many errors, was absent too often, and so on and so forth, and *I* must do something about that. Thus, performance feedback can become personal, in spite of the best efforts of the person giving the feedback to make it nonpersonal, when it comes down to me and something I need to do.

CONSEQUENCES OF FAILURE

We now turn our attention to two types of PA failures to consider: failure to have a PA system and failure to carry out a PA review process properly. Most U.S. management writers who publish in the PA field believe having a system in place is crucial to organizational success. Dick Grote (2002), a prolific writer about performance appraisal processes, says, "Yes, performance appraisal is really necessary. And, no, there is no better way to obtain the benefits" (p. 19). Both Grote and John Lubans (1999) take exception to W. Edwards Deming's claim that PA is an organizational "evil" and should be eliminated. The supporters of PA, and there are many, are firm believers in the many goals of the process, both administrative and behavioral. Thus, for them the failure to have a system will mean, at the most extreme level, organizational failure, and at the very least it will result in an organization that performs poorly.

On the other hand, I know from first-hand experience in Nordic country libraries, where PA does not exist, that these libraries are as well run and productive as U.S. libraries that have the system in place. Tom Coens and Mary Jenkins (2000) published a book with the title *Abolishing Performance Appraisal*, in which they make the case that PA is ineffective as we know it in the United States. Their premise is that though there may be some benefits from the system overall, it is a failure and needs to be radically changed. My personal belief is they are correct. We have a system that tries to accomplish too many things, some of which are diametrically opposed to one another, in a single process. Coens and Jenkins (2000) make the point:

> Due to its inherent design flaws, appraisal produces distorted and unreliable data about the contribution of employees. Consequently, the resulting documentation is not useful for staffing decisions and often does not hold up in court (p. 18).

TIP: Positive feedback and feedforward can be useful in encouraging and motivating staff and may be two of the only techniques available to the rater in some situations.

No matter what we may believe about PA's effectiveness, the vast majority of us must work with the system and do our best to offset its shortcomings. The last clause of the above quotation raises the very real consequences of failing to handle the PA process properly. Raters about to conduct a review session addressing performance shortcomings and who have years of experience in conducting PA reviews always have in the back of their minds the possibility that the session may lead to a formal compliant by the ratee, in the form of appeals, grievances, and perhaps even legal action ending in court. Thus, "doing it right" is very important for everyone in terms of time, morale, and overall unit/organizational productivity.

It should be noted that only a very small percentage of all appraisals lead to any type of postmeeting action, and only a tiny fraction of those end up in court. Nevertheless, when a situation does escalate beyond the ratee filing a written rebuttal for attachment to the rater's evaluation, nothing can be more disruptive for a unit. Not only is productive time lost on the part of both the rater and ratee while dealing with the case, but also other unit staff become involved, if for no other reason than they are being asked to listen to their fellow ratee's "side of the story." In some cases, they may be called upon to contribute statements about what they saw, heard, experienced, and so forth and so on.

Though this is a book about performance appraisal, not about how to handle discipline in the workplace, a few more comments about the latter are necessary as the two concepts are interrelated. On page 45 I discussed "progressive discipline" for handling long-term performance/behavior issues. The documentation from appraisal sessions becomes an element in the progressive discipline process.

An important fact for supervisors to keep in mind is the fact that the sooner a "discipline" problem is addressed, the less likely it is to lead to major confrontations. Grievances are a little like trying to dam the flow of water. There is no great challenge in checking the flow from a seeping spring. A brook is not much more challenging. When the water becomes a stream, the situation can be testing, and when it becomes the size of the Mississippi, it may be almost impossible to control. With some quick coaching throughout the review period, one may be able to resolve the "problem." Waiting until a PA review session to really address the concern is starting to tempt fate, and a rebuttal by the person may result. Rebuttals to the appraisal are a danger signal that this is a serious concern that needs more attention on the part of both rater and ratee. Failing to give it attention increases the chances of having to deal with a formal grievance. Lack of resolution at the grievance level often means arbitration/mediation or even court action. As the problem escalates through the various stages, time passes and positions harden, making resolution increasing complex and difficult to achieve. Thus, the sooner one confronts the small, but perhaps uncomfortable task, of correcting a performance/behavior problem, the less likely it is to get "out of hand."

LEGAL CONSIDERATIONS OF PA

Although there can be legal consequences for mishandling PA assessments, there is *no* requirement for an organization to have such a process. However, employers and supervisors face potential liability from a variety of federal and state laws when there is a system in place. Just to name a few of the federal laws and regulations that can impact the PA process: Title VII of the Civil Rights Act of 1964 (42 U.S.C. Chapter 21), Civil Rights Act of 1991 (Pub. L. 102-166), Age Discrimination in Employment Act (29 U.S.C. §§ 621-634), the Americans with Disabilities Act (42 U.S.C. Chapter 126), and the Equal Pay Act (29 U.S.C. § 206). There are also tort issues such as negligence, misrepresentation, and defamation. Note: None of the following should be viewed as legal advice; it is just a "heads-up" that there are legal issues associated with PA.

Few of us who go through the annual PA ritual review give much, if any, thought to any legal implications for what we are about to do or experience. Those that do are most likely doing so because the upcoming review has to go over serious performance shortfalls. However, even favorable reviews may, at some point, become factors in legal action, especially when a termination is at stake.

How is it that PA reviews can become elements in legal actions? The underlying answer is that courts hold that a PA review is a form of *test* and is a key element of the employment relationship. Remember the long list (see pp. 4–5) of beliefs about what PA is to accomplish? They cover a host of employment topics—pay, training, promotion, demotion, discipline, transfer, and even retention—essentially, almost any decision regarding an employee after the person is hired.

There are two major grounds that cause PA reviews to become subject to legal or arbitration consideration. The first consideration is the accuracy or validity of assessments in predicting future performance or promotability. The second consideration is the accuracy or validity of assessment(s) in terms of past performance/behavior.

The majority of organizations, including libraries, have a policy of "employment at will." That means there is no *formal* contract that exists covering the relationship between the employee and employer. (Most employment contracts cover a relatively short time period; seldom are they longer than 5 years.) The concept of "employment at will" allows either party to end the relationship at any time without regard to contractual concerns. (As an employee in such an environment, I can accept a position elsewhere, give 2 weeks' notice of my leaving, and my current employer cannot stop me from leaving. Even the frequently used "2 weeks' notice" is a matter of custom rather than law. Likewise, the employer can terminate my employment with little or no notice.)

The following is a real, first-hand example of "employment at will" with which I had some experience at a university (it was not with the library, fortunately). Eight hours before the beginning of the last workday in a month (a Friday), all the employees of computing services received a notice they were to attend a mandatory meeting at 8:00 A.M. the next morning. The university's president and vice president for business affairs greeted them. The group walked into the meeting as university employees; within 5 minutes, they knew they only remained so until 5:00 P.M. that day. Their choice was sign a contract with a technology outsourcing company (the contract specified a person signing could not resign and take a position of *any* type with the university for 5 years) by 5:00 P.M. the following Monday or be unemployed. (The technology firm was taking over the computer services for the university and would be responsible for paying the salary for the 8 hours worked on Monday for those electing not to sign the contract.) This is an example of the two standard types of employment in the United States: "at will" for the university and contractual with the technology firm. Had the university just wanted to let all the employees go, it probably could have done so, perhaps with more lead time, but with little or no appeal possibilities for the employees.

Employment at will does not, however, give employers unlimited discretion over terminations. One major limitation, at least in some courts, is the existence of what is termed an "implied contract." A second major exception to the "at will" concept is when the termination is a violation of "public policy" (discrimination or harassment for example).

Discrimination cases are the most common "public policy" challenges to employer decisions regarding an employee and which involve PA reviews. Such challenges require that, first, the employee or a governmental agency establish a *prima facie* case. Once that occurs, the burden of proof falls on the employer to show that there was no violation. When, or if, an employer fails to demonstrate that its PA process is fairly designed and administered, courts can and do make the employer liable for costs such as legal fees, back pay, training program costs, and promotions.

Demonstrating that the system is appropriately designed and administered can be challenging, especially the latter factor. One of the things courts look for is the use of multiple raters rather than the single rater—because multiple raters are not that often used, for reasons noted in Chapter 2, this poses a problem. Certainly, the discussion in Chapter 2 made the point that multiple raters are more likely to produce the most accurate assessments in terms of reliable and valid assessment, which is the key issue for courts. However, the cost of engaging in such a process on a regular basis is high and few do it. One reason for not doing so is that courts do tend to treat reviews done by a single, but different, supervisor over time as multiple raters.

A second element in a court's decision regarding the "fairness" aspect of the process is the presence or absence of a system whereby the employee can appeal a PA review. Lacking such a mechanism there is little likelihood the PA system will be judged "fair."

IMPLIED CONTRACTS

What is an implied contract? If there were a simple answer to that question, there would be many fewer lawsuits for wrongful termination. Courts have ruled an implied contract existed on the basis of material contained in employee handbooks, verbal statements, the manner in which PA reviews are used, and other behaviors on the employer's part. Essentially, an *implied contract* can be almost any nonexplicit agreement/behavior that affects the relationship between the employer and employee in some manner. Thus, a series of positive PA reviews during many years could be a determining factor in a wrongful termination suit because the employee had no reason to believe their performance was unsatisfactory, and thus an implied employment contract existed.

Though almost all of the implied contract issues that end up in court are the result of allegations of "wrongful termination," a few have related to other issues such as promotion and transfer. As noted earlier in this chapter, hinting, implying, or doing anything else that the ratee could view as a "promise" of some future positive outcome is not only inappropriate in general, it can get the rater and the organization into legal trouble. Certainly, the most common fallout from unfulfilled hints is a loss of respect, trust, or confidence in the rater on the part of the ratee. Such actions also have a way of undermining the level of trust in the rater on the part of all employees they supervise. Although rare, such vague "promises" do result in grievances and arbitration, if not in litigation.

TORT LIABILITY

Three of the most common PA-related tort civil liability cases are negligence, defamation, and misrepresentation. Most *negligence* cases arise from the employer's (supervisor's) failure to follow the established procedures, especially in terms of progressive discipline, collective bargaining agreements, or employee contract issues. Some of the most common failures, based on court cases, are:

- Failure to have standardized procedures for all ratees
- Failure to have rater training
- Failure to communicate deficiencies to the ratee
- Failure to provide ratee access and input to the ratings
- Failure to allow for opportunities to correct deficiencies
- Failure to provide an appeal process
- Failure to use multiple, diverse, unbiased raters
- Failure to require consistent documentation across all the raters
- Failure to have a system for monitoring for potentially discriminatory actions or system abuse.

As one can see, the list is long, and many of the "failures" start with the rater's actions.

Defamation torts can arise from negative PA reviews in three ways. First, errors/misrepresentation of *facts* is an obvious issue. In the PA process, emphasis is on facts rather than subjective elements. For example, saying "Evans' cataloging error rate was over 6%" when it was actually 4.3% could be ruled defamation (factual error), whereas saying "Evans should improve his cataloging accuracy" probably would not be. Second, communicating ("publishing") a defaming statement to a third party; and third, that such communication injured the employee/ratee. (Note: "Third party" does not include those individuals required to take some action in the PA process; for example, the rater's supervisor and staff in HR who handle the reviews.) In most instances, the third-party exception also extends to outside agencies that the employer is expected to cooperate with, such as state and federal bodies.

Misrepresentation is a complicated issue, especially when it comes to former employees. Withholding negative information about performance unless the information supplied suggests performance was acceptable *and* there is no foreseeable risk of harm to the new employer or a third party is acceptable to courts. Examples where withholding problem performance information could lead to a misrepresentation case would be where the former employee had been disciplined for fighting with coworkers or a school media specialist who had been reprimanded for inappropriate touching of students and the individual engages in the same type of behavior with the new employer. Courts have ruled against the former employee in such cases. Many employers have a policy of not providing information beyond the dates of employment in part because of the problem of misrepresentation.

ACHIEVING SOUND PA DATA

Though few court decisions, as reported, hinged on reliability or validity issues surrounding the PA review, a study of 295 federal appellate court decisions that involved performance appraisal reviews as a significant element in the case suggested that such factors are a consideration (Werner and Bolino, 1997).

Werner and Bolino identified job analysis, written instructions, employee review of the assessment, and multiple raters as some of the key elements that judges considered. Performance standards, validity, and reliability of the data in the reviews as well as due process were also significant concerns for the courts. The essential "bottom line" is appraisal criteria should be objective, job related, behavior based, employee controlled; specific functions should be appraised and not generalities; and the criteria should be discussed with the employee.

The bottom line items appear to be self-evident; however, viewing the number of court cases that involve one or more of the above as failures, it appears we still have a long way to go to implement the self-evident criteria. One of the elements the reader will see in the appraisal forms that accompany this book are frequent examples of checklists, boxes to fill out that are "general" rather than specific in character. Although frequently done, incorporating too many general and/or subjective factors in the PA process can be a disaster waiting to happen.

Terms used in checklists such as "initiative," "resourcefulness," "judgment," and so forth, are nonspecific and open to widely varying individual interpretations. That in turn leads to different raters assigning rather different meanings, and even for a single rater assessing different ratees. Such variations can be a major problem, especially when the terms do not appear in the performance standards for a ratee. Clearly, such ratings can be, and usually are, highly variable comparisons— something courts do not like. As the authors of an article entitled "Improving Comparability in Performance Appraisal" (Edwards, Wolfe, and Sproull, 1983) pointed out, "people do not like to make comparisons, and comparisons among people are especially disliked" (75). The article goes on discuss why, if people in general do not like such comparisons, courts take a very dim view of comparisons unless there is *clear* evidence of validity and reliability in such comparisons.

Two key methods for assuring some degree of validity and reliability in the comparisons are rater training and having established definitions that raters employ in the assessment process. Figures 3.1 and 3.2 are illustrations of a checklist of definitions and a broader based guidance document that are helpful in achieving library/institution-wide reliable/valid data/comparisons. (The full set of guidelines appears in Part III and on the CD-ROM that accompanies this book, as do the entire appraisal forms.)

At Loyola Marymount University (LMU) (Figure 3.1), librarians are "Administrative & Professional" (A&P) personnel whereas the support staff are "Office & Technical" (O&T). The guidelines start with a short explanation of what LMU means by the word or phrase used in the checklist followed by definitions of how to employ the five performance levels (outstanding, highly effective, effective, needs improvement, and unacceptable) associated with the word or phrase.

LMU PERFORMANCE DEFINITIONS

QUALITY OF WORK

Thoroughness, accuracy and neatness of work produced
[Applies to both O&T and A&P.]

- (Outstanding) Work is consistently error free, thorough, neat, correct, logically organized and statistically accurate.

- (Highly Effective) Work is nearly always error free (with a few very minor errors), thorough, neat, correct, logically organized, and statistically accurate.

- (Effective) Work contains some acceptable errors that may require some review and editing by supervisor.

- (Needs Improvement) Work reflects errors that require careful review and correction by supervisor or partial reworking/revision.

- (Unacceptable) Work is frequently not acceptable or useable.

LMU SERVICE STANDARDS

Effectiveness of demonstrating the LMU Service Standards to the LMU community, including students, parents, faculty, staff, and outside guests.
[Applies to both O&T and A&P.]

- (Outstanding) Exceptional service orientation; exceptionally friendly and helpful toward others.

- (Highly Effective) Good service orientation; friendly and helpful toward others.
- (Effective) Regularly meets service expectations.
- (Needs Improvement) Sometimes forgets service orientation and serves at a substandard level.
- (Unacceptable) Rarely demonstrates LMU's service standards. Often rude and offensive toward others.

PRODUCTIVITY

OFFICE & TECHNICAL
Volume of work produced.

- (Outstanding) Amount of work produced is exceptional and exceeds expectations.
- (Highly Effective) Output is frequently more than required and regularly exceeds expectations.
- (Effective) Volume of work produced meets expectations and sometimes exceeds expectations.
- (Needs Improvement) Productivity and volume of work produced occasionally falls below expectations.
- (Unacceptable) Unacceptable level of productivity; often below expectations.

ADMINISTRATIVE & PROFESSIONAL

Meets established deadlines; sets new goals upon task completion.

- (Outstanding) Exceeds expectations with regard to volume and deadlines; sets new goals upon completion of task; is cooperative, energetic and resourceful; develops new ideas or approaches to problems.
- (Highly Effective) Meets deadlines and volume expectations; does more than is required; sets new goals, is constructive, energetic and develops new ideas and approaches to problems.
- (Effective) Meets performance expectations of a reasonable proportion of deadlines; does what is required; sets new goals and develops new ideas or approaches to problems.
- (Needs Improvement) Performs below expectations, frequently misses deadlines and is not goal oriented.
- (Unacceptable) Amount of work produced is unacceptable. Does not meet deadlines or set goals.

PUNCTUALITY

Reporting to work or appointments on time; frequency of leaving work before end of shift.
[Applies to both O&T and A&P.]

- (Outstanding) Always on time for work and/or appointments and remains at work as needed.

- (Highly Effective) Rarely tardy in reporting for work and for appointments; very rarely leaves work early.

- (Effective) Seldom tardy for work or for appointments; seldom leaves work early.

- (Needs Improvement) Sometimes tardy for work or for appointments; sometimes leaves work early without a valid reason.

- (Unacceptable) Often tardy for work or for appointments; often leaves work early.

DEPENDABILITY

Degree and amount of supervision required and reliability exhibited in following established procedures and completing assigned work.
[Applies to O&T only.]

- (Outstanding) Exceptional degree of independence and reliability; continuously follows established procedures in completing assigned work without much follow up.

- (Highly Effective) Exhibits a high degree of independence; follows established procedures; rarely requires follow up.

- (Effective) Meets expectations of following established procedures and completes regular assignments with minimum supervision. May need supervision on critical projects.

- (Needs Improvement) High degree of direction needed. Occasionally fails to establish procedures or requires checking on routine work assignments. Marginal reliability.

- (Unacceptable) Fails to follow established procedures and requires supervision on all assignments and procedures. Totally unreliable.

Figure 3.1 Performance Definitions: Loyola Marymount University

Even with definitions, one can see where various interpretations can arise. For example, in the first definition in Figure 3.1 (Quality of Work), what constitutes a performance that is "consistently error free" and one that is "nearly always error free"? Though the definitions/guidelines help raters, individuals can and do have varying ideas about the exact meaning of "consistently" and "nearly always." Note that the top rating does not call for perfection, although some raters view the "top" as requiring just that. Training the raters in the use of the definitions helps, but long-held personal views about what level of performance warrants "outstanding" and warrants "highly effective" are difficult to change in one or two training sessions. However, having such definitions and training are very important in terms of creating an appraisal process that is more effective and fair to employees throughout the organization.

MCPAI-R	Observation Issues	Documentation Sources	Typical Questions for Conferences
1.3. Works with the principal and school leadership team to provide flexible access to the instructional services of the school library media coordinator	"Flexible access allows any student, teacher, or staff member to access the services of the school library media coordinator when needed to support and enhance teaching and learning, thus impacting student achievement. Flexible access enables the school library media coordinator to plan with teachers and staff for instructional purposes." *(IMPACT for Administrators: A Resource for Evaluating Media and Technology Programs and Personnel, p. 8)* **Please note** that 1.3 refers to the instructional services of the school library media coordinator rather than the media center facility which is covered in 2.2.	**Look For:** Presentations and memos providing input to the school leadership team and principal in planning the school-wide schedule; documents such as media coordinator's schedule, plan book that shows opportunities for every student to use the media center; teacher request forms for provision of instructional services.	**Interview Question:** How do you ensure/ advocate for flexible access to your instructional services?

Figure 3.2 PA Process: North Carolina Department of Public Instruction, Media Coordinator Performance Appraisal Instrument—Revised (MCPAI-R)

Figure 3.2 is an example from the North Carolina Department of Public Instruction's PA process and which provides more detailed guidance. It goes beyond relatively short definitions of terms and essentially creates a structure within which the rater is to operate, by suggesting what to look for, how to approach each element, and what sources of documentation might be useful to examine. (The full document appears in Part III and on the CD-ROM accompanying this book.) Again, as long as people are doing an assessment, there will always be a subjective element. However, the approach taken by the NC Department of Public Instruction's structuring and guidance document reduces the risk of too highly variable ratings. Think about all the ways the statement "Works with the principal and school leadership team to provide flexible access to instructional services of the school library media coordinator" could be interpreted. Even with documentation of the above type, training of raters is a crucial step. It is a factor the courts consider when a PA review has really gone wrong and resulted in legal action.

SUMMARY

"Completing the process" and getting it done properly are more complex than it may seem, as this chapter pointed out. There are many places where one can slip-up from failing to plan a session through mishandling a ratee's concern about an evaluation as well as otherwise missing apparently straightforward steps. Even positive appraisals can, under certain circumstances, lead to legal action.

Though the sessions addressing unsatisfactory performance are difficult/unpleasant, they tend to be the ones that raters do spend some time planning. It is the positive review sessions where circumstances are such that rewarding the performance is almost impossible that too little planning takes place and problems can arise.

Because few of us look forward to the PA process, it is rather surprising that there are not more problems than currently exist. Preparation for the sessions, all too often, is minimal or nonexistent both on the part of the rater and ratee. Failure to prepare adequately at best leads to an assessment that does nothing more than complete the necessary paperwork. At worst, lack of preparation becomes a court case. As Andy Marken (2003) wrote,

> HR people go to great lengths to guide and counsel managers on what to and what not to cover in the review and what to write and not write down. Lawyers love to spend hours and days going over the reviews for innocent comments, statements, observations that will produce fat settlements for their clients . . . and fees for them (p. 5).

Some examples of the HR guidelines reviewed in this chapter, accompanied by the full text, appear in Part III and on the CD-ROM. However, guidelines are good only as long as one follows them and even then there are no guarantees. Reviewing the guidelines, taking training when it is offered, and planning the PA review sessions in advance are the best ways to avoid problems.

REFERENCES

Coens, Tom, and Mary Jenkins. 2000. *Abolishing Performance Appraisals: Why They Backfire and What To Do Instead.* San Francisco: Berrett-Koehler Publishers.

Edwards, Mark R., Michael Wolfe, and J. Ruth Sproull. 1983. "Improving Comparability In Performance Appraisal," *Business Horizons* 26(5): 75–80.

Goldsmith, Marshall. 2003. "Evaluating Performance Evaluating Individual Performance?" *New Zealand Management* 50(3): 34–37.

Grote, Dick. 2002. *The Performance Appraisal Question and Answer Book: A Survival Guide for Managers* (New York: AMACOM).

Johnson, Robert G. 1979. *The Appraisal Interview Guide* (New York, AMACOM), 72.

Lubans, John. 1999. "I've Closed My Eyes to the Cold Hard Truth I'm Seeing—Making Performance Appraisal Work." *Library Administration & Management* 13(2): 87–89.

Marken, G. A. 2003. "The #1 Guide to Performance Appraisals…Doing It Right!" *Public Relations Quarterly* 48(1): 5–6.

Mercer Human Resources Consulting. 2002. "Employees Are Better At Appraising Than Coaching Employees." Available at: www.mercerhr.com/pressrelease/details.jhtml?idContent=1078240 (accessed 3 September 2003).

Philp, Tom. 1990. *Appraising Performance for Results,* 2nd ed. New York: McGraw-Hill.

Werner, Jon M., and Mark C. Bolino. 1997. "Explaining U.S. Courts of Appeals Decisions Involving Performance Appraisal: Accuracy, Fairness and Validation," *Personnel Psychology* 50(1): 1–24.

II. APPRAISAL METHODS YOU CAN USE

4 OUTCOME-ORIENTED METHODS

Anyone looking at the history of performance appraisal (PA) might think that the key to a successful system resides in what assessment methods one uses, at least based on the volume of research performed to date. Between the end of World War II and the early 1980s, hundreds of research papers appeared exploring which format was best; "best" in the sense of getting the most accurate, unbiased assessments for the organization. In 1980, Frank Landy and James Farr published a review of the formal research done to date. Their overall conclusion was that no one method was consistently better than another. Since the time this article appeared and the field accepted their findings, very little new research on the topic has occurred. It is also one of the reasons that most of today's appraisal forms incorporate several approaches to assessing performance rather than just one.

However, the research prior to the Landy and Farr article was extensive, varied in approach, and most assessment methods can still be found on some appraisal forms in some organizations. How one attempts to summarize or categorize the formats also varies. I prefer one of the more common approaches for grouping these available formats: outcome, scaling, and ranking. This chapter covers the outcome formats (essay/narrative, critical incident, direct index, standards of performance and management by objectives), and the next two chapters discuss the other two formats.

ESSAYS/NARRATIVES

Essays are the oldest of the appraisal techniques in the United States. As noted in Chapter 1, the concept of performance appraisal in organizations arose from the military practice of assessing individuals for their potential for promotion. The concept started to "take off" after World War II, when thousands of military personnel returned to the civilian workforce.

The original methodology required the superior/supervisor to prepare an essay describing the ratee's strengths and weaknesses. Generally, such essays are, or should be, very candid and provide a mechanism for feedback that can allow for good dialogue to occur between the ratee and rater. A limitation is, in the absence of guidance about what one should cover, the rater has almost unlimited scope for what to or not to include in the narrative. Obviously, the essay can be, and often is, highly subjective as well as being potentially biased for either positive or negative reasons. Within the military, this was somewhat less problematic, as an individual usually had a number of superiors "weighing in" on performance issues before any promotion decision occurred.

For organizations where a long-term association exists between ratee and rater, the essay/narrative format, when used alone, can be tricky in terms of producing useful assessments. When used as the only assessment method, and without having multiple raters, the approach probably would carry little weight from a legal perspective. Thus, it is not surprising to find few organizations that rely solely on this technique. However, because the essay/narrative format does allow the rater to address special situations not covered in a typical "one size fits all" appraisal form, it is frequently used in combination with other appraisal techniques.

The original method of narrative assessment involved the rater preparing the essay/narrative, which is still the most common usage. However, some organizations now use it for self-assessment purposes. For self-assessment, the open-ended nature of this format allows individuals the freedom/opportunity to address the special aspects of their position as well as any unusual activities that may have occurred since the last review. Figure 4.1 (RAND Library) is an example of the essay self-assessment format from a special library setting. Figure 4.2 (Huntington Library) is an example of an essay supervisor assessment form.

ANNUAL ACTIVITY REPORT & SELF-ASSESSMENT—RAND LIBRARY

Name:

Unit:

Position:

Period Evaluated:

Overview of Job Responsibilities:

Major Accomplishments During This Period (relate to previous year's goals):

Professional Development Activities (classes, seminars, conference attendance):

Uncompleted Goals:

Goals for the Coming Year (give metric for measuring progress):

Overall Self-Assessment

_____   _____
Signature   Date

(Courtesy of RAND Corp 2000)

Figure 4.1 Essay/Narrative: Annual Activity Report and Self-Assessment, RAND Library

---

HUNTINGTON LIBRARY—PERFORMANCE APPRAISAL

Name: _____   Appraisal Date: _____

Title: _____   Date of Hire: _____

Department:_____   Supervisor:_____

INSTRUCTIONS: Refer to "*Guidelines for Supervisors*" for information. Please type or print legibly using black or blue ink. Use the reverse of the page if necessary.

1. **GENERAL PERFORMANCE RESULTS:** Evaluate the employee's work performance and accomplishments over the review period. If appropriate, include a discussion of specific goals and objectives established during the year and the extent to which these goals and objectives were met or not met. SAFETY ISSUES: Comment on the employee's safety record (e.g., attendance at training sessions, safe work habits, use of personal protective equipment, etc.). Was the employee involved in any work-related accidents? Were they avoidable? For a supervisory staff member being appraised, also comment on the safety record of his/her staff.

2. **GENERAL PERFORMANCE CHARACTERISTICS:** Consider characteristics and attitudes of the employee which are relevant to job performance, such as interpersonal skills, attitudes, initiative, judgment, teamwork, adherence to deadlines, meeting commitments, following instructions and willingness to learn. Comment only on how such characteristics have affected the employee's job performance and give examples.

3. PLANS FOR IMPROVEMENT: Comment on specific ways in which the employee's performance might be improved. Consider both what the employee may need to do to improve and what the supervisor could do to help the employee improve performance. Include agreed-upon actions, target dates and expected results. SAFETY IMPROVEMENTS: Comment on specific ways the employee's safety behavior might be improved. (Additional training? Use of personal protective equipment?) For a supervisory staff member, what must he/she do to keep his/her staff free of future injuries? (Conduct "tail-gate" or "just-in-time" training? Monitor safety behavior of staff?).

4. CHOOSE OPTION (1) OR (2) TO COMPLETE:

A. Overall performance rating:

Superior: _____   Good: _____   Satisfactory: _____

Needs Improvement: _____   Unacceptable: _____

B. Narrative summary of performance:

5. ADDITIONAL COMMENTS:

_____

Supervisor   Date

_____

Personnel   Date

_____

Next Level of Management   Date

_____

Employee   Date

*Employee's signature does not necessarily indicate agreement with this performance appraisal, but rather that the appraisal has been received and understood. Written comments by the employee may be made on a separate sheet.

SUPPLEMENTAL PERFORMANCE APPRAISAL (FORM A) FOR MANAGERIAL STAFF

Name: _____ Date: _____

In addition to the standard Performance Appraisal, this supplement should be completed for all staff members with supervisorial responsibility. Please comment on the staff member in terms of:

- **Leadership:** Effectiveness in gaining commitment and inspiring teamwork and accomplishment among subordinates; communication of departmental and institutional goals.
- **Development of Staff:** Effectiveness in training and coaching staff; giving performance feedback and encouraging improvement; supporting professional development; conducting effective performance reviews.
- **Administration:** Effectiveness in planning, organizing and executing departmental work; delegation and follow-up skills.
- **Budget Management:** Effectiveness in planning and managing the department, program and/or project budget.
- **Interpersonal Relationships and Professional Conduct:** Effectiveness in interacting with staff throughout the institution; extent to which the employee's conduct meets the institution's standards of professionalism.

APPRAISAL COMMENTS:

(Courtesy of the Huntington Library)

Figure 4.2 Essay/Narrative: Huntington Library

SCHOOL LIBRARY MEDIA SPECIALIST EVALUATION—EVALUATION FORM

Focus Area:

Performance Criteria:

Commendations:

Recommendations for Improvement:

Strategies for Improvement:

Date

_____   _____
Library Media Specialist Signature   Administrator's Signature

(Courtesy of Maine Association of School Libraries, www.maslibraries.org)

Figure 4.3 Essay/Narrative: School Library Media Specialist Evaluation, Evaluation Form

SCHOOL LIBRARY MEDIA SPECIALIST EVALUATION—ACTION PLAN

Sample of one of several focus areas developed during initial supervisor and Library Media Specialist conference. See also related Sample Action Plan for magazine use, designed by Library Media Specialist to assist goal.

Focus Area: Curriculum development and implementation—the use of magazines within the information literacy framework.

Performance Criteria:

- Demonstrates depth of knowledge of the research process.
- Integrates specific research skills and strategies within social studies discipline.
- Demonstrates collaborative skills with teachers.
- Maintains good interpersonal relationships with students.
- Employs appropriate teaching practices, including
    a. Sets high, measurable expectations, communicated clearly to students.
    b. Uses a variety of tools to measure individual student performance.
    c. Incorporates relevant elements of Maine Learning Results.
    d. Involves students in goal setting and assessment design.

Commendations:

Recommendations for Improvement:

Strategies for Improvement:

Date

_____

Library Media Specialist Signature   Administrator's Signature

(Courtesy of Maine Association of School Libraries, www.maslibraries.org)

Figure 4.4 Essay/Narrative: School Library Media Specialist Evaluation, Action Plan

Figure 4.3 (Maine Association of School Libraries) is a typical essay section from a PA form that employs several assessment methods such as checklists and Behavioral Anchored Rating Scale (BARS). Figure 4.4 illustrates the type of guidance that is, or should be, provided to the rater in preparing the narration. Other examples of ways to structure a narrative section in a PA form are available on the CD-ROM that accompanies this book.

GENERAL PROS OF THE ESSAY/NARRATIVE METHOD

- ✔ Observed behaviors/performance can be described/ detailed.
- ✔ If accurate, can be useful for feedback.
- ✔ Can list specific skills, accomplishments, shortcomings—which may not come through in other methods.
- ✔ Good for final selections for personnel actions.
- ✔ Flexibility—can be adapted for any job description.
- ✔ Good for reviewing unique positions.
- ✔ Supervisors can rate/evaluate according to individual's specific tasks, instead of all being evaluated using same scale.
- ✔ Good with jobs in situations with changing customer needs—as needs change, elements of job change—with essay, appraisal can be tailored, adjusted.
- ✔ Can answer question, "does employee meet changing needs?"

GENERAL CONS OF THE ESSAY/NARRATIVE METHOD

- ✔ No way to differentiate between employees' performance.
- ✔ Subject to human error.
- ✔ Supervisor's words can be interpreted differently by different people.
- ✔ Review depends on supervisor's writing/expressive skills almost more than performance.
- ✔ Employees described by skilled writers may be perceived as more effective than employees described by unskilled writers even though they may be equally effective.
- ✔ Supervisors may measure different criteria for different employees, so no means of comparison exists.
- ✔ Does not provide numerical data.
- ✔ Not good for identifying candidates for personnel actions or for validating other selection criteria.

✔ Unstructured, so results can vary widely between supervisors.

✔ Most researchers are critical of this method.

✔ Different styles of reviewing on the part of raters—the review may be favorable, but given differences in writing styles, it can be hard to determine extent of favorability.

✔ Because of limited guidelines for raters, the appraisal can be influenced by non-performance-related factors (race, sex, age, and so forth).

✔ Flexibility benefit can be found with other methods as well.

Despite the negatives associated with this assessment method, the fact remains that it is extremely popular, as witnessed by the many examples of this approach in the forms that accompany this book. It is also the one method that consistently appears in all types of libraries—academic, public, school, and special.

CRITICAL INCIDENTS

The *critical incident* method is a variation of the essay/narration approach. Here, the focus shifts from overall performance to one or more activities in which the ratee was particularly successful or unsuccessful. What is necessary to make this an effective methodology is that the rater creates a record at the time the "incident" occurs, rather than trying to remember events at the end of the PA cycle. When it is time for the review, the year's "incidents" are summarized in a narrative essay. Some organizations that make extensive use of this technique prepare a form/booklet for the rater that provides space for areas of performance deemed "critical," such as decision making, planning, fiscal management, and so forth.

The underlying concept is that critical incidents force supervisors to observe subordinates throughout the PA cycle for the specific purpose of assessing performance. Theoretically, the approach should also lead to immediate feedback, both positive and negative. The recording of the behavior/activity provides data that goes beyond the assessment of performance. In cases of disagreement about the assessment, such a record can be useful to third parties in making their judgment(s) about the situation.

Researchers such as Baker (1988), Eichel and Bender (1984), and Smither (1998) all suggest that this methodology can lead to "oversupervision," or micromanaging. Also, for some employees, in organizations using the booklet technique, there is a sense of the supervisor maintaining "a little black book" on everyone. Occasionally, supervisors just write-up "sample" work activities rather than "critical incidents" because there is an emphasis on keeping records with this method. A recent article outlining the use of this method is by Hagner, Noll, and Donovan (2002).

Figures 4.5 and 4.6 illustrate the use of the critical incident concept to address the special or unexpected aspects of performance that can and do arise. The Virginia form (see Figure 4.5) is very open-ended and is incorporated within a larger "Management by Objective" style performance plan seen in Figure 4.10. The hypothetical "generic" form (see Figure 4.6) focuses on the unexpected aspects of performance. Clearly, the two forms call for the rater to consider very different performance issues. The "special assignments" seen in Figure 4.4 implies some degree of planning or anticipation that calls on one set of skills, whereas the "unanticipated events" section of Figure 4.6 would call on a rather different skills set. In the first case, skills such as planning, time management, and decision making can be highlighted. The second example is useful for such characteristics as flexibility, tolerance for change, and perhaps leadership.

21. Special Assignments	22. Measures for Special Assignments
G.	
H.	

Optional	
23. Agency/Departmental Objectives	**24. Measures for Agency/Departmental Objectives**
I.	
J.	
K.	
L.	

(Courtesy of Commonwealth of Virginia)

Figure 4.5 Critical Incidents, Virginia

PERFORMANCE PLAN AND EVALUATION
(FOR OTHER THAN MANAGERS)

Name	Performance Period To
Department	Unit/Function
Title	

OVERALL PERFORMANCE EVALUATION		PERFORMANCE RELATIVE TO EXPECTATIONS			
(Check appropriate rating)	Far Exceeds	Exceeds	Fully Meets	Marg. Meets	Does not Meet

AGREEMENT APPROVAL	DATE	FINAL PERFORMANCE EVALUATION	DATE
Rater:		Rater:	
Participant:		Approved By:	
Approved By:		Discussed with Participant on:	
Interim Review Dates:		Participant's Signature Affirming Discussion Held:	

PART I: BASIC MANAGEMENT OBJECTIVES/JOB RELATED BEHAVIOR
–List Objectives/Behaviors to be Rated

OBJECTIVE/BEHAVIOR	PERFORMANCE RATING				
	Far Exceeds	Exceeds	Fully Meets	Marg. Meets	Does not Meet
Job Knowledge					
Problem Analysis					
Planning and Organizing					
Initiative and Resourcefulness					
Responds to Department Goals/Public Need					
Decision Making					
Adaptability					
Interpersonal Effectiveness					
Personal Management					

PART II: OVERALL JOB PERFORMANCE (Check appropriate rating)					
Notable Unanticipated Events	Far Exceeds	Exceeds	Fully Meets	Marg. Meets	Does not Meet
Comments on Overall Performance: (List 3 greatest strengths and 3 greatest weaknesses)					

Figure 4.6 Critical Incidents: Generic, Performance Plan and Evaluation (For Other Than Managers)

GENERAL PROS OF THE CRITICAL INCIDENT METHOD

✔ Theoretically, this method forces the supervisor to observe performance, collect data, and give feedback throughout the PA cycle.

✔ Employees get meaningful feedback—information on specifics (behavior and results).

✔ Accomplishments, skills, shortcomings.

✔ Clear identification of things done wrong/right.

✔ When a large enough number of incidents are collected/categorized, they can be used in training programs such as time management, or improving decision-making skills, or for selecting or classifying employees.

✔ Good for performance development—clearly identifies job areas where training is necessary.

✔ Gives employees a sense of how performance relates to new positions when thinking about career planning/direction.

GENERAL CONS OF THE CRITICAL INCIDENT METHOD

✔ Time consuming on the part of supervisors, who must record behaviors for all employees on a daily or weekly basis.

✔ Can lead to oversupervision.

✔ Ironically, the method does not usually involve *timely* feedback—supervisors often wait until end of period to give feedback because this method emphasizes record keeping, not results sharing.

✔ Different incidents will occur for different employees—no numerical scores to compare; no scale to put value on incidents.

✔ Not good for rewards assessment.

✔ Not very good for selecting candidates or validating other criteria for selection.

✔ Doesn't address patterns of performance in comparing individual employees.

✔ Subject to bias—raters can know to record incidents to support any personnel action (positive or negative).

✔ Not good for determining the most "promotable" employees—need something more comparative.

✔ Not useful in defining jobs, because incidents are recorded after (or during) the fact.

✔ For career planning, can distort expectations of employees for a new position's required performance.

DIRECT INDEX

Direct index is one of three methodologies that focus on very specific outcomes or results of a ratee's performance—the other two, performance standards and management by objective, are covered next. All three methods were developed between the late 1950s and mid 1980s as a result of two concerns about existing appraisal methods—especially the essay/narrative method. First, there were considerable doubts about the value of methods that were subjective, nonspecific (in the sense that the rater decided what to address), variable from ratee to ratee (rater[s] freedom to decide what to cover made ratee comparisons difficult), and qualitative in character. The second concern related to the qualitative nature of PAs at the time. After years of rapid productivity gains in U.S. organizations, there was a noticeable "leveling off" of employee performance efforts. There was the hope that by emphasizing results during the PA process, employee productivity would regain an upward movement.

The direct index (DI) approach's only concern is with identifiable outputs. Each job is studied in order to identify suitable output measures. Once identified, the outputs are combined with a numerical index that reflects the "value" of an output. The "value" of outputs would vary, although some could be the same. Supervisors normally assign the numerical value; however, in a setting where the staff are all professionals, a joint setting of values is probably the best approach.

An example of the direct index method would be as follows: say Evans performs original cataloging of Danish materials and handles reference questions related to Denmark; one output measure could be "the number of items processed per unit of time or average time to process an item." Another output measure might be "errors per item." A third measure could be the "number of reference questions answered." Obviously, the ideal is high output with zero errors and a large number of queries resolved. However, there are some trade-offs. The higher the production goes, the more likely errors will occur. Likewise, perfection on every item will probably mean a relatively low production. Handling reference questions would draw time away from cataloging activities, which again would conflict with the "number of items processed" measurement. To counter this, the supervisor might believe that error-free records are twice as important as productivity—thus each record produced might have a value of 2, whereas a perfect record might have a value of 4. Because most of Evans' time is spent on cataloging, similarly, reference questions might only have a value of 1.

Evans' DI performance appraisal would reflect the overall numerical value of all the outputs achieved during the PA cycle. One obvious drawback of DI is it only addresses activities that are measurable. Trying to measure such things as work relationships, decision making, time management, and so forth, is almost impossible on any meaningful basis. Also, there are jobs, especially in library public-service areas, where it is very difficult to identify enough outcomes to make this a useful methodology by itself.

GENERAL PROS OF THE DIRECT INDEX METHOD

✔ Reduces rater error in perception and bias.
✔ Reduces PA tension, as both rater and ratee know what the data are.

GENERAL CONS OF THE DIRECT INDEX METHOD

✔ Changes in index number may not always represent changes in the employee's performance.
✔ Not very useful for giving feedback.
✔ Takes time to identify appropriate outcomes.

STANDARDS OF PERFORMANCE

Chapter 2 has a major section that covers the importance of establishing performance standards and how to develop them. For some individuals, such standards are a form of management, and they seldom think of using the material in the formal evaluation process. Certainly, they understand the standards come into play, at least indirectly, during the PA process—most often during feedback sessions.

When used in an appraisal form, *standards of performance* represent a list of performance measures that exist when the job is properly done. Naturally, the more items that are suitable for expression in quantitative terms, the more objective the results are viewed by ratees. However, performance standards can address qualitative concerns as well, which is why it is a more commonly employed method than DI.

Figure 4.7 (Colorado State University; CSU) illustrates a typical "blank" form one might use with performance standards. The levels in the CSU form go from 1 being the poorest performance to 4 being the best performance. Using material drawn from the book by Carol Goodson (1997), I have created samples of how a form ready for making the assessment might look. Figure 4.8 is for a department head and Figure 4.9 is for an acquisitions assistant. The examples are only meant as samples; as most jobs would have many more standards listed.

PLANNING AND EVALUATION FORM
STANDARDS/GOALS/OBJECTIVES ASSOCIATED WITH SUCCESS IN THIS POSITION

"Standards/Goals/Objectives" are specific statements or requirements and agreed upon by the supervisor and the employee. "Measurement Method" reflects the evaluation basis for the expected results. "Results achieved" are the accomplishments of the employee during the evaluation period.

	Standard/Goal/Objective:	Results Achieved:
		_____ Level 4
1	Measurement Method:	
		_____ Level 3
		_____ Level 2
		_____ Level 1

Standard/Goal/Objective:	Results Achieved:
	_____ Level 4
2 Measurement Method:	
	_____ Level 3
	_____ Level 2
	_____ Level 1
Standard/Goal/Objective:	**Results Achieved:**
	_____ Level 4
3 Measurement Method:	
	_____ Level 3
	_____ Level 2
	_____ Level 1
Standard/Goal/Objective:	**Results Achieved:**
	_____ Level 4

4	Measurement Method:	
		_____ Level 3
		_____ Level 2
		_____ Level 1
	Standard/Goal/Objective:	Results Achieved:
		_____ Level 4
5	Measurement Method:	
		_____ Level 3
		_____ Level 2
		_____ Level 1

Figure 4.7 Standards of Performance: Planning and Evaluation Form, Colorado State University

---

S.M.A.R.T. GOALS

Specific—they precisely define the work involved

Measurable—quantitative, qualitative, and timely

Agreed—both supervisor and employee are committed

Realistic—an acceptable but stretching challenge

Timed—specify completion and review dates

There are five types of standards/goals/objectives:

- To achieve routine work assignments
- To resolve identified problems
- To support innovation
- For professional development
- To support institutional or departmental goals

(Courtesy of Colorado State University, Human Resource Services, Fort Collins, Colorado)

STANDARDS OF PERFORMANCE PLANNING AND EVALUATION FORM

DEPARTMENT HEAD—NAME: _____

STANDARDS/GOALS/OBJECTIVES ASSOCIATED WITH SUCCESS IN THIS POSITION

	Standard/Goal/Objective:	Results Achieved:
	Unit/department's plan is updated annually	
	Plan is clear	_____ Level 4
	Plan is thorough	
1	Measurement Method:	
	Copy of plan	_____ Level 3
		_____ Level 2
		_____ Level 1
	Standard/Goal/Objective:	**Results Achieved:**
	Motivates and mentors department staff	
	Provides regular feedback	_____ Level 4
	Encourages/suggests development activities	

2	Measurement Method:	
	Peer/staff feedback	_____ Level 3
	Staff participation taking part in training opportunities	
		_____ Level 2
		_____ Level 1
	Standard/Goal/Objective:	**Results Achieved:**
	Acts as communication channel for department	
	Meets regularly with department members	_____ Level 4
	Brings departmental issues to appropriate administrators	
	Communicates with other unit heads in open manner.	
3	Measurement Method:	_____ Level 3
	Minutes of staff meetings	
	Agendas for meetings with senior managers and other department heads	
		_____ Level 2
		_____ Level 1

Figure 4.8 Standards of Performance: Planning and Evaluation Form, Department Head

STANDARDS OF PERFORMANCE
PLANNING AND EVALUATION FORM

ACQUISITIONS ASSISTANT—NAME: _____

STANDARDS/GOALS/OBJECTIVES ASSOCIATED WITH SUCCESS IN THIS POSITION

	Standard/Goal/Objective:	Results Achieved:
	Handles invoices promptly and correctly	
	Processes invoices daily	_____ Level 4
	Has invoices from past week ready for approval by noon Friday	
1	Measurement Method:	
	Records showing dates of processing	_____ Level 3
	Supervisor observation	
		_____ Level 2
		_____ Level 1
	Standard/Goal/Objective:	**Results Achieved:**
	Handles pre-order searching quickly and accurately	
	Requests searched within 10 working days of receipt	_____ Level 4
	Error rate at 1 or less per 100 items searched	
2	Measurement Method:	
	Order requests showing data of receipt and completion of pre-order searching	_____ Level 3

		_____ Level 2
		_____ Level 1
	Standard/Goal/Objective:	**Results Achieved:**
	Changes order status to received promptly and accurately	
	Changes made within 1 working day	_____ Level 4
	No errors	
3	Measurement Method:	_____ Level 3
	Records from packing slips/online shipping lists/invoices	
		_____ Level 2
		_____ Level 1

Figure 4.9 Standards of Performance: Planning and Evaluation Form, Acquisitions Assistant

GENERAL PROS OF THE STANDARDS OF PERFORMANCE METHOD

✔ Employees and supervisors both have input into job description, identifying ways to achieve desired results.

✔ The employee is more likely to try to meet goals, because he/she had a part in forming them.

✔ Supervisor also more committed to providing support for achieving goals.

✔ The employee is not surprised by the results of the review.

✔ Has chance to correct standards not being met, because he/she knows standards from beginning.

✔ Feedback more objective—based on specific standards to be met rather than personal attributes.

✔ Favorably viewed—many think this is an important appraisal method—and is useful for performance development.

✔ If time can be spared to develop standards and use this method, it is a good/thorough process—which pays off because job goals/results clearly specified.

GENERAL CONS OF THE STANDARDS OF PERFORMANCE METHOD

✔ Requires significant time/effort to develop standards.

✔ Supervisors and employees must cooperate/talk/discuss standards, which need to be identified for each part of job.

✔ Must have clearly defined standards.

MANAGEMENT BY OBJECTIVE

Today, few people think of management by objectives (MBO) in relation to performance appraisal. Management by objectives is instead thought of as a form/style of management. Frequently, MBO is also associated with Peter Drucker (1954), who first used the phrase. However, Douglas McGregor (1957) was the person who provided the impetus to this concept, at least in terms of performance appraisal, although he never used the term.

MBO, at least in its purest form, requires the careful defining of goals, objectives, and priorities in a three-layered approach. Individuals and their supervisors establish personal goals, objectives, and priorities for a given time frame, usually a year. However, those must be linked to the unit/department's set of goals, and so forth, which in turn are linked to the overall organizational set. The personal goals are where one can see the link to performance appraisal.

Typically, the MBO process operates as follows:

✔ Senior management identifies overall organizational goals, objectives, and priorities.

✔ Unit/department heads in turn create their plans based on what is in senior management's plan.

✔ Unit level plans are coordinated to assure that none of senior management's plan is overlooked.

✔ Supervisors and staff are then expected to create individual plans.

✔ Supervisors work with staff members in making adjustments to individual goals, and so forth, to assure all tasks/activities identified by senior management have proper coverage. Supervisors and department heads engage in a similar process.

✔ Review sessions are performed frequently in order to gauge progress, identify problem areas, and adjust goals to meet changing circumstances and needs.

✔ End-of-cycle reviews identify areas of success and failure and attempt to identify ways to correct/address areas that failed or were less successful than desired.

Figure 4.10 (from Virginia), although not an MBO form, does represent a form that links individual performance to organizational/unit objectives. This particular example is a two-part form. Information contained within the work description/performance plan is completed at the beginning of the evaluation cycle and becomes the basis for the performance evaluation, which is completed at the end of the evaluation cycle. In such a way, elements identified in sections 19 and 20 early in the year are then "reported out" at year-end in sections 34 and 35.

One way in which boxes 19 and 20 could be completed for one job element for a library administrative assistant is:

% Time	19. Core Responsibilities	20. Measures for Core Responsibilities
45%	B. Coordinates and monitors all support services of the Associate Director, overseeing and controlling workload so the office runs smoothly, ensuring all deadlines are met and problems are handled and resolved promptly. Acts as liaison between administrative departments, individual faculty, campus and college-wide staff to ensure that all aspects of support duties are handled in compliance with the rules and regulations that govern the institution. Maintains copies of position descriptions and performance plans for all library personnel. Keeps records of materials for statistical purposes. Coordinates joint-unit travel arrangements. Pursues professional development and is actively involved in library, and college-wide committees and activities to ensure currency of all policies.	• Maintains library administrative files, budget files, IPEDS reports and other reports, and compiles and/or procures statistics as necessary. • Prepares accurate, neat, consolidated statistical reports and library annual reports in a timely fashion. • Coordinates responses to requests for library personnel information, including updates and revisions to the library telephone directory; submissions made in a timely fashion. • Maintains updated copies of position descriptions/performance plans for all classified staff, providing copies upon request. • Participates in professional development activities as appropriate.

This element would then be "reported out" in the accompanying performance evaluation as:

| B.

☒ Extraordinary Contributor

☐ Contributor

☐ Below Contributor | Ms. X continues to respond to requests for information and assistance in a timely manner. She revised the Library In-Service brochure and compiled statistics from the LRS In-Service, and her assistance with this activity was much appreciated. She maintains the Home Phone Directory, and other personnel listings, which she keeps up-to-date, pending information provided by unit supervisors. She has assisted other unit supervisors with completion of paperwork, so that deadlines were met. She communicated with Library staff on issues relating to archives and is encouraged to continue her work toward organizing the library archives. Personnel records are maintained in order and are filed promptly. She is commended for her work to complete staff meeting minutes in a timely fashion and is encouraged to continue these efforts. |

The "organizational objective" (box 15) is frequently the mission statement, which reinforces how the employee's work directly fits within the goals of the organization.

EMPLOYEE WORK PROFILE WORK DESCRIPTION/PERFORMANCE PLAN	Parts I, II, III, and IV are written or reviewed by the supervisor and discussed with the employee at the beginning of the evaluation cycle.

PART I—Position Identification Information	
1. Position Number:	2. Agency Name & Code; Division/Department:
3. Work Location Code:	4. Occupational Family & Career Group:
5. Role Title & Code:	6. Pay Band:
7. Work Title:	8. SOC Title & Code:
9. Level Indicator: ☐ Employee ☐ Supervisor ☐ Manager	10. FLSA Status: ☐Exempt ☐ Non-Exempt
Employees Supervised: Does employee supervise 2 or more employees (FTEs)? ☐Yes ☐ No	Exemption/Partial Exemption Test (if applicable):

11. Supervisor's Position Number:	12. Supervisor's Role Title & Code:
13. EEO Code:	14. Effective Date:

PART II—Work Description & Performance Plan

15. Organizational Objective:

16. Purpose of Position:

17. KSAs and or Competencies required to successfully perform the work (attach Competency Model, if applicable):

18. Education, Experience, Licensure, Certification required for entry into position:

% Time	19. Core Responsibilities	20. Measures for Core Responsibilities
%	A. Performance Management (for employees who supervise others)	Examples of Measures for Performance Management: • Expectations are clear, well communicated, and relate to the goals and objectives of the department or unit; • Staff receive frequent, constructive feedback, including interim evaluations as appropriate; • Staff have the necessary knowledge, skills, and abilities to accomplish goals; • The requirements of the performance planning and evaluation system are met and evaluations are completed by established deadlines with proper documentation; • Performance issues are addressed and documented as they occur. • Safety issues are reviewed and communicated to assure a safe and healthy workplace.
%	B.	
%	C.	
%	D.	

%	E.
%	F.

100%

21. Special Assignments	22. Measures for Special Assignments
G.	
H.	

Optional

23. Agency/Departmental Objectives	24. Measures for Agency/Departmental Objectives
I.	
J.	
K.	
L.	

ADDENDUM—ORGANIZATIONAL CHART

This page is printed separate from the remainder of the Work Description/Performance Plan because it contains confidential employee information.

PART III—Employee Development Plan
25. Personal Learning Goals
26. Learning Steps/Resource Needs

PART IV—Review of Work Description/Performance Plan		
27. Employee's Comments:	Signature: Print Name:	Date:

28. Supervisor's Comments:	Signature: Print Name:	Date:
29. Reviewer's Comments:	Signature: Print Name:	Date:

EMPLOYEE WORK PROFILE PERFORMANCE EVALUATION	Parts V, VI, VII, VIII, and IX are written or reviewed by the supervisor and discussed with the employee at the end of the evaluation cycle.

The following pages are printed separate from the remainder of the EWP because they contain confidential employee information.

PART V—Employee/Position Identification Information	
30. Position Number:	31. Agency Name & Code; Division/Department:
32. Employee Name:	33. Employee ID Number:

PART VI—Performance Evaluation	
34. Core Responsibilities—Rating Earned	**35. Core Responsibilities—Comments on Results Achieved**
A. ❏ Extraordinary Contributor ❏ Contributor ❏ Below Contributor	

B. ❑ Extraordinary Contributor

   ❑ Contributor

   ❑ Below Contributor

C. ❑ Extraordinary Contributor

   ❑ Contributor

   ❑ Below Contributor

D. ❑ Extraordinary Contributor

   ❑ Contributor

   ❑ Below Contributor

E. ❑ Extraordinary Contributor

   ❑ Contributor

   ❑ Below Contributor

F. ❑ Extraordinary Contributor

   ❑ Contributor

   ❑ Below Contributor

36. Special Assignments—Rating Earned	**37. Special Assignments—Comments on Results Achieved**

G. ❑ Extraordinary Contributor

   ❑ Contributor

   ❑ Below Contributor

H. ❑ Extraordinary Contributor

   ❑ Contributor

   ❑ Below Contributor

38. Agency/Department Objectives— Rating Earned	39. Agency/Department Objectives— Comments on Results Achieved
I. ❑ Extraordinary Contributor ❑ Contributor ❑ Below Contributor J. ❑ Extraordinary Contributor ❑ Contributor ❑ Below Contributor K. ❑ Extraordinary Contributor ❑ Contributor ❑ Below Contributor L. ❑ Extraordinary Contributor ❑ Contributor ❑ Below Contributor	

40. Other significant results for the performance cycle:

Part VII—Employee Development Results

41. Year-end Learning Accomplishments:

Part VIII—Overall Results Assessment and Rating Earned

- An employee receiving an overall rating of "Below Contributor" must have received at least one Notice of Improvement Needed/Substandard Performance form during the performance cycle.

- An employee who earns an overall rating of "Below Contributor" must be reviewed again within three months.

- An employee receiving an overall rating of "Extraordinary Contributor" must have received at least one Acknowledgment of Extraordinary Contribution form during the performance cycle. However, the receipt of an Acknowledgment of Extraordinary Contribution form does not guarantee an overall performance rating of "Extraordinary Contributor" for that performance cycle.

42. Overall Rating Earned

- ❑ Extraordinary Contributor

- ❑ Contributor

- ❑ Below Contributor

Part IX—Review of Performance Evaluation

43. Supervisor's Comments:	Signature: Print Name:	Date:
44. Reviewer's Comments: ·	Signature: Print Name:	Date:

45. Employee's Comments:	Signature:	Date:
	Print Name:	

EMPLOYEE WORK PROFILE
AGENCY OPTIONAL SECTIONS

Confidentiality Statement:

I acknowledge and understand that I may have access to confidential information regarding [employees, students, patients, inmates, the public]. In addition, I acknowledge and understand that I may have access to proprietary or other confidential information business information belonging to [Agency]. Therefore, except as required by law, I agree that I will not:

- Access data that is unrelated to my job duties at [Agency];
- Disclose to any other person, or allow any other person access to, any information related to [Agency] that is proprietary or confidential and/or pertains to [employees, students, patients, inmates, the public]. Disclosure of information includes, but is not limited to, verbal discussions, FAX transmissions, electronic mail messages, voice mail communication, written documentation, "loaning" computer access codes, and/or another transmission or sharing of data.

I understand that [Agency] and its [employees, students, patients, inmates, public], staff or others may suffer irreparable harm by disclosure of proprietary or confidential information and that [Agency] may seek legal remedies available to it should such disclosure occur. Further, I understand that violations of this agreement may result in disciplinary action, up to and including, my termination of employment.

_____   _____
Employee Signature   Date

Annual Requirements:		
Activity	**Current? If so, date completed?**	
Required In-Service or Other Training	❑ Yes _____Date	❑ No N/A
Valid Licensure/Certification/Registration	❑ Yes _____Date	❑ No N/A
Employee Health Update	❑ Yes _____Date	❑ No N/A

Essential Job Requirements (Indicate by each E = essential, M = marginal, or N/A)

Physical Demands and Activities:

___ Light lifting <20 lbs.	___ Standing	___ Sitting	___ Bending
___ Moderate lifting 20-50 lbs.	___ Lifting	___ Walking	___ Climbing
___ Heavy lifting 50 lbs.	___ Reaching	___ Repetitive motion	
___ Pushing/pulling	___ Other		

Emotional Demands: **Mental/Sensory Demands:**

___ Fast pace ___ Avg. pace	___ Memory	___ Reasoning	___ Hearing	
___ Multiple priorities	___ Reading	___ Analyzing	___ Logic	
___ Intense customer interaction	___ Verbal communication			
___ Multiple stimuli	___ Written communication			
___ Frequent change	___ Other			

(Courtesy of Commonwealth of Virginia)

Figure 4.10 Management by Objectives: Employee Work Profile, Virginia

Figure 4.11 is an illustration of what an MBO form might look like for a professional working in an archives or special collections environment, again drawing upon material in Goodson's (1997) book.

MBO GOALS FOR FISCAL YEAR 20__
SPECIAL COLLECTIONS/ARCHIVES

Name _____

Date _____

- Obtain/conduct one oral history.
- By 30 June, conduct three workshops on the use of primary resources making use of the Goldsmith collection.
- By 15 November, submit a proposal to NEH for the digitizing of the _____ collection.
- Increase visits to Special Collections by 12%.
- Add at least two collections to the department's Web page.
- Mount two exhibitions during the year.

Figure 4.11 Management by Objectives: MBO Goals for Fiscal Year

---

GENERAL PROS OF THE MANAGEMENT BY OBJECTIVE METHOD

- ✔ Provides structure for planning/recording performance standards.
- ✔ Encourages employee participation in setting standards.
- ✔ Employer and employee can "share thoughts" about job duties/priorities.
- ✔ Identifies what is expected in behaviors and results.
- ✔ Excellent for feedback; employee not surprised by feedback at end of period and has a chance to correct deficiencies before final review.
- ✔ Employee more likely committed to achieving goals; supervisor more likely committed to give support—better motivation.
- ✔ Feedback/appraisals more objective.
- ✔ Good for organizations or jobs undergoing change.
- ✔ Set of MBO statements can be prepared quickly because they focus on new accomplishments/activities.
- ✔ If productivity is down, setting goals/standards can bring it back up.

✔ When the same goals are used for all, the method lends itself to comparison, and distribution of rewards/promotion/job placement.

✔ Great for job definition—especially good when employee and employer work together to do so.

✔ If training involves setting goals/plan, then this is useful.

✔ Can be good in career planning—as goals are set, and specifics to accomplish are identified, this method can help make self-evaluation possible.

GENERAL CONS OF THE MANAGEMENT BY OBJECTIVE METHOD

✔ No numerical scores for comparing employees; different areas measured for different employees.

✔ Goals set for one employee may be easier or harder to achieve than those set for another.

✔ Not good for determining pay/rewards when goals/plans different for different employees.

✔ Subjective, can involve human error/bias.

✔ Implies a comparison between employees' performance, but doesn't define what to compare.

✔ Emphasis on small number of specifics—ignores effectiveness/ineffectiveness in other areas.

✔ Most objectives are often short-term—long-term tasks/effectiveness can be overlooked.

✔ Usually need a way to monitor ongoing objectives in addition to those that are more short-term in nature.

✔ Usually do not adequately address employee potential.

✔ Only partially good for feedback – the objectives identified are specific to performance, but the method does not really focus on methods/behavior used to obtain results/outcomes—hard to know what to change to get better results.

✔ Not always useful for training—focus on end rather than means.

SUMMARY

In writing about PA developments, Kenneth Wexley and Richard Klimoski (1984) used a heading "Person, Process, or Product Measures?" (p. 37). That heading sums up the content of this chapter rather well. Essays/narratives did and do tend to focus on personality traits more than anything else, and as such do not really provide much useful data from a behavioral point of view. When used in conjunction with other methodologies, however, they do provide a more well-rounded and individualized picture of a person's performance. Critical incidents tend to focus on processes/events. The last three methods reviewed in this chapter—direct index, standards of performance, and MBO—all emphasize products. A recent handbook by Edwards, Scott, and Raju (2003) provides an excellent overview of PA methods. Another useful book is Langdon's *Aligning Performance* (2000).

The primary message of this and the next two chapters (if not the entire text) is: There is no single "best" method of PA. Each has its pluses and minuses, as was seen throughout the chapter. However, when used in thoughtful combination, outcome-oriented assessment methods can be beneficial tools for both "management" and employees.

REFERENCES

Baker, Joe. 1988. *Causes of Failure in Performance Appraisal and Supervision.* New York: Quorum Books.

Drucker, Peter. 1954. *The Practice of Management.* New York: Harpers.

Edwards, Jack E., John C. Scott, and Nambury S. Raju. 2003. *The Human Resources Program—Evaluation Handbook.* Thousand Oaks, CA: Sage Publications.

Eichel, Evelyn, and Henry E. Bender. 1984. *Performance Appraisal: A Study of Current Techniques.* New York: AMA Research and Information Service.

Goodson, Carol F. 1997. *Complete Guide to Performance Standards For Library Personnel.* New York: Neal-Schuman.

Hagner, David, Ann Noll, and Lara Donovan. 2002. "Identifying Community Employment Program Staff Competencies: A Critical Incident Approach," *Journal of Rehabilitation* 68(1): 45–51.

Landy, Frank J., and James L. Farr. 1980. "Performance Rating," *Psychological Bulletin* 87(1): 72–107.

Langdon, Danny G. 2000. *Aligning Performance: Improving People, Systems, and Organizations.* San Francisco: Jossey-Bass/Pfeiffer.

McGregor, Douglas. 1957. "An Uneasy Look at Performance Appraisal," *Harvard Business Review* 35(3): 89–94.

Smither, James W. 1998. *Performance Appraisal: State of the Art in Practice.* San Francisco: Jossey-Bass.

Wexley, Kenneth, and Richard Klimosky. 1984. "Performance Appraisal: An Update," in *Research in Personnel and Human Resources Management,* edited by Kendrith Rowland and Gerald Ferris, 35–79. Greenwich, CT: JAI Press.

5 SCALING METHODS

Finding the balance between work traits (decision making and attendance, for example), work outcomes, and "job dimensions" (behaviors) was and is an ongoing challenge for human resource (HR) departments. In Chapter 1, I noted some of the challenges when I listed the beliefs about what performance appraisal (PA) can/should accomplish and the division between administrative and behavioral purposes. Another challenge, equally complex in character, is to have a PA process that is valid and reliable. Scaling is one broad category of techniques for assessing performance that emphasizes behaviors and results.

By way of definition, a job dimension/*behavior* would be ratee "resolves problem correctly without direction." A job dimension/*result* would be ratee's "quality and quantity of work." One of the advantages of scaling methods is they can be used with any job that one can define comprehensively. Although it seems simple at first, it is the definition issue that makes the development of appropriate scales so time consuming. The key to developing a useful scaling form is the use of "anchors." Anchors are statements—on the form—that indicate the degree to which the ratee exhibits the behavior. Graphic rating scales are widely used because they provide a good basis for feedback and selecting individuals for personnel actions. We will now review several of the most common types of scales, including weighted checklists, and Behaviorally Anchored Rating Scales.

WEIGHTED CHECKLISTS

The *weighted checklist* method requires the rater to actually observe the behavior in question; any behavior not observed is left blank on the form. Some organizations make use of a "hidden value" for each behavior; hidden in the sense neither rater nor ratee know the weight/value of the behaviors. Some readers may wonder why the value(s) are "secret." The reason is to help counteract possible bias (halo/horns effect). If the rater and ratee do not know the value, presumably they will focus on actual performance issues rather than achieving either more positive or negative results than is warranted by the performance.

Staff Performance Review

Employee's Name

Job Title

Unit

Supervisor's Name

	4 points	3 points	2 points	1 point	0 points
Quality of work	Work is consistently error free, thorough, neat, correct, logically organized and statistically accurate.	Work is nearly always error free (with a few very minor errors), thorough, neat, correct, logically organized and statistically accurate.	Work contains some acceptable errors that may require some review and editing by supervisor.	Work reflects errors that require careful review and correction by supervisor or partial reworking/revision.	Work is frequently not acceptable or usable.
Productivity	Exceeds expectations with regard to volume and deadlines; sets new goals upon completion of task; is cooperative, energetic and resourceful; develops new ideas or approaches to problems.	Meets deadlines and volume expectations; does more than is required; sets new goals, is constructive, energetic, and develops new ideas and approaches to problems.	Meets performance expectations of a reasonable proportion of deadlines; does what is required; sets new goals and develops new ideas or approaches to problems.	Performs below expectations, frequently misses deadlines and is not goal oriented.	Amount of work produced is unacceptable. Does not meet deadlines or goals.
Oral communication	Oral communication is exceptional; engages the recipient; concise, logical and clearly understandable.	Oral communication is consistently concise and understandable.	Meets expectations of oral communication in a concise and logical manner.	Oral communication is sometimes confusing and misunderstood by others.	Oral communication is not acceptable. Expressed ideas must be passed onto other personnel for presentation and understanding.
Knowledge of job	Has an exceptionally thorough grasp of all facets of the job; understands nuances of the university, the office, and the job.	Has a good grasp of the job; rarely requires assistance.	Has grasp of the job; requires minimal supervision; some opportunities for additional knowledge, experience or training do exist.	Needs improvement to perform the job; requires supervision and additional training.	Lacks knowledge and skills to effectively perform duties and responsibilities of the job. Training required may be excessive.

Figure 5.1 Hypothetical Weighted Checklist

Figure 5.1 is a sample of a hypothetical weighted checklist. Each of the four categories could have a "weight" assigned to it by HR and/or the department head and which is unknown to the person doing the rating or to the ratee. Table 5.1 illustrates how the "weighting" system *might* operate with a supervisor rating three staff members (A, B, and C). The rater and ratees would see the form (Figure 5.1) as it appears. HR or the department head might assign a weight of 3 for quality, 2 for productivity, 1 for communication, and 4 for knowledge of the job. The results are different between the weighted and unweighted values, which could make a difference in what personnel decision might be made: unweighted results, A = 12, B = 10, and C = 13; weighted results, A = 29, B = 26, and C = 35.

	4	3	2	1	0	Unweighted Value	Weighted Value	Weighted Total
Quality								
A	X					4	3	12
B			X			2	3	6
C		X				3	3	9
Productivity								
A		X				3	2	6
B		X				3	2	6
C	X					4	2	8
Communication								
A		X				3	1	3
B			X			2	1	2
C			X			2	1	2
Knowledge								
A			X			2	4	8
B		X				3	4	12
C	X					4	4	16
Table 5.1 Hypothetical Results of Weighted Checklist								

GENERAL PROS OF THE WEIGHTED CHECKLIST METHOD

✔ Good for feedback—specific observed behaviors are documented throughout the review cycle.

✔ Good for comparisons because of the presence of scores.

✔ Useful in collecting data to help in personnel decisions.

GENERAL CONS OF THE WEIGHTED CHECKLIST METHOD

✔ Supervisors unable to show employees their "real" score.

✔ No way to assess degree of positive or negative behaviors.

GRAPHIC RATING SCALES

The *Graphic Rating Scales* (GRS) method is one of the most widely employed PA formats. They are relatively easy to develop and have a high degree of acceptance by ratees as being valid. Eight of the sample forms that accompany this text incorporate some type of graphic rating scale. Most of them use a five- to nine-point scale with five points being the most common.

GRS is the oldest of the quantitative PA techniques, and according to Eichel and Bender (1984), almost 60% of the organizations contacted used some variation of GRS and believed it to be useful/important. Essentially, GRS forms contain a list of job performance qualities/behaviors for which the rater then selects a place along a continuum believed to represent the ratee's performance/behavior relative to each unit.

Figure 5.2 (Cerritos Community College), Figure 5.3 (City of Mountain View), and Figure 5.4 (North Carolina Department of Public Instruction) all illustrate some of the variations found in GRS forms. However, none of the three contain "anchors." (Note: The weighted checklist seen in Figure 5.1 is also a variation of GRS.) Scales can use either numbers or words; for example, 5/ "one of the best" to 1/ "one of the worst" or 1/ "below average," 2/ "average," 3/ "above average," 4/ "well above average," and 5/ "outstanding."

CERRITOS COMMUNITY COLLEGE DISTRICT
FACULTY EVALUATION CRITERIA FORM

Evaluatee: Area of Responsibility:

(print name)

Division/Area: Semester/Year:

Tenured: ☐

Probationary: ☐ First Contract (year one)   ☐ Third Contract (year three)

              ☐ Second Contract (year two)   ☐ Third Contract (year four)

Part-Time: ☐

*If the evaluatee is either a contract (probationary) or a part-time faculty member, this completed form must be forwarded with the appropriate Decision Sheet to the Personnel Services Office for placement in the evaluatee's personnel file.

I. KNOWLEDGE OF SUBJECT MATTER

a) Has a comprehensive knowledge of the subject/area of responsibility (degrees and experience)

    ☐ Satisfactory   ☐ Needs Improvement   ☐ Not Applicable

b) Maintains currency in the discipline/area of responsibility

    ☐ Satisfactory   ☐ Needs Improvement   ☐ Not Applicable

c) Is well informed on available materials

    ☐ Satisfactory   ☐ Needs Improvement   ☐ Not Applicable

d) Knows basic methods of testing, evaluating, test interpretation and assessment of students' skills, issues and concerns

    ☐ Satisfactory   ☐ Needs Improvement   ☐ Not Applicable

Comments:

II. TECHNIQUES OF INSTRUCTION AND/OR PERFORMANCE:

PRESENTATION/INTERACTION WITH STUDENTS/STUDENT EVALUATIONS

a) Adheres to content and objectives of course outline of record

[ ] Satisfactory [ ] Needs Improvement [ ] Not Applicable

b) Follows objectives appropriate to area of responsibility

[ ] Satisfactory [ ] Needs Improvement [ ] Not Applicable

c) Organizes lessons/activities to meet student needs

[ ] Satisfactory [ ] Needs Improvement [ ] Not Applicable

d) Presents the material and information with clarity

[ ] Satisfactory [ ] Needs Improvement [ ] Not Applicable

e) Shows interest in subject/area of responsibility

[ ] Satisfactory [ ] Needs Improvement [ ] Not Applicable

f) Makes effective use of time

[ ] Satisfactory [ ] Needs Improvement [ ] Not Applicable

Comments:

III. TECHNIQUES

a) Maintains an environment conducive to student learning/participation and development

[ ] Satisfactory [ ] Needs Improvement [ ] Not Applicable

b) Uses appropriate methods, materials and techniques responsive to needs of students and consistent with department/area practices

[ ] Satisfactory [ ] Needs Improvement [ ] Not Applicable

c) Uses appropriate methods of evaluation

[ ] Satisfactory   [ ] Needs Improvement   [ ] Not Applicable

Comments:

IV. EFFECTIVENESS OF COMMUNICATION

a) Demonstrates proficiency in written and oral English enabling clear, effective communication

[ ] Satisfactory   [ ] Needs Improvement   [ ] Not Applicable

b) Explains fully objectives, procedures and methods of evaluation

[ ] Satisfactory   [ ] Needs Improvement   [ ] Not Applicable

c) Explains fully alternatives, approaches, responsibilities and methods for success

[ ] Satisfactory   [ ] Needs Improvement   [ ] Not Applicable

d) Communicates interest in the subject matter/area of responsibility

[ ] Satisfactory   [ ] Needs Improvement   [ ] Not Applicable

e) Shows pose, confidence and occasional humor

[ ] Satisfactory   [ ] Needs Improvement   [ ] Not Applicable

f) Maintains appropriate role in students/faculty relationship

[ ] Satisfactory   [ ] Needs Improvement   [ ] Not Applicable

g) Manifests good rapport with students/staff

[ ] Satisfactory   [ ] Needs Improvement   [ ] Not Applicable

Comments:

V. ACCEPTANCE OF RESPONSIBILITY

a) Is punctual and meets scheduled obligations

[ ] Satisfactory   [ ] Needs Improvement   [ ] Not Applicable

b) Follows up on responsibilities to students and staff

☐ Satisfactory   ☐ Needs Improvement   ☐ Not Applicable

c) Maintains records satisfactorily

☐ Satisfactory   ☐ Needs Improvement   ☐ Not Applicable

d) Attends assigned meetings

☐ Satisfactory   ☐ Needs Improvement   ☐ Not Applicable

e) Is cooperative and willing to accept constructive criticism, when it is given in an appropriate manner

☐ Satisfactory   ☐ Needs Improvement   ☐ Not Applicable

Comments:

VI. ADDITIONAL COMMENTS

Signatures of Evaluation Team Members:

_____	_____	_____
Signature	Signature	Signature
_____	_____	_____
Date	Date	Date

NOTE: The evaluatee may respond in writing in respect to the accuracy, relevance, and completeness of the evaluation by submitting such written response to the Personnel Services office within 20 work-days following the date he/she receives the evaluation. Such response (if any) shall become a part of the evaluation report and be placed in the evaluatee's personnel file.

Acknowledgement of review/receipt by evaluatee (Evaluatee's signature does not necessarily imply agreement)

| _____ | _____ |
| Evaluatee's Signature | Date |

(Courtesy of Cerritos Community College)

Figure 5.2 Graphic Rating Scales: Faculty Evaluation Criteria Form, Cerritos Community College District

CITY OF MOUNTAIN VIEW
PERFORMANCE EVALUATION
MANAGEMENT AND PROFESSIONAL EMPLOYEES

Employee: _____   Evaluation Period: _____

Position/Dept.:_____   Date: _____

I.   Evaluation of Employee's Standards: *(See description of ratings.)*

	Exceptional	Very Good	Good	Needs Improvement
1. Customer Contact and Service Skills				
2. Interpersonal Effectiveness (Internal)				
3. Job Knowledge, Skills and Abilities				
4. Decision Making, Problem Solving				
5. Organizing and Planning				
6. Personal Responsibility and Initiative				
7. Communication Skills				
8. Flexibility and Adaptability				
9. Supervisory Skills (*If Applicable*)				

	Exceptional	Very Good	Good	Needs Improvement
Job-Specific Standards (Defined by Employee and Supervisor as part of annual goal setting)				
Comment:				

(Courtesy of Mountain View Public Library)

Figure 5.3 Graphic Rating Scales: Performance Evaluation, City of Mountain View

Function/Practice Planning and Facilitating Information Access and Delivery, Evaluation, and Use	Date of Conference/ Observation	Data Source if applicable	Comments
Creates and maintains a learning environment			
Works to provide flexible access to resources			
Organizes school library media facilities and resources			
Encourages use of print and electronic resources and services			
Works cooperatively with other libraries and agencies to share resources			
Adheres to and communicates copyright and ethical use of all resources			
Advocates for intellectual freedom			

Summary Comments:

Above Standard _____   At Standard _____

Below Standard _____   Unsatisfactory _____

(Permission to reprint granted by the Division of Instructional Technology, the North Carolina Department of Public Instruction)

Figure 5.4 Graphic Rating Scales: North Carolina Department of Public Instruction

GENERAL PROS OF THE GRAPHIC RATING SCALES METHOD

✔ Good for feedback, as specific behaviors/actions are documented.

✔ Helpful in choosing candidates for personnel action and for validating selection criteria.

✔ Provide information for status of human resources.

✔ Useful when they closely describe behaviors/results as outlined in organizational or departmental standards.

✔ Less time-consuming overall.

✔ Time-consuming but easy to draw up, but can then be used/adapted to many different jobs.

✔ Provides simple, quantitative results.

✔ Good for employee comparison.

✔ Considered dimensionally heterogeneous.

✔ Easy to do when supervisor has to evaluate many employees.

✔ Associated with high levels of user acceptability and face validity.

GENERAL CONS OF THE GRAPHIC RATING SCALES METHOD

✔ Usefulness depends on how accurately job aspects defined.

✔ Subject to human error.

✔ Do not provide as much depth as methods such as the essay.

✔ Some think adaptability to many different jobs makes this method too generic—not specific enough to be useful.

✔ Anchors, when used, are often ambiguous and are not behaviorally defined.

✔ Difficult to compare between raters (especially across different departments).

✔ Raters and employees can interpret anchors differently.

✔ Supervisors forced to evaluate all based on same dimensions/aspects of job.

✔ Cannot tailor to individual employees, specific job duties.

✔ One solution to this problem: include both core rating dimensions, plus an additional section that a supervisor can tailor .

BEHAVIORALLY ANCHORED RATING SCALES

Behaviorally Anchored Rating Scales, or BARS, are an updated version of graphic rating scales. P. C. Smith and L. M. Kendall (1963) usually receive credit for introducing the BARS concept. The use of behavioral statements (anchors), in theory, removes/reduces the ambiguity of GRS. (Compare GRS Figures 5.2 to 5.4 without anchors to Figure 5.5 [Hayward Public Library] and Figure 5.6 [Colorado State University] with anchors.) Use of anchors should improve the quality/accuracy of the ratings. Notice that the illustrated anchors are in terms of job behaviors, which makes it effective for feedback purposes. In Figure 5.6 (Colorado State University), the levels go from Level 1, the lowest category, to Level 4, the highest.

LIBRARY PAGE PERFORMANCE EVALUATION

Name: Date of Hire:

Date of Last Evaluation: Supervisor:

O = Outstanding   G = Good   A = Average   N = Needs Improvement   U = Unsatisfactory

TASK PERFORMANCE		O	G	A	N	U
Following : Directions	Demonstrates ability to learn new tasks, and retains instruction.					
Efficiency:	Speed and accuracy. Uses time wisely.					
Dependability:	Rarely needs reminding. Follows through with tasks.					
Initiative:	Seeks work assignments. Wants to learn.					
WORK HABITS						
Attendance:	Always at work or advises library of absence.					
Punctuality:	Always on time. Works to end of shift.					
Attitude:	Cooperation and courtesy towards public and staff.					
Conduct:	Keeps idle conversation to a minimum and does not disrupt the work of others.					

Special Assignments or Skills:	Outstanding	Good	Average	Needs Improvement	Unsatisfactory
1.					
2.					
3.					

Employer Comments:

Overall Evaluation: Outstanding   Good   Average   Needs Improvement   Unsatisfactory

(Library Page Evaluation Form provided Courtesy of the City of Hayward and the Hayward Public Library, Hayward, California)

Figure 5.5. BARS: Library Page Performance Evaluation: Hayward Public Library

BEHAVIORS ASSOCIATED WITH SUCCESS IN THIS POSITION

Check behaviors that will be evaluated. As with standards/goals/objectives, careful discussion of expectations should occur. Use the blank spaces to weigh job specific behavior:

E = Essential   I = Important   N = Not Applicable

Then, Please rate according to the following levels for performance:

_____

_____ **Job Knowledge/Potential**: Possesses knowledge of established policies and procedures. Possesses sufficient skills and knowledge to perform all parts of the job effectively and efficiently. Provides technical assistance to others and is consulted by others on technical matters. Pursues professional development. Displays innovation.
Level 1_____ Level 2_____ Level 3_____ Level 4_____

_____

_____ **Accountability**: Meets changing conditions and situations in work responsibilities. Accepts constructive criticism and suggestions and makes appropriate changes. Handles conflict in a constructive manner. Seeks solutions acceptable to all. Willingness to accept supervision. Can consistently be relied on to perform job. Seldom needs to be reminded. Is fully ready to work at beginning of work schedule and continues until workday is done. Does not abuse leave practices.
Level 1_____ Level 2_____ Level 3_____ Level 4_____

_____

_____ **Interpersonal Relations**: Maintains smooth working relations, support and respect of others. Demonstrates tact and diplomacy in negotiations or confrontations with others. Contributes to employee morale and motivations. Is accessible to others and responsive to their questions, needs and concerns. Supports and appreciates the diversity of coworkers, students, customers, and visitors. Shares information, credit and opportunities. Displays an appropriate balance between personal effort and team effort.

Level 1_____ Level 2_____ Level 3_____ Level 4_____

_____ **Communications**: Demonstrates effective listening skills. Uses appropriate language and terminology. Speaks in a manner that is understood, courteous and effective. Seeks and considers ideas from others on issues that affect them. Keeps supervisor and coworkers informed. Prepares written documents that are complete, clear and understandable. Is considerate of the communication skills of others.

Level 1_____ Level 2_____ Level 3_____ Level 4_____

_____ **Customer Service**: Provides prompt and friendly service to internal and external customers. Helps identify customer needs through courteous questioning and a sincere desire to be helpful. Follows up with customers, as appropriate, to insure satisfaction. Considers and recommends alternatives to costumers when needed.

Level 1_____ Level 2_____ Level 3_____ Level 4_____

_____ **Competence/Responsibility**: Maintains quality/quantity standards. Accepts responsibility for all areas of job. Uses time effectively with minimal errors. Completes work thoroughly in a reasonable amount of time. Meets or surpasses established goals. Works accurately, neatly, and attends to detail.

Level 1_____ Level 2_____ Level 3_____ Level 4_____

_____ **Motivation/Commitment**: Displays drive and energy in accomplishing tasks. Handles several responsibilities concurrently. Conveys positive and professional image of work unit to others. Puts forth extra effort when needed. Agrees to modify schedule or adapt Programs when necessary. Self-starter. Displays positive attitude in work assignments and interactions with others.

Level 1_____ Level 2_____ Level 3_____ Level 4_____

_____ **Problem Solving/Reasoning**: Recognizes and analyzes work related problems. Uses available resources to evaluate and recommend potential solutions. Ability to use good judgment to arrive at sound conclusions. Ability to take timely action.

Level 1_____ Level 2_____ Level 3_____ Level 4_____

_____ **Safety**: Aware of job safety procedures. Keeps abreast of changes in safety procedures. Practices safety work habits. Reports possible safety hazards to supervisor. Attends safety-training programs, as appropriate.

Level 1_____ Level 2_____ Level 3_____ Level 4_____

_____ **Supervision/Performance Management**: Employees supervised demonstrate productivity, competence and high morale. Provides supervision, feedback and training for employees. Utilizes employee's skills and abilities. Conducts performance Planning and evaluations for employees in a timely manner. Develops goals, objectives and deadlines and communicates them to employees. Resolves routine personnel issues or problems.

Level 1_____ Level 2_____ Level 3_____ Level 4_____

Additional benchmarked behaviors/competencies available on the web at:
www.colostate.edu/Depts/HRS/cpp/index.html

Level 1_____ Level 2_____ Level 3_____ Level 4_____

Level 1_____ Level 2_____ Level 3_____ Level 4_____

Level 1_____ Level 2_____ Level 3_____ Level 4_____

Training and Development Programs

_____

_____

_____

(Courtesy of Colorado State University, Human Resource Services, Fort Collins, Colorado)

Figure 5.6. BARS: Colorado State University

One drawback of BARS, in addition to the time it takes to create them, is that as jobs change revisions are necessary, as frequently job behaviors are added and/or cease to exist for a position. Typically, developing a BARS assessment form involves six steps:

- Identify job dimensions.
- Identify appropriate behavioral anchors.
- Assign anchors to job dimensions.
- Assign a value to anchors.
- Create a rating scale.
- Test scale using several raters all rating the same job. It should be noted that raters should *not* be the ones who developed the form.

When raters use BARS as intended and they select the appropriate behavior level, the technique is very effective. However, the meanings are clear to a rater as they will know how each selection will impact the final overall assessment. Thus, the technique can do nothing about rater lenience or harshness. A variation of the technique to counter this issue is to use a "mixed-standard scale." This method takes the BARS format and, rather than presenting the material in a scaled form, it mixes all the items for all job dimensions. Raters then respond to each item indicating whether the ratee's performance is better, worse, or equal to the behavior described. The final results are compiled by HR where the scales are "reassembled" in the scaled format. Because of the time and effort involved, the mixed method is not often used.

GENERAL PROS OF THE BARS METHOD

✔ Reduces ambiguity—rater helps develop scales; using their own terminology—resulting in more careful/honest evaluation.

✔ Specific feedback for employee—the method provides an outline of expected and discouraged behaviors and indicates where the employee is weak/strong.

✔ Results can be expressed numerically, so data is useful for making comparisons of employees and validating selection criteria.

✔ Focus on behavior rather than personality traits.

✔ Relatively good for determining pay/rewards and placement/promotion—defines the kinds of performance to be rewarded and can be used for many employees doing same/similar job.

✔ Can help in forming job descriptions/definitions—defines effective/expected behavior for individual jobs.

✔ Good when employees know what behaviors are being evaluated.

✔ Good in training/development—identify specific job behaviors to focus on.

✔ Relatively useful for career planning/guidelines/direction—provides feedback about behavior.

✔ Raters are required to think of specific behaviors in order to determine effectiveness, not subjective impressions or vague recollections.

✔ Helps reveal/determine performance requirements for a job—then provides measure of how effectively tasks performed.

✔ Reduces human error, according to some studies.

✔ Useful in getting raters to give accurate ratings, because it gives a fair and accurate portrayal of what is required on the job; also provides concrete benchmarks for evaluation.

✔ Stronger method of assessment in regards to qualitative criteria.

✔ Negative feedback easier to present to an employee; also more specific.

✔ Helps improve communication between employer and employee—expectations clearly defined.

✔ Provides incoming candidates with good idea of expectations of job.

GENERAL CONS OF THE BARS METHOD

✔ If using different forms for different job descriptions/levels, new scales often need to be developed—this process can be time consuming.

✔ Even though superior to other scales, there is a high cost in terms of time and effort to put BARS together successfully.

✔ Large task to develop, requires expertise.

✔ Need to be worded clearly, widely accepted/interpreted the same way.

✔ Scales often need continuous updates to remain relevant.

✔ Majority of employers say BARS is not useful or applicable in their companies—thus it is not widely used.

✔ No matter how BARS dimensions are worded, still allows for human error and bias.

✔ Like graphic scales, rater knows how to use scale to get desired rating/personnel actions.

✔ Not very useful for human resources planning/assessment—results are based on specific jobs, not much room for generalization across jobs.

✔ Can be good for feedback, but some think it is limited—results only generally describes employee's actual behavior.

✔ Often hard to equate actual behaviors with scale behaviors to determine how to rate—scale anchors sometimes can be too specific.

✔ Rater has to determine that this is the kind of behavior employee would take.

✔ Can be an awkward judgment.

✔ BARS not necessarily more effective at rating than other methods.

✔ Still susceptible to bias, leniency, inconsistency between raters.

✔ Still hard to determine the real value of BARS—has potential, but still unknown/undetermined by critics.

SUMMARY

Behavioral-based assessment methods are moderately good for decisions relating to pay/rewards, promotion, and job definitions as well as in providing feedback and career planning. Though they are of little help to HR in terms of staff planning, they are valuable when used for decisions regarding training and development. As noted in Chapter 4, a truly effective PA system employs a mix of methods: behavioral and outcome oriented. Two useful books that provide additional information about the methods in this and other methodology chapters are Bacal (2004) and Edwards, Scott, and Raju (2003). The latter title contains detailed information on a variety of evaluation/assessment programs.

REFERENCES

Bacal, Robert. 2004. *Manager's Guide to Performance Reviews.* New York: McGraw-Hill.

Edwards, Jack E., John C. Scott, and Nambury S. Raju. 2003. *The Human Resources Program—Evaluation Handbook.* Thousand Oaks, CA: Sage Publications.

Eichel, Evelyn, and Henry Bender. 1984. *Performance Appraisal: A Study of Current Techniques.* New York: AMA Research and Information Service.

Smith, Patricia C., and Lorne M. Kendall. 1963. "Retranslation of Expectations: An Approach to the Construction of Unambiguous Anchors for Rating Scales," *Journal of Applied Psychology* 47(2): 149–155.

6 RANKING METHODS

When in the midst of the performance appraisal (PA) process, one often forgets that there is a difference, at least in terms of PA, between rating (scaling) and ranking. When *rating* a person during a PA session, the comparison is, or should be, drawn between the individual's performance and a performance standard. (As noted at a number of points throughout this book, having fully developed performance standards *is* important.) *Ranking*, on the other hand, compares an individual's performance with that of their work colleagues within the unit. It is a method that is better suited to meeting the administrative side of PA than it is to addressing behavioral issues.

Many Europeans think the United States has a fixation with ranking, and to a degree they are correct. It is difficult to pick up a daily newspaper that does not contain at least one story that does not mention rank or rankings—especially if it has a sports section. The popular press is full of the "Top Ten" this or that covering everything from places to live, doughnut shops, best school districts, bestsellers, and almost anything else one can think of. Though we have little difficulty in ranking job applicants, when it comes to ranking people one works with, there are problems.

Because job applicants probably never will know if they were first of fifteenth, one does not have to be *as* ready to justify ranking. In the workplace, ratees quickly determine who was number one and who was last. Having clear-cut standards that are observable becomes essential in ranking workplace situations. Some people refer to it as a "rank and yank" process (Sears and McDermott, 2003).

Ranking is a procedure that uses an ordinal scale that sets limits on the rater. Normally, there can only be one ratee per rank. This can be a challenge when the rater thinks there are good ratees but none that should be in the first rank. One concern for raters and ratees is "employers who force-rank generally align employee evaluations with predetermined performance distribution percentages. Evaluators end up making determination a person-versus-person basis rather than person to established standards basis" (Sears and McDermott, 2003: 7). Robert Bacal (2004) suggested that though ranking contributes to employee competition and perhaps increases productivity, its downsides are important to consider. "But the disadvantages of such a system…are almost always going to outweigh any performance improvement" (Bacal, 2004: 62).

In a simple ranking system, a supervisor must determine how each subordinate performs from the very best to very worst. When the number of ratees is small, the task may be relatively simple; however, even if there are only four or five, the fact there can be no ties can create challenges. There can only be one person per "slot." Even with five individuals, questions can arise. For example, let's assume a rater ranked five people as follows:

1. Jackson
2. Peterson
3. Anderson
4. Erickson
5. Evans

We can assume that Jackson is the "best" performer and that Evans is the "worst." But what we do not know is how much difference there is between the two and is Evans' work acceptable. Such rankings do not work well when the work unit staff were selected because they were all top performers. It is rather like ranking astronauts; yes one can probably do it, but the fact of the matter is they are all highly capable people and more than able to do the job. Simple ranking differentiates staff members but does not provide information about by *how much* do they differ.

When the number of employees undergoing PA is large, it is usually easy to sort out the "tops" from the "bottoms." However, handling the midrange performers can be *very* difficult. How does one determine, with some degree of accuracy, who is ranked 9th, 10th, or 11th out of, say 14 people? The answer is, with great difficulty. It is easier when there are quantifiable performance standards. Lacking those, the rater will be hard pressed to give solid justifications for the middle ranks. This is especially difficult when the review(s) become a matter of mediation or a court case.

The process clearly needs to look at overall performance rather than segments, except in special circumstances such as work teams that are not ongoing, in order to avoid the "halo" and "horns" effect (see pp. 19–20). Having multiple rankers improves the validity and reliability of the rankings. However, that requires the rankers to have equal observation time, which few, if any, organizations can put into place.

Clearly, major shortcomings of ranking in a library setting are staff size and job types. Few libraries have staffs large enough, 100 or more employees, to have more than 2 people performing an identical job.

Further Thought

- Do you think there is a psychological difference in the PA meeting, both for the rater and ratee, when a review is based on ranking? For rating?
- As a ratee, would you have more or less difficulty accepting a rater's ranking of your performance?
- As a rater, how comfortable are/would you be in having sessions in which you must compare one ratee with all the other ratees and discuss that assessment with each person?

(Note: Remember a job is not the same as a position; one job may have more than one position assigned to it.) When there are only two or three people performing a job, formalized ranking makes little sense. One area where it might be useful is with part-time staff such as pages/shelvers. (It is interesting to note that only one library, Hayward Public Library, that contributed appraisal forms had a PA system in place for its pages.)

GENERAL PROS OF THE RANKING FORMAT

✔ Very good for "order-of-merit" lists, especially when more than one supervisor ranks the same group.

✔ Can help keep appraisals consistent with actual performance.

✔ Supervisors often find this method easy to use—popular method.

✔ Helps minimize human error—including leniency.

✔ Only a small number rated at the top/outstanding.

✔ Helpful in putting employees in performance categories—supervisors do not have to put specific number in each or use all categories.

✔ Helpful in finding inconsistencies in ratings/narrative descriptions and finding human error in other methods.

✔ Simple and natural way to evaluate performance.

✔ Ideal for rewards/pay determination when people rewarded differentially according to performance.

✔ Good for determining who should be eligible for promotion—easily identifies best performers.

✔ Can sometimes be good for human resources planning—direct comparison of employees clearly identifies levels of performance—needs to be combined with other absolute methods for best results, though.

✔ Helpful in career planning/development—employees see where they compare to other employees in line for a job/position—provides realistic look at employee's prospects.

✔ Easy to implement—no form that needs to be adapted to a variety of different jobs/categories.

GENERAL CONS OF THE RANKING FORMAT

✔ Impossible to determine how much difference exists between employees on the list.

✔ Not useful for comparing employees in different job groups.

✔ Not useful for giving feedback to employees.

✔ Can lead to conflict.

✔ Legally, feedback is needed in appraisal, so this method cannot be used alone.

✔ Specifics of behavior/performance not measured.

✔ Does not give an accurate picture of the diversity of human resources, skills, and abilities that are available in the workforce of the organization.

✔ Does not provide measure of where development is needed.

✔ Can identify candidates for training, but does not specify areas where training is needed.

✔ More difficult with larger number of employees to rank—tends to produce less valid results.

✔ Only useful for administrative purposes.

✔ Cannot measure performance absolutely—those high on the list may only be moderate performers or those low on list may still be high performers if all on the list are high performers.

✔ Subject to bias.

✔ Not useful for job definition.

✔ Can measure hierarchy of employees, but not degree of skill.

✔ No way of determining values of workers in acceptable/unacceptable performance levels.

✔ Although intended to focus on overall performance, it becomes tedious to repeatedly rank same group of employees in various dimensions/areas of job performance.

✔ If job content frequently changes, list can become outmoded.

✔ Prevents leniency, but leniency not always an inaccurate measure of performance.

PAIRED COMPARISON

The paired comparison method addresses some of the issues of the simple ranking approach. Here, the rater/supervisor must rank every possible combination of ratees. The process can simply be done by the rater or, as is often the case, either someone from human resources (HR) or an outside consulting firm prepares cards for each pair of employees. That person then "administers" the process by showing the rater each pair in a deliberately random manner. The process covers all appropriate combinations of work activities so the cards are used several times. Cards are shuffled so that the same name is not always on top of the pair. The supervisor/rater then picks or identifies which of the pair has better job performance in a given activity. A personnel specialist counts how many times each employee is picked and then ranks employees by these numbers.

An advantage of this process is that it is more systematic than basic simple ranking; employees are compared more directly to one another. Sometimes, employees are compared generally (with all staff regardless of job category), but more often the process is for specific job areas/criteria. With specific categories, in some cases the criteria apply to both employees equally, and because the supervisor can so indicate this, both persons can be given the same "value" for that item. Supervisors are usually required to consider overall performance and make relative judgments on each pair.

THINGS TO CONSIDER IN ARRANGING PAIRS

- All employees should be about equal in where they appear (right/left or top/bottom) to help prevent bias.
- In a long list of pairings, a name should alternate from one side to another.
- No person to appear in two pairs in a row and should be as far apart as possible.

Scoring results is complex when outsiders handle the process. When doing it on a more informal basis, one can simply assign a value for each ranking, say five for a "better," a three for a "tie," and one for a "poorer." Using the earlier simple ranking of five people (p. 126), one might get the following results from a paired assessment on six criteria.

	Better [X5]	Tie [X3]	Poorer [X1]	Total
Jackson	5		1	26
Peterson	4		2	22
Anderson	4	1	1	24
Erickson	2	1	3	16
Evans	1		5	10

In the above example, the paired result is just slightly different from the simple ranking, and assuming all five are performing competently, the variation could be insignificant. However, the gap between the top three and bottom two might suggest that Erickson and Evans may need additional attention (training, motivation, and so forth).

There is a danger in putting a numerical value on something that is a subjective assessment. When the criteria assessed are all quantitative in character, there is really no issue. However, lacking solid performance standards (error rates, quantity produced, and so forth), the "value" can take on more significance than it should.

The formalized process of calculating values is very complex, as noted above, and well beyond the scope of this book. An interested reader can find a detailed description of the process in J. P. Guilford's book *Psychometric Methods* (Guilford, 1964).

PROS OF THE PAIRED COMPARISON RANKING METHOD

✔ Can develop interval scales not possible with basic ranking.

✔ Supervisors find this method relatively easy/natural.

✔ Have often done this before, informally.

✔ Same forms can be used for multiple job titles.

✔ Reduced subjectivity somewhat.

See also discussion of "Ranking" above (many of the same pros/cons also apply to paired comparison).

CONS OF THE PAIRED COMPARISON RANKING METHOD

✔ Larger number of employees makes this difficult.

✔ Like ranking, no absolutes—hard to determine exact performance level.

✔ One solution: sometimes throw in a standard instead of a name (e.g., Nancy vs. Outstanding)—standards given a rank along with employees.

✔ *See also* discussion of "Ranking" above (many of the same pros/cons also apply to paired comparison).

FORCED DISTRIBUTION

As stated earlier, one of the shortcomings of simple ranking or even paired rankings is they do not identify *how much* variation exists between the individuals so ranked. The *forced distribution* method addresses that problem. A rater must divide ratees into a specified number of categories. Most often, five categories are developed, based on the "normal curve" concept. In some cases, the rater *must* place a preset percentage of ratees into a category. Sometimes, the categories just have labels such as "outstanding," "above average," "average," "below average," and "unacceptable." Regardless of the category label chosen, the assumption is the raking should reflect the bell-shaped curve, with percentages assigned as 10%, 20%, 40%, 20%, 10%.

Because the method rests on the assumption of the normal curve, forced distribution has limited validity when applied to groups of less than 30 people. That being the case, one can see that it has almost no value in library PA assessment. This is because there are few library supervisors who have thirty or more direct reports. Baker (1988: 97) suggested that "the rankings developed by this method should be considered *rough* estimates rather than true measures of performance" (emphasis added). Another issue that arises is due to the nature of a group selected because of their great skill, knowledge, or performance level. These individuals should not be forced into a "normal curve" system. I have worked at an institution where HR required this approach, even for small groups. In my case, there were just 14 people to evaluate, well below the recommended "threshold" for this method. Nevertheless, each year it was expected that I rate one employee in the bottom 10%. There was one year when that was easy to do because of nonperformance and a dismissal, but most years this system only caused staff unhappiness, as it should.

The institution where I experienced a variation of the forced distribution/ranking system did not employ the method as a means of selecting people for dismissal as is sometimes the case in a for-profit setting ("Rank and Yank" as noted earlier in this chapter). Sears and McDermott (2003) noted forced ranking probably "played its own small part in the company's demise (p. 8)." The company they were referring to was Enron, an organization that made extensive use of forced ranking. It may be a technique to use if forced with the unpleasant task of laying off personnel if there are no other guidelines such as contracts or seniority to guide decision making. Raters must keep in mind, even with sound standards against which one measures performance, the number assigned *is* subjective and the middle groupings are most suspect. *HR Focus* had two articles in 2002 that looked at forced rankings (February and April 2002).

PROS OF THE FORCED DISTRIBUTION METHOD

✔ Addresses the problem of leniency (too many staff get the top rating).

✔ Reduces socially desirable response (present rater with equally socially desirable options rather than just one).

✔ Sends a clear message that raters must be more candid in their ratings.

CONS OF THE FORCED DISTRIBUTION METHOD

✔ More rough estimate of performance.

✔ Conformity to normal curve not always true.

✔ Categories imply there is a big degree of difference between employees' performance; in reality, the difference may not be that big.

✔ Difficult to place people in categories and in pre-established percentages.

✔ Rater and ratee acceptance is very low.

SUMMARY

Comparisons/ranking methods are especially useful for administrative personnel decision-making situations such as promotions and staff reductions. There have been times when I have used ranking informally, not because it was requested by HR, but because it helped me make recommendations regarding salary increases when confronted with a fixed pool of funds to distribute. One time I tried to get the department heads (the direct supervisors) to make the recommendations with no success. They were too uncomfortable to recommend person *x* get this amount and person *y* that amount—they wanted everyone to get the same increase. That would be possible to do, but it would also make the label "merit increase" meaningless. There was a minimum base percentage for satisfactory performance—a type of cost-of-living increase. Using unit head feedback both at the time of having to make the decision and from comments about staff throughout the year, I used the paired comparison method to make the recommendations. This process does take a substantial amount of time, but it at least gives one the sense of being as fair as possible and recognizing good performance.

One clear drawback of these methods is the high degree of subjectivity when there are few, if any, clear performance standards in place. Another limiting factor is that ranking is not very helpful with the behavioral aspects of PA. Saying "I ranked you below others in the department" really does not tell the person what needs to be done to improve. Furthermore, by the time the rater starts to explain the way of the ranking, the ratee has usually stopped listening

Comparisons/ranking methods are in fact used infrequently in most organizations. Evelyn Eichel and Henry Bender (1984) reported on a survey they conducted on the types of methods used for PA. Out of ten methods available, simple ranking came in 6th place (41.7% of the organizations indicated they used it), whereas paired comparisons ranked 10th (with only 16.3% usage). The low use is largely due to concerns about validity and reliability if there is a formal (legal) challenge to the ranking.

REFERENCES

Bacal, Robert. 2004. *Manager's Guide to Performance Reviews.* New York: McGraw-Hill.

Baker, Joe. 1988. *Causes of Failure in Performance Appraisal and Supervision.* New York: Quorum Books.

Eichel, Evelyn, and Henry E. Bender. 1984. *Performance Appraisal: A Study of Current Techniques.* New York: AMA Research and Information Service.

Guilford, J. P. 1964. *Psychometric Methods,* 2nd ed. New York: McGraw-Hill.

HR Focus. 2002. "Forced Rankings: Tough Love or Overkill?" 79(2): 11–12.

———. 2002. "Kinder, Gentler Reviews: A Forced Ranking Backlash?" 79(4): 7–8.

Sears, David, and Don McDermott. 2003. "The Rise and Fall of Rank and Yank," *Information Strategy: The Executive's Journal* 19(3): 6–11.

7 TEAM METHODS

Performance appraisal has been an individual matter for most of its history. Though individual performance is still a significant issue, teams are increasingly becoming a factor for all types of organizations. (It is interesting to note that none of the libraries contacted for copies of their appraisal forms indicated they had any form for assessing team performance.)

Starting in the early 1990s, an ever increasing number of both the largest and smallest companies in the United States started making use of teams. There are many factors driving the shift from individual to team-centered work. Perhaps the origin of this shift was the performance of the Japanese economy during the 1970s and 1980s and Deming's (1986) and Juran's (1989) work in the area of "quality management." In any event, customer satisfaction as well as effective and efficient use of resources became significant for U.S. organizations. There was also a "flattening" and "downsizing" of a number of organizations, which called for the remaining staff to become more flexible and able to handle a variety of duties. That in turn suggested that cross-trained staff and work teams would be appropriate approaches. More often than not, it also resulted in the creation of self-directed teams responsible for deciding how to accomplish tasks.

A "team" in a business/organizational sense is a nebulous term that has had a number of definitions. In one sense, every organization is a team, as there is always a need for worker interaction and coordination of activities. One of the better definitions of a *work team* as we use the term today is from Guzzo and Dickson (1996): "A 'work group' is made up of individuals who see themselves and who are seen by others as a social entity, who are interdependent because the tasks they perform as members of a group, who are embedded in one or more larger social systems, and who perform tasks that affect others" (pp. 308–309). Perhaps adding that workgroups/teams develop a shared commitment to one another and the tasks the group/team carries out helps distinguish such groupings from traditional work units. Another difference is teams, in the current management usage, are empowered to make many decisions regarding how and when work gets done as well as who does it.

For all their advantages, teams do present human resources (HR) and the traditional peformance appraisal (PA) process with some basic challenges. The obvious fundamental challenge is the typical PA process focuses on the individual not a group. Looking at the PA literature, one finds that material on team appraisal is almost nonexistent prior to 1992. Thus, efforts to try to reconcile how to reward groups rather than individuals are relatively recent.

Another challenging factor is the permanency of a team, which can vary from a few weeks to an indefinite period. Special project teams of short duration (4 to 6 weeks) are relatively easy to handle in a traditional PA process through the use of a narrative. Longer term teams are more challenging, even when they last for less than a full PA cycle, because in most cases some aspects of each team member's "real job" does not get done. In the case of a short-term team consisting of existing staff members, there can be concerns regarding what part(s) of the "real job" should receive limited attention because of the team project. Though their supervisors are well aware of the need for the team project, some resentment may arise due to the "lost" work for the team members' home unit. The resentment can come out in the appraisal process when the rater uses the "lost work" as a reason to slightly downgrade the ratee.

With any team, there is always the question of how to assess its efforts beyond "did it or didn't it accomplish its goal/purpose." If it was considered a successful team, should all team members receive equal "credit," whatever that might be? Even more difficult, does everyone share equally in any failure of a team? Richard Reilly and Jack McGourty (1998) suggest using a three-pronged assessment program for teams: competencies, individual performances, and team performance. By competencies, they are referring to "a collection of behaviors that contribute to the performance of organizationally valued work" (p. 249). Just having the proper combination of competencies on the team does not ensure team success, but lacking them does ensure failure.

Like any other organizational activity, team tasks require a careful definition of what the team is to accomplish, what skills, knowledge, and abilities are necessary to achieve success, and how the task(s) relate to overall organizational goals and objectives.

Research in the United States has demonstrated that one issue in implementing self-directed teams in organizations for the first time is *competition*. The traditional PA system with its focus on the individual reinforces the concept of individual competition. In an organization that has made regular use of PA rankings, the environment is one with relatively low levels of trust, little emphasis on cooperation, and high competitiveness. Essentially, rankings and other traditional PA techniques pit individuals against one another for salary increases, promotions, and other rewards.

Thus, simply creating teams in an organization does not guarantee desired outcomes would be accomplished. This is especially true if there is no change in existing PA methods. There is, however, a need to appraise both team and individuals within the team and in ways that reward cooperation among team members. Examining the system/process for barriers to cooperation accomplishes this goal.

There are a number of factors/issues that characterize effective teams. Some or all of them can be incorporated into a team assessment system. One factor is team members must understand and accept the concept of *mutual accountability*. That is, they all are accountable for both successes and failures of the team, even when only one or two members were the most significant factor(s) in the outcome. For most team members, this may be the most challenging aspect of being part of a team. In the United States, schools and workplaces, although shifting toward team/collaborative work, still are more or less based on individual effort and accountability. This factor complicates the team assessment process, as learning to work as a part of a team is a behavior that must be learned and developed. Careful thought must be given for how to address it early in the team's development—well before any PA assessment takes place.

One way that mutual accountability is more acceptable is when all the members "buy into" the common purpose(s)/goal(s) for the team. Here, as is true for accountability, early training/team development activities are one of the keys to having a successful team.

Another key to team success is *consensus decision-making*. Consensus decision-making requires substantial and free team discussions. Encouraging open and frank team discussions may prove to be challenging, if the team selection process did not take personality issues into account. Some level of "conflict" is likely to arise in the process of reaching a consensus. There are three modes for handling conflict: fight, flight, and flow. Some understanding of team members' typical mode for handling conflict will assist the team supervisor(s)/leader(s) both in creating a functional group and in assessing performances.

Fighters see issues/ideas as black and white, right and wrong, and so forth, and whatever the position the fighter takes is the "correct" one. They frequently push for an "I win, you lose" outcome. This can be a serious barrier to consensus decision-making, as frequent conflict can diminish team effectiveness as team members acquiesce to this behavior. *Flighters* represent the opposite approach; they much prefer "comfort" over fighting for a position/view. They typically "give in" rather than take a stand, even when they have evidence to support their position. This approach is also problematic for good team performance, as important ideas may fail to receive proper attention. "Going with the *flow*" is what teams need, especially when that means working through issues to reach a consensus and then working with that decision/plan/process/and so forth.

Recently, Clancy and colleagues (2003) conducted an interesting study on team decision-making. The research group found there was a significant improvement in performance when the team leader used an "intention" rather than "command" style of decision making. Their results match up with the generally held position that mutual decision-making is what teams should strive to achieve. Essentially, the "intention" approach means the team leader communicates intentions to the team member, who in turn decides what actions and behaviors need to be taken to accomplish the intentions.

A successful team must have good conflict management skills, either through the team leader or from the team's supervisory staff. As noted above, there needs to be recognition of team members' individualized preferred mode of handling conflict. Additionally, long-term teams, in order to be successful, must develop team conflict management strategies rather than depending on outside intervention.

Building mutual respect and support is fundamental to the success of long-term teams. Establishing this takes time and effort. The "time" factor can become a problem during the early stages of the team's existence. Frequent team meetings are a hallmark of effective teams and is one of the crucial ways of developing mutual respect and support. This has implications for PA in that during the early years of a team's existence, assessment should focus more on team building factors than on productivity.

Once mutual respect and support exist within a team, mutual goal setting, mutual planning, and task assignment becomes easier and more rapid. There will also be more willingness to accept peer assessments as valid and something to act upon.

Essentially, the areas of concern in the PA process for teams, beyond productivity, are trust, open/honest communication, conflict management, mutual decision-making, problem solving, and so forth, and collaboration. The team should view their activities as mutually supportive win–win processes rather than individual successes/failures.

Another step to ensure that teamwork barriers are minimal is to use PA methods that do not emphasize the individual. Even "small" rewards such as "employee of the month" can cause teamwork problems. Robert Crow (1995: 53) listed eleven problem areas for effective teamwork.

- Institutionalized competition is any system which forces one person or group to lose so that another can win. This includes:
- Performance appraisals that are rated numerically and used for rankings . . .
- Forced distributions . . .

- Pay for performance . . .
- Employee of the month/year programs . . .
- Contests between shifts, and departments . . .
- Poorly defined internal promotion policies . . .
- Ranking plants best to worst . . .
- Quotas . . .
- Profit centers . . .
- Managing by the numbers . . .

Developing team-based competencies that draw on middle/senior management, team leader(s), team members, team customers both internal and external, and other "stakeholders'" ideas/assessments serves a sound basis for designing team assessment programs. Internal customers' assessment is a very important concept for continually improving internal cross-departmental processes and productivity. Once agreed upon, the competencies can be linked to team behaviors/processes/activities. Ideally, there is a rating of the importance of the various competencies to each behavior/process. Figure 7.1 represents a hypothetical database management team in a library. It also illustrates the relative importance of the competencies for each of the behaviors.

Behavior	Selecting Databases	Negotiating Licenses/ Contracts	Handling Service Calls	Assessing User Needs	Assessing Database Usage
Competency					
Communication	3	4	2	5	1
Knowledge of databases	5	3	4	2	1
Knowledge of networking	3	1	5	2	4
Knowledge of contracts	2	5	1	4	3
Decision making	4	5	1	3	2
Self-direction	5	1	4	3	2
Fiscal management	4	1	2	3	5
(5 = highest importance; 1 = lowest importance)					

Figure 7.1 Hypothetical Database Management Team Competencies

Developing and applying performance standards for teams is just as important as it is for individuals. Table 7.1 illustrates some performance standards for a hypothetical database management team. With such information, it becomes possible to create an assessment process that can cover both the entire team and its individual team members.

Database selection

- Feedback from users and staff incorporated into selection process.
- Selection decisions based on local trial of database/product.
- Selection decisions will balance fiscal and service issues.

Negotiating licenses/contracts

- Issues of library responsibility/liability of end-user usage deleted from license/contract.
- All licenses/contracts reviewed and changes negotiated prior to final selection decision.
- Usage of database material for Interlibrary Loan (ILL) purposes negotiated, if necessary

Remote access service calls

- Service calls responded to within 10 minutes during service hours
- Ninety percent of service calls resolved during first callback.
- User complaints less than 1 per 200 calls.

Assessing user needs

- Annual survey of user satisfaction performed.
- Four or more demonstration sessions of possible new products/services held annually.
- Four or more database usage training sessions held annually.

Assessing databases

- Usage data for database review analyzed before each renewal.
- Each database's coverage reviewed to determine additions/deletions in coverage.
- Databases compared annually to determine degree of overlap.

Table 7.1 Performance Standards: Database Management Team

In *When Teams Work Best*, LaFasto and Larson (2001) identified two categories of factors that differentiate successful and unsuccessful team members: working knowledge and teamwork. Within the *knowledge* category they included two factors: experience and problem-solving ability. They also grouped four factors under the *teamwork* heading: openness, supportiveness, personal style, and action orientation. Using their factors and the hypothetical database management team material seen earlier, let us consider for a moment what a reasonable assessment system could look like.

The "who" in the assessment process would probably be multiple raters. Peers within teams should rate one another. Customers of the team's output should rate the team. Other potential raters would be the person to whom the team reports, team members might rate the team leader, and, if multiple teams exist, they could rate one another as teams. Given the nature of the database management team's performance standards (see Figure 7.1), a Behaviorally Anchored Rating Scales (BARS) format (as reviewed in Chapter 5) would work for both the team and its members. Figure 7.2 illustrates some possible team assessment items using the BARS approach. Translating such items over for individual team members would be relatively easy.

Remote Access Service Calls	5	4	3	2	1
Response within 10 minutes	More than 90% responses within 10 minutes	90–80% responses within 10 minutes	79–70% responses within 10 minutes	69–60% responses within 10 minutes	Under 60% responses within 10 minutes
First response call success rate	More than 95% of the time	94–90% of the time	89–85% of the time	84–80% of the time	79–75% of the time
Complaints over 200 calls	One or less on average	Two on average	Three on average	Four on average	Five or more
Teamwork – meetings	Always open and frank	Sometimes open and frank	Occasionally open and frank	Sometimes guarded	Often guarded and defensive
Decision making	All team members participate and accept decisions	Almost all team members participate and accept decisions	Majority of team members participate and accept decisions	Some decisions have limited participation and acceptance	Few decisions are fully accepted by all team members

Figure 7.2 Hypothetical Database Management Team Assessment

There is a commercially available form (the *Campbell-Hallam Team Development Survey* [TDS]; Pearson Reid London House, 2002) that can be helpful for the team to use in assessing itself. It is not intended to serve as a traditional PA format; however, many of the components in it are areas of interest in the formal PA process. The TDS is a paper-and-pencil assessment that measures nineteen dimensions of team functions, focusing around the themes of resources, improvement, team success, and improvement. Results of the assessment provide the team members with data that can be used to improve performance.

SUMMARY

Teams are more and more frequently becoming the way organizations manage work and fulfill their priorities. In preparing this chapter, I found a fairly large body of literature on team assessment from a research/theoretical point of view but very little illustrating the application on an ongoing basis in an organization. None of the libraries I contacted that shared copies of their PA forms had any designed for team assessment. The best resource I encountered was a book edited by Michael Brannick, Eduardo Salas, and Carolyn Price (1997) entitled *Team Performance Assessment and Measurement*, but again this was research-based material. I expect over the next few years we will see more material from the application point of view as the use of teams continues to grow. In the meantime, methods we have explored in earlier chapters, such as BARS, can be adapted to a team-based organization. The key in team assessment is to look at factors such as mutual accountability and consensus decision-making and to develop team-based performance standards. It should also be remembered that team leaders should receive some sort of formal training in the assessment process. Such training is discussed in Chapter 9.

REFERENCES

Brannick, Michael T., Eduardo Salas, and Carolyn Price, eds. 1997. *Team Performance Assessment and Measurement: Theory, Methods, and Applications*. Series in Applied Psychology. Mahwah, NJ: Lawrence Earlbaum Associates.

Clancy, Julia H., et al. 2003. "Command Style and Team Performance in Dynamic Decision-making Tasks," in *Emerging Perspectives on Judgment and Decision Research*, edited by Sandra Schneider and James Shanteau, 586–619. Cambridge, UK: Cambridge University Press.

Crow, Robert. 1995. "Institutionalized Competition and Its Effects on Teamwork," *Journal for Quality and Participation* 18(3): 46–53.

Deming, W. Edwards. 1986. *Out of the Crisis.* Cambridge, MA: Massachusetts Institute of Technology, Center for Advanced Engineering Technology.

Guzzo, Richard A., and Marcus W. Dickson. 1996. "Teams in Organizations: Recent Research on Performance and Effectiveness," in *Annual Review of Psychology*, edited by Janet T. Spence, 307–338. Palo Alto, CA: Annual Reviews, Inc.

Juran, Joseph M. 1989. *Juran on Leadership for Quality: An Executive Handbook.* New York: Free Press.

LaFasto, Frank M. J., and Carl E. Larson. 2001. *When Teams Work Best: 6000 Team Members and Leaders Tell What It Takes to Succeed.* Thousand Oaks, CA: Sage Publications.

Pearson Reid London House. (2002). "TDS: Campbell-Hallam Team Development Survey." Available at: www.pearsonreidlondon-house.com/brochures/tds.pdf (accessed October 27, 2003).

Reilly, Richard R., and Jack McGourty. 1998. "Performance Appraisal in Team Settings," in *Performance Appraisal: State of the Art in Practice*, edited by James W. Smither, 244-277. San Francisco: Jossey-Bass.

8 MANAGER/EXECUTIVE APPRAISAL

Though any of the performance appraisal (PA) methods covered in this text can be applied to employees at any level of the organization, we will now turn our attention to PA at the "managerial" level. Although every employee can benefit from a well-executed PA process, senior and middle managers traditionally have been appraised on an irregular basis. Whereas in 1996 Vinson reported less than 26% of such appraisals employed the *360° process*, which is the focus of this chapter, the usage is going up. In today's environment, with CEOs of major corporations facing charges of fraud and other illegal behaviors, there is a substantial interest in making senior/top management appraisal a normal part of the organization's PA system and in using the 360° process. Some countries, such as Australia, have successfully used the 360° for many years.

The most appropriate method for such assessments is the aforementioned 360° assessment. There is a tendency to think of this solely as a "managerial assessment method." However, it can be useful at all levels of an organization and can be successful in countering the always-present concern that supervisor/subordinate assessments can be overly biased—either negatively or positively. Where it is used, it is usually done sporadically for managerial staff. However, as we will see, 360° assessment can be used as a regular methodology by the entire organization or, in a recent development, as a self-directed process.

WHY USE A 360° ASSESSMENT?

There are several reasons why the 360° method can be valuable to an organization. One of the most obvious reasons is that coworkers (both above and below the ratee on the organizational chart) are in the best position on a day-to-day basis to observe long-term performance. (Note: For the most senior managers—CEOs—there are some serious drawbacks to this approach, as I will discuss later in this chapter.) Another important reason is the fact that multiple raters provide input to the process. Using multiple raters, as noted at various points throughout this book, is one of the best methods for assuring fairness and accuracy. Given today's emphasis on staff involvement as a means of motivation, yet another reason appears; it requires the staff take part in a significant organizational process. The involvement can lead to an increase in morale and a sense of empowerment. Despite these advantages, it can, unfortunately in some cases, lead to a sense of fear when the rater is assessing their supervisor. This is more likely when participation is mandatory and staff have reason to doubt the organization will maintain confidentiality of the names of those who submitted ratings.

In 1985, R. E. Walton published an article that reported on the use of "commitment strategy" in U.S. organizations. He emphasized the importance of creating ways for staff "to be heard" on organizational issues including human resources (HR) policies and practices. Walton indicated that supervisors on the "front line" should facilitate rather than direct subordinates and assist them in becoming self-managers (p. 82). Any organization moving into "commitment" or "quality" model should at least carefully consider using an "upward" appraisal processes, if not the 360° technique.

ISSUES IN SUBORDINATE APPRAISAL

As covered in Chapter 2, there are a number of issues that can affect subordinate appraisal of supervisors. Probably the one that arises most frequently is "how much do subordinates know about the supervisor's duties/job description?" A related issue is the amount of training subordinates have for conducting a performance appraisal. Will there be game playing—"I got a good review from you so I'll do the same for you"—or just the opposite? In this case, PA becomes essentially a game of "tit for tat" between rater and ratee, as roles reverse over time.

As mentioned above, there is a fear issue or "paranoia" on the part of many subordinates about providing anything but the most positive assessment. Anonymous rating systems help address this concern. However, that approach raises a "fairness" issue for the ratee. "How can I trust anonymous assessments, either positive or negative, as I don't know the source?" On a personal level, from my teaching days, I always thought more carefully about suggestions from good students who signed their evaluations than I did an anonymous comment. Facing one's accuser(s) is a major factor in any "due process." Thus, if anonymous appraisals are the norm, there needs to be a process in place to address these concerns.

If the subordinate appraisal is a significant factor in promotion decisions regarding supervisors, there is the possibility supervisors may "play to the house." That is, they may focus too much on trying to please staff at the expense of carrying out their duties as a supervisor.

This is one reason why the 360° appraisal is useful. It brings into play assessment from above as well as from peer supervisors.

Sometimes, there is a concern that the supervisor's authority becomes undermined/reduced because of subordinate appraisal. To date, there is no research evidence that supports this concern. Nevertheless, some supervisors do worry about this possibility. Certainly, few subordinates will have the full picture of the supervisor's duties and performance. In highly participatory organizations that make extensive use of committees, for example, it may be necessary for the supervisor to be away from the unit to participate in committee work. Subordinates will have little or no idea of how well the person performs committee assignments. They may also resent the supervisor being "away so much" and perhaps feel that the time spent does not represent "real work."

WHAT SHOULD BE APPRAISED?

Given the issues outlined above, what should a subordinate and the 360° appraisal cover? Perhaps a good starting point draws upon the work of one of my favorite management authors, Henry Mintzberg. His classic book *The Nature of Managerial Work* (1973) outlines ten roles for a manager: figurehead, leader, liaison, monitor, disseminator, spokesperson, entrepreneur, disturbance handler, resource allocator, and negotiator. It is relatively easy to see how one could develop a very reasonable appraisal format using these roles as the starting point.

H. John Bernardin (1986) reported the results of a survey asking supervisors and subordinates how qualified they thought they were to evaluate managerial performance (p. 428) using the Mintzberg roles. There was a high degree of agreement between the two groups on roles subordinates would have first-hand knowledge of: leadership, liaison, monitor, disseminator, entrepreneur/innovator, crisis/dispute handler, resource allocator. The areas of difference of opinion were the figurehead/organizational representation, spokesperson, and negotiator roles. However, supervisors thought themselves well qualified to make such judgments, thus giving support to the value of peer review and the 360° process.

SELF-DIRECTED 360° APPRAISAL

Kate Ludeman (2000) discussed the issue of self-directed 360° appraisals. One of the essential elements for a successful 360 program is that HR or an outside consultancy handle the process. Another factor is that there are multiple raters in both subordinate and peer categories as well as, if at all possible, from above. This means multiple raters in each category for each review cycle. Most consultants recommend at least five subordinates in order to assure some degree of anonymity.

A typical 360° system does not include "face-to-face" feedback. Rather, HR or the consultant provides the feedback to the ratee. Figure 8.1 is an example of one way in which multiple-level feedback may be presented to the ratee. When the rater wants clarification, HR or the consultant gets in touch with the rater(s) seeking further information and then gets back to the ratee. With a self-directed system, the intermediary is bypassed, allowing faster and unfiltered feedback. Lacking the anonymity of the "traditional" 360 does increase concern about some of the issues discussed on pp. 151–153.

Ratings of Individual Leadership Behaviors				
This is a display of ratings for individual leadership behaviors, as rated by the ratee, his/her supervisor, and a sampling of his/her subordinates (direct reports). The numbers in these categories are then averaged to find the ratee's overall score.				
(1 = Inadequate, 3 = Average, 5 = Superior)	**Self**	**Supervisor**	**Direct Reports**	**Overall**
Measures/Evaluates Work ____ The supervisor used acceptable workload efficiency and effectiveness measures to gauge the performance of work and its organization.	**3.8**	**3.0**	**3.4**	**3.3**
Plan/Assign/Direct Work ____ Prior to beginning a project, the supervisor effectively planned and assigned work for the most efficient use of personnel resources and equipment. ____ The supervisor's estimated times for completion of projects were generally correct.	**4.0** 4.0 3.5	**3.5** 4.0 3.0	**3.9** 4.0 3.7	**3.8** 4.0 3.6
Organizes/Coordinates ____ During a project, the supervisor effectively organized and coordinated people and resources to meet or exceed performance objectives. ____ The supervisor executed plans and activities within the budget appropriation.	**3.8** 4.0 3.5	**3.3** 3.5 3.0	**3.3** 3.3 3.3	**3.5** 3.6 3.3
Decisions/Judgment ____ The supervisor effectively applied logic and decision making principles.	**3.3** 3.5	**3.0** 3.0	**3.2** 3.5	**3.2** 3.3

(1 = Inadequate, 3 = Average, 5 = Superior)	Self	Supervisor	Direct Reports	Overall
___ The supervisor selected the most appropriate decision from among options, shared the decision with others as appropriate, and followed through with decisions.	3.0	3.0	2.8	2.9
Training/Development ___ The supervisor maintained high performance by initiating timely employee training, performance evaluations, and assisted employees with career planning.	**4.0**	**3.6**	**3.0**	**3.5**
Cost Reduction Activities ___ The supervisor aggressively worked to find and implement effective methods to reduce the expense of achieving the City's goals.	**3.5**	**2.8**	**3.0**	**3.1**
Delegation of Authority ___ The supervisor assigned responsibility to others and "stepped away" from assignments yet still maintained control; used delegation as a means of time management.	**4.0** 4.0	**3.0** 3.5	**2.7** 3.3	**2.9** 3.6
___ The supervisor accepted the work responsibility for negative results of delegated work.	4.0	2.5	2.0	2.8
Technically Aware ___ The supervisor remained aware of current developments and writings related to the job.	**3.3** 3.0	**3.0** 3.0	**3.3** 3.0	**3.2** 3.0
___ The supervisor had an ongoing program of self-improvement to expand job related knowledge and skills.	3.5	3.0	3.5	3.3
Negotiate/Settle Disputes ___ The supervisor effectively settled disputes without engendering employee hostility and grievance procedures.	**4.0**	**3.5**	**3.5**	**3.7**
Meets Budget Goals ___ The supervisor developed and achieved relevant objectives, translated goals and objectives into useful activities and effectively dealt with barriers to meeting agreed upon goals and objectives.	**3.5**	**2.7**	**3.0**	**3.1**

Figure 8.1 Example of Self-Directed 360° Appraisal

Another, and important, feature of the self-directed 360 is that it can be personalized in a way that is impossible for organizational-wide assessments. This is because it is initiated by a person rather than the organization. Naturally, it also personalizes the feedback while focusing on specific areas of interest to the ratee. For example, a library director might seek feedback on their ability as a communicator or crisis handler or a supervisor of branch operations might want feedback on resource allocation skills.

Another difference in the self-directed approach is the ratee meets with each of the raters to go over their comments. That brings up Ludeman's first and most crucial point, that is, a commitment to hearing the truth. She notes that listening to areas where we need to improve is never easy but can prove valuable. Because the ratee determines what the raters are to address, there is strong interest on the ratee's part to strengthening/improving in the area(s) considered and presumably a commitment to hearing some negative things. Nevertheless, a person should think long and hard about the need for such a commitment before starting a self-directed 360.

Doing a self-assessment of area(s) of interest is the first planning step for a self-directed 360. Being able to honestly face weakness or areas needing development is difficult, but doing so will allow the raters to comment more freely and make the feedback that much more useful.

Take the hypothetical library director's interest in doing a self-directed 360 on their crisis handling skills. Though the occurrence of such crises as floods, earthquakes, hurricanes, or sprinkler pipes breaking in the stacks are rare, they are significant when they do take place. Most directors who have been in place for many years have probably experienced one or more such occurrences and have staff who went through the experience as well. What might be some areas of concern for feedback? Six possible areas are communication, delegation, setting priorities, leadership, problem solving, and teamwork. The director would do a self-assessment of these areas and ask the raters identified to do the same using a past crisis as the background. Even if a supervisor has not had to deal with a catastrophic incident, there are still the daily challenges that must be faced in terms of balancing budgets or possibly dealing with difficult personnel issues. These can also be used as the focus of feedback gathering efforts.

Ludeman (2000) suggests that becoming ready for the feedback requires both mental and emotional preparation. She suggests it may be helpful to keep in mind that the areas explored and questions asked are for your benefit. Furthermore, "once you have the answers, they're like broccoli and liver: like them or not, they're good for you and will help you grow" (p. 45).

The final steps, after securing the feedback, are to analyze the information and create a development plan based on the analysis. Your development plan should indicate the desired goal, what steps you will take to reach the goal, and what resources will be needed to make the outcome possible. Communicating the development plan to the raters gives them a sense of your openness and desire to improve and may motivate them to undertake a similar process.

PROS AND CONS OF THE 360 METHOD

There are two basic ways of using the 360 process. One is where everyone goes through the process—organization-wide or perhaps just an identified unit. The other is where an individual, either through self-directed or management decision, undergoes the process alone. Self-directed 360s are difficult enough; being singled out or being one of a few identified by management as needing this process can be worrisome. Although the individual may be aware that the reason is to gather data to assist in a major promotion decision, they also know some people not involved in the process may believe it is being done

Pros of 360° Appraisal	Cons of 360° Appraisal
• Multiple simultaneous raters. • Better accuracy, greater validity. • Less likely to be susceptible to bias. • Very useful in promotion decisions. • Very useful for development and training purposes. • Self-directed 360 focuses on self-identified areas of concern. • Highly useful in team environments.	• Potential for "getting even." • Being "singled out" by management for whatever reason(s) may have adverse impact on the individual due to staff misunderstanding the reason for the assessment. • Anonymous feedback may be nonconstructive. • Leaks or lack of confidentiality can make feedback hazardous for the rater. • May cause overall good employees to leave the organization because they dislike the process, especially where requests for additional information either fail to materialize or are overly slow in coming. • Some raters may/will not have background or training for doing an appraisal. • Some raters may/will not have an adequate knowledge/experience base for making meaningful assessments on all aspects of performance.

for negative reasons. This in turn can become grist for the "rumor mill." Though people may know rumors are just rumors, such negative talk can cause lasting damage to work relationships and even careers. Before instituting the 360 appraisal method with selected employees, it is important to weigh the benefits and these potential costs.

Figure 8.1 illustrates how one might compile data from a hypothetical self-directed 360 appraisal. The text in the form is drawn from the Hayward Public Library Management Unit Supplement form.

360 AND CEO APPRAISAL

Appraising the most senior managers is in some ways the most complex of the PA processes. To some degree, senior management appraisal has been mysterious and, often in the minds of staffers, nonexistent. Yet we read about senior managers and CEOs "resigning" due to the poor performance of the unit/organization for which they were responsible. *Library Journal*'s news section occasionally has notices of the departure of a library director due to "disagreements" between the director and the governing board. There is seldom much in the way of "hard" information as to the hows and whys of such resignations/departures. Certainly, some type of performance appraisal/assessment took/takes place in some instances.

Two 1995 documents provide some insights into the "whats" and "hows" of assessing organizational and senior managerial performance. One, from the Conference Board, outlined organizational issues (Broncato, 1995). The other, from the National Association of Corporate Directors (1995), covered the senior staff side—CEOs, governing boards, directors. No doubt, much of this work grew out of ever louder concern in the press and among the general public about what appear to be excessive compensation packages for senior managers and governing boards. The 2003 "resignation" of the CEO of the New York Stock Exchange is but one example of the doubts about pay and performance at the top.

Longenecker and Gioia (1992) suggested there was (is) an executive/senior management appraisal paradox. Their paradox is that whereas organizations value performance, including executives, the chances of securing valid appraisals decrease as responsibilities increase. In part, the paradox rests on several myths:

- Senior managers neither want nor need a formal PA process.
- Prestige/"dignity" of senior managers is damaged by a formal PA process.

- Organizational demands make it impossible for senior managers to engage in the PA process either as rater or ratee.
- Organizational outcomes (profits, productivity, customer satisfaction) are the only means of assessing senior managerial performance.
- Senior managers' responsibilities are too broad and complex to be handled in a formal PA process.
- Senior managers' autonomy, creativity, entrepreneurial abilities are hampered/curtailed by feedback.

Though research has dispelled all of these myths completely or to some degree, there are at least two facts that do enter into senior management PA that create major concerns. Few would disagree with the fact that an inaccurate/invalid appraisal of senior managers, especially the CEO, has much greater consequences for the organization than for other members of the organization. Making certain the process will be valid is complex, as the position(s) targeted are complex in nature.

The second "fact" is that as one moves up in the organization, the advancement and operations become increasingly political and nothing has more potential for becoming politicized than senior management PA. Overcoming this potential adds to the complexity of developing an assessment process that is fair and valid. So where does one begin the process?

LEADERSHIP COMPETENCIES

"Leadership" is a concept with almost as many definitions as there are writers on the topic. What everyone agrees on is that without it, whatever "leadership" means, an organization will fail. From a PA perspective, perhaps the efforts to define "leadership competencies" are most valuable. J. P. Brisco (1996) identified four distinctive approaches to identifying competencies: data-based, value-based, strategy-based, and learning-based. *Data-based* competencies are behavioral data and work best for organizations with needs that are continuous and relatively predictable (most libraries would fall into this category). *Value-based* competencies arise formally or informally in which "values" are key to its success. *Strategy-based* competencies relate to anticipated future needs of the organization to meet competition and work best where there are clear needs for new strategic directions when the future is uncertain. *Learning-based* competencies emphasize abilities a person has in relation to their ability to learn new competencies as well as their capacity to adapt to changing circumstances. This competency is most appropriate for organizations operating in a rapidly changing environment.

A later study by B. M. Bass (1997) suggested that successful transformational leaders all possessed four important characteristics: charisma, inspirational motivation, intellectual stimulation, and individualized consideration. The characteristics' broad labels are of little assistance in assessing performance; however, the elements making up the grouping are useful. For example, some of the elements included within "intellectual stimulation" are questioning of old assumptions, stimulating others to seek out and implement new ways, providing new and/or innovative perspectives, and encouraging the expression of new ideas. In essence, this type of leader is a "change agent" not so much by personally doing something, but by encouraging and facilitating others to see change as necessary. A careful review of the Brisco and Bass publications is worthwhile for anyone thinking about doing a senior management PA process.

Although leadership is a key area of performance consideration, there are other significant areas as well. A leader with a vision of the organization's future is highly desirable, but if the person cannot, at least in broad terms, translate that vision into a plan, the vision is of little value. Thus, another area for appraisal is planning and, more specifically, strategic planning.

Almost every definition of management contains some verbage that it requires people to "get things done." Although senior managers will not handle day-to-day HR operations, an effective CEO/senior manager will monitor its policies and practices. They "set the tone" for an organization both through policies and behavior that impacts everything from diversity to morale.

Though "front-line" staff has the day-to-day contact with customers and, more often than not, represents the organization, for better or worse, in the minds of the customer, senior management also sets the tone. If they do not implement quality assessment measures, front-line staff will assume that quality is not a significant issue and act accordingly. Even the type and frequency of the assessment activities speak to senior management's quality concerns.

Obviously, fiscal management is one of the primary responsibilities of senior management both in securing and expending financial resources. Issues such as how accurate and well-controlled budget plans were, how much and how effective fund-raising activities were, and the degree of cost-effective employment of resources (people, equipment, and money) are all suitable appraisal areas.

For libraries, senior management is usually the sole source for advocating and promoting the library and its services to the parent organization—university, city, corporation, and so forth. Assessing performance in these two areas is extremely important, as weak performance in either area will lead to significant problems for the library.

Major Areas of Senior/CEO Manager Appraisal for Libraries

- Leadership
  - o Charisma/vision
  - o Change agent
  - o Conflict resolution

- Planning
  - o Short term
  - o Long term
  - o Strategic

- HR management
  - o Utilization
  - o Turnover/absenteeism
  - o Morale
  - o Motivation

- Quality of services
  - o User assessment
  - o Outside agency assessment
  - o Assessment mechanisms in place

- Fiscal management
  - o Value-added
  - o Budgetary control
  - o Cost control

  - o Fund raising

- Advocacy
  - o Spokesperson within parent organization
  - o Spokesperson to professional and service community
  - o Negotiation skills

- Compliance to standards/regulations
  - o Support of professional standards
  - o Health and safety
  - o Support/implementation of legal requirements and privacy

- Organizational promotion
  - o Marketing program
  - o Public-relations program
  - o Community involvement

Compliance with standards, regulations, and laws are not always viewed as significant issues for libraries. Decisions that senior management makes about the degree of compliance with professional standards such as MARC may not have an immediate impact on the library but can come back to haunt the library years later. Today's legal environment regarding user privacy and legislation such as the Patriot Act make senior management decisions about how to comply complex. For libraries in educational institutions, there are a variety of accreditation compliance issues that usually fall to senior managers to oversee.

COACHING SENIOR MANAGERS

There may be a few paragon managers who are talented in all aspects of management; however, most excellent/effective managers still have one or two areas that could use improvement. Starting in the early 1990s, even large corporations began hiring "executive coaches." Such coaches are external specialists who come in to assist a senior manager with a specific issue—a critical downsizing, starting a marketing program, or helping with behavioral/style short-comings. Some of the typical broad areas of "flaws"/short-comings are:

- Problems with interpersonal relationships
- Difficulty molding a staff/team
- Difficulty making strategic transitions
- Lack of follow-through
- Overdependence
- Strategic difference with higher management

For further details on these areas, see the work by M. M. Lombardo and C. D. McCauley (1998) included in the References list for this chapter.

As with athletic teams, the coach provides guidance, advice, and assists in developing an action plan and methods for carrying out the plan, but the senior manager is the one who executes the plan. Coaching usually lasts 3 to 9 months but can last a year or more. Such services are not inexpensive; however, they may be a good investment in the long run. I have paid for such coaching for department heads on several occasions. In each case, the manager was good in all but one but crucial aspect of their job, and the "problem" area was suitable for short-term coaching—3 or 4 months. Was it a success and worth the cost? From a success point of view very definitely in two cases and in the other there was substantial improvement, and all the units ceased to perform poorly. From a cost perspective, it is difficult to say because in a library setting it is difficult to set a dollar value on lost productivity. One can put a value on absenteeism and turnover, but these are a small part of the real costs. I believe the use of external coaches is a worthwhile approach when the senior manager has only one or two areas to address.

The use of coaches brings us back to one of the major purposes for the PA process: staff development. Just as most managers have some weakness, few supervisors have great skills in coaching/teaching. Use of external coaches is an area that more organizations should incorporate into the PA process.

SUMMARY

Whether an entire organization adopts the process or only selected managers opt to participate as a self-directed activity, 360 appraisals provide a more complete picture of an individual's performance, when done properly, than does the traditional supervisor-rating-subordinate method. The method has been growing in usage for all levels of organizations, not just senior managers/CEOs. Self-directed 360s provide an opportunity to tailor the process to a person's area(s) of concern. From a legal perspective, the 360 method provides the multiple raters that courts prefer to see. When the 360 PA method is used in conjunction with coaches, true gains in professional development and organizational effectiveness can be realized.

REFERENCES

Bass, Bernard M. 1997. "Does the Transactional-Transformational Leadership Paradigm Transcend Organizational and National Boundaries?" *American Psychologist* 52(2): 130–139.

Bernardin, H. John. 1986. "Subordinate Appraisal: A Valuable Source of Information About Managers," *Human Resource Management* 25(3): 421–439.

Briscoe, Jon P. 1996. *Competency-Based Approaches to Selecting and Developing Executives.* Boston, MA: Executive Development Roundtable, Boston University.

Broncato, Carolyn Kay. 1995. *New Corporate Performance Measures: A Research Report.* New York: Conference Board.

Lombardo, Michael M., and Cynthia D. McCauley. 1988. *Dynamics of Management Derailment.* Technical Report 34. Greensboro, NC: Center for Creative Leadership.

Longenecker, Clinton O., and Dennis A. Gioia. 1992. "The Executive Appraisal Paradox," *Academy of Management Executive* 6(2): 18–28.

Ludeman, Kate. 2000. "How to Conduct Self-Directed 360," *Training and Development* 54(7): 44–48.

Mintzberg, Henry. 1973. *The Nature of Managerial Work.* New York: Harper and Row.

National Association of Corporate Directors. 1995. *Performance Evaluation of Chief Executive Officers, Boards, and Directors.* Washington, DC: NACD Blue Ribbon Commission.

Vinson, Mary N. 1996. "The Pros and Cons of 360-Degree Feedback: Making It Work," *Training and Development* 50(4): 11–13.

Walton, Richard E. 1985. "From Control to Commitment in the Workplace," *Harvard Business Review* 63(2): 77–84.

9 TYING METHODS TOGETHER

Throughout this text, I have examined various aspects of assessment from developing assessment methods to preparing for the evaluation meeting. Together we have explored performance appraisal (PA) from the point of view of assessing the individual and have reviewed the special challenges associated with evaluating team performance. This final chapter gives me an opportunity to address several additional important issues that relate to PA: "pay for performance," training the raters, and perceptions of fairness. It will end with some thoughts and suggestions for raters.

PAY FOR PERFORMANCE

Robert Heneman and Maria Gresham (1998) opened their essay on *pay for performance* by noting, "a revolution is taking place in compensation and incentive systems....New pay-for-performance plans are used to compensate employee performance at all levels in the organization" (p. 496). Their definition of *performance-based pay* is very broad, starting with the old familiars such as "piece rate," commissions, employee suggestions, and "merit pay." Some of the others may be less familiar, such as skill based, competency based, standard hour, team-based merit, and gainsharing compensation.

Very few books on performance appraisal contain little more than a passing mention of compensation and how it *is* related to PA. Perhaps it is because there is, or has been, a tendency to emphasize the "development" behavioral aspects of PA on the part of human resources (HR) departments. Perhaps using a more straightforward approach and clearly linking PA and compensation would help reduce the tensions surrounding PA reviews.

When the organization talks about "merit pay," everyone knows that the "merit" will be linked to what is in the annual performance review documents, perhaps not totally—but certainly to a significant degree. Any discussion of "pay-for-performance" makes the connection between PA and compensation crystal clear. I have not seen any research about which—if any—PA assessment techniques work best with the various pay-for-performance plans. When, or if, such research is done, we may have a better understanding of what we need to do to make PA fulfill the many expectations organizations have for the process.

Most discussions by academics of pay for performance suggest it is a mechanism for compensating people for things *beyond* those found in the job description. There are five broad categories that usually appear in such discussions. One of the most frequently mentioned categories is for an *accomplishment* that goes beyond the job description. Mastering a *new skill or competency* not covered in the job description is another. Perhaps the most common application is for *exceeding goals*. Another common approach is for compensation for ideas/suggestions that result in *organizational improvement* or savings. The last approach, the least often mentioned, is for *team compensation* when the team exceeds its goals. Two good books to consult on pay for performance are Steven E. Gross' (1995) *Compensation for Teams* and Thomas B. Wilson's (1995) *Innovative Reward Systems for the Changing Workplace.*

Heneman and Gresham (1998) concluded their essay by stating, "Performance-based pay plans should only be used for organizational change under limited circumstances" (p. 519). Their point is well taken, and yet my experience in several organizations has been that merit pay *is* the system. Comparing the organizations' application of merit pay, which is the oldest of the pay-for-performance systems, to what the literature suggests it should be indicates that the organizations may be misusing the term or during the years the process changed significantly from its original design. Heneman and Gresham noted that when such compensation plans become *the* system used, employees and even the organization cease to view the process as "additional" or a "privilege" and it becomes a "right."

My personal view is organizations should be more open about the linkage between performance reviews and compensation while continuing to acknowledge the behavior aspects of the process. By trying to disassociate the two, the organization creates an environment of at least mild distrust.

Further Thought

- If you had to implement a performance-based pay method, how would you guard against it becoming a "right" in the minds of employees?
- How would you administer performance-based pay in a team environment?
- Do you think establishing an open linkage between compensation and PA would reduce tension?

TRAINING THE RATERS

If there is a single theme of this text, it is that the PA process should strive for reviews that are valid and reliable. Books such as *Abolishing Performance Appraisals* (Coens and Jenkins, 2000) and research findings implying that they are ineffective (Dorfman, Stephan, and Loveland, 1986) raise questions about the process. Furthermore, articles such as "Behind the Mask: The Politics of Employee Appraisal" (Longnecker, Sims, and Gioia, 1987) suggesting it is nothing more than an exercise in organizational politics or Ilgen's (1993) essay indicating rating accuracy is not always the rater's objective, raise further questions about the what and why of PA systems. Despite all of the above, PA is still a fact of life in most U.S. organizations, and there should be a major effort to avoid the pitfalls the above references, as well as others, point out. One of the ways to do this is through *rater training*.

In some ways, the effort to achieve bias-free, valid, reliable assessments is like searching for the Holy Grail; a noble objective, but probably one that will never end. Putting this into the library context, it is like achieving and maintaining an absolutely error-free Online Public Access Catalog (OPAC). There are, however, some practical reasons for having training programs. One reason is that, as noted in Chapter 3, PA reviews can become a central element in legal actions. Untrained raters are an invitation to and a primary factor in losing a lawsuit. Another factor is, given the political element in PA, that by providing training, the organization sends a message that "fairness" in the reviews does matter. Well-trained raters will provide ratees with more accurate feedback, especially in behavioral aspects of performance, and in providing coaching and development opportunities. That in turn should mean their units are more effective and productive, thus enhancing the organization's overall performance. Though most organizations provide some training, the emphasis is on "some." Time and "people power" are always limiting factors in most organizational activities, and when it comes to rater training, the resources are scarce indeed. Very few training programs do more than 1 or 2 hours of the "basics" for new raters while perhaps spending minimal time and effort updating "established" raters on changes in the format or processes. Because of this, it is important to consider some practical suggestions for what the library might do to supplement standard HR training, beyond paying for an outside consultant to come in to do a half- or full-day workshop.

One step is to spend time on what HR people refer to as *performance dimension training* (PDT). Though that process can be complex at a basic level, the library raters could/should devote sufficient time to reviewing the definitions of each performance dimension to achieve a relatively high degree of agreement among raters in the library. For example, Figure 5.1 (p. 106) includes "Quality of work" as a job dimension, with a set of five definitions:

- 4 points: Work is consistently error-free, thorough, neat, correct, logically organized, and statistically accurate.
- 3 points: Work is nearly always error-free (with a few very minor errors), thorough, neat, correct, logically organized, and statistically accurate.

- 2 points: Work contains some acceptable errors that may require some review and editing by supervisor.
- 1 point: Work reflects errors that require careful review and correction by supervisor or partial reworking/revision.
- 0 points: Work is frequently not acceptable or usable.

Another example is from the Loyola Marymount University (LMU) performance factors guidelines (p. 56). In this case, the "LMU Service Standards" are:

- **(Outstanding)** Exceptional service orientation; exceptionally friendly and helpful toward others.
- **(Highly Effective)** Good service orientation; friendly and helpful toward others.
- **(Effective)** Regularly meets service expectations.
- **(Needs Improvement)** Sometimes forgets service orientation and serves at a substandard level.
- **(Unacceptable)** Rarely demonstrates LMU's service standards. Often rude and offensive toward others.

A training session for the Figure 5.1 material would work toward rater understanding of what "consistently error-free" or "frequently not acceptable" means so that at least the raters within the library had a shared understanding of these meanings. In the case of the LMU Standards, there would/could be two elements to the training. First, the definitions would be discussed, with a goal of improving interrater consistency. Second, a review would be completed of just what the "LMU Service Standards" are and how they apply to a given unit within the library. The last aspect is particularly important, as some units (technical services, for example) have staff who may have little or no contact with the public while doing their work but still represent the university to outside vendors and other contacts.

Such training may not have a profound impact on the assessments, at least at the library's parent organizational level; however, it should improve the employee's perception of the fairness of raters across units within the library.

One way to enhance the training process is to include some "hands on" exercises, such as having the raters either alone or divided into small teams apply the definitions to some hypothetical cases. There are some cases available that one could use, although they were not produced for the use I'm suggesting. For example, Patricia Belcastro (1998) published a book on performance appraisal through American

Library Association (ALA), entitled *Evaluating Library Staff*. This work contains a number of cases covering various categories of library employees. With some minor modification, they could become the basis for a training exercise. Part of the exercise should also be to identify the job dimensions covered and then make a judgment about what level of performance was achieved.

If the raters do the exercise/practice independently, one can add a further element to the training. One common assessment problem is inflated ratings, especially when there is a long-term work relationship between rater and ratee. The added element would be to compare the level of rating given in the cases to actual ratings of ratees by the rater. It is likely the actual rating will be higher than the case ratings. Though there are a host of variables in the actual rating that cannot be replicated in a case study, such comparisons do raise the rater's awareness of the need to be objective and the need for greater accuracy.

Another type of desirable training focuses on reducing bias. Such training is often identified as *rater error training* (RET). RET training rests on the idea it is difficult for raters to differentiate among ratees and that there are three broad categories of errors: leniency, severity, and central tendency. Of the three, the most common error is *leniency*. This error occurs when the rater tends to give everyone a high or relatively high rating in order to avoid conflict and/or confrontations. Few of us enjoy confrontations, and certainly the PA review has great potential for confrontation, especially if it suggests the ratee is "average" or below. However, if appropriate feedback has been given *throughout* the entire review cycle, the prospect of the annual or semiannual assessment meeting turning into a conflict-filled "ordeal" should be lessened. Another source of this type of error is concern on the rater's part for their staff. The rationale for this goes along the lines of, "If other raters give their staff high ratings, perhaps mine will not get good raises if I don't rate them highly." This is where the value of PDT comes into play. Of course, to assure the PDT sessions are translated into practice, the raters' supervisor must engage in some careful monitoring of the reviews. Two other factors can be issues: fear of a grievance/retaliation on the part of the ratee and/or having low performance standards. In addition, *severity*—the opposite of leniency —and *central tendency*—attempting to avoid either extreme by not rating employees in the "Excellent" or "Needs Improvement" categories—can also cause problems in staff morale and are not effective means of employee development. Raising awareness of the sources of error and how to avoid them is the objective of RET programs.

There are other training programs, but they require more time and effort than most libraries can afford to develop in-house; however, there are consultants that are willing to provide such training. Some of the other programs are FOR (*frame-of-reference*), which developed from

Bernardin's (1986) research, and whom I have cited several times in this text, which assists in improving rater accuracy. RVT (*rater variability training*) is a combination of RET and FOR training. BOT (*behavioral observation training*), which as its name suggests is designed to improve rater observational skills in the area of performance assessments by enhancing the detection, perception, and recall powers when looking at/for performance behaviors. An interesting program is SLT (*self-leadership training*), which, in spite of its name, is for developing raters' self-confidence in their ability to carry out PA reviews. This is done through exercises emphasizing "positive self-talk, mental imagining, and developing positive belief/thought patterns."

One obvious issue to consider is what training is appropriate for a given assessment technique. Neil Hauenstein (1998) developed a four-element matrix for thinking about what training and appraisal purpose worked together most effectively. In Chapter 1, I noted PA had two purposes: administrative and behavioral. Hauenstein uses the term "developmental" instead of "behavioral" for his matrix. He divides assessment techniques into frequency or subjective evaluations and thus creates his matrix of frequency-administrative, frequency-developmental, subjective-administrative, and subjective-developmental. He includes checklists, BOS, and productivity scales as well as management by objective (MBO) in the frequency-based category. His subjective category covers Graphic Rating Scales (GRS), behaviorally anchored scales, as well as "mixed" standards. He suggests that all training involve PDT as a baseline. For both the frequency-administrative and frequency-developmental categories, he suggests BOT as the most appropriate technique for training. In his view, RVT is the best approach for subjective-administrative purposes and FOR for subjective-developmental needs. Figure 9.1 is a visual representation of *some* of Hauenstein's ideas.

	Frequency Assessment Methods	**Subjective** Assessment Methods
	Checklists, BOS, Productivity, MBO	GRS, BARS, "mixed standard"
Administrative	Training methods: PDT, BOT	Training methods: PDT, RVT
Developmental	Training methods: PDT, BOT	Training methods: PDT, FOR

Figure 9.1 Hauenstein Matrix

There is a second area where additional training for raters is beneficial. That is in improving their feedback skills. The primary objectives of such training are to improve motivational feedback and task-level conversations. Other elements should emphasize the need for fairness and the necessity of letting the ratee have an active voice during the review session. The skill of giving effective feedback takes time to cultivate, but two articles by Simonsen (1998) and Swinburne (2001) have been included in the References list as a starting point. There is also a Web site worth looking into that can be found at www.t2ed.com/index.html. The site contains the Employee Performance Appraisal and Development System (EPADS), which is designed to provide feedback on work performance. Another short but useful article is Anita Rowe's (1993) "Understanding Diversity Blind Spots in the Performance Review." In this article, she addresses the need to consider "diversity" issues when engaging in PA sessions.

FAIRNESS

Fairness is a small word but one filled with complexity. What is "fair," more often than not, is in the eye of the beholder. Differences in perceptions of fairness abound in PA. Research suggests there are three primary elements that make up a person's perception of PA fairness (Greenberg, 1986). One element is *justice*, which has two aspects in terms of PA: fair/just in pay increases (outcomes) and fair/just in the procedures used in the process. The other two elements of fairness are consistency and appropriateness.

Organizations benefit from having a fair PA system in several ways. First, employee attitude and reactions to the process are more positive. Second, employee motivation and performance improve. Third, employee attitudes toward the organization improve. Finally, there is a reduced chance of legal actions arising from the process.

Are there things one can do to improve the perception of fairness in regard to the PA process? Of course. One step is to have employees prepare self-evaluations and *incorporate* portions of the evaluations into the overall PA process. Another step is ensuring that ratees have ample opportunity to talk during the review sessions and giving evidence that their feedback to raters is taken seriously. Insuring the appraisal process is year-round with at least one or two reviews between the formal annual review also improves perceptions, as employees see raters more along the lines of a "coach," as I covered in Chapter 2. Monitoring the system for consistency and having training programs for raters that focus on consistency also contribute to the perception of fairness.

Having employees involved in assessing the system and in making adjustments in the system further improves the perception of fairness. Joint development of performance standards is also a plus as this will help insure the appraisal is job related.

FINAL THOUGHTS

At the beginning of this text, I outlined the many beliefs about PA and noted the fact it is a process that, in a great many organizations, is a dreaded procedure. It is probably unlikely that an assessment session will ever be something the rater or ratee will look forward to; however, there are things one can do to make it less stressful/painful. Most of the following items are things a library can implement on its own; however, having the assistance of HR would make it easier.

- Develop realistic job-related performance standards with staff input.
- Meet with ratees at least once or more between the formal/required session(s) to review their performance.
- Consider using some additional assessment methods such as self, peer, or 360 in addition to the primary assessment tool chosen to check on possible bias, accuracy, and fairness.
- Checking boxes on a form that suggest a problem exists does nothing to determine what or why the problem exists. Spend time investigating the situation.
- Focus on developmental issues in appraisal sessions.
- Listen as much or more than you talk as the rater in appraisal sessions.
- Share the assessment with the ratee prior to session, if allowed, in order to make the session more useful.
- Spend time with raters going over guidelines in an effort to get more interdepartmental consistency in ratings.
- Practice methods of both giving and receiving feedback effectively. It is not enough to "say the right thing at the right time in the right way," but you must also be open to comments or reactions from the individual being evaluated.

- Use the forms included on the accompanying CD-ROM to develop or improve upon existing assessment forms.

As mentioned in Chapter 1, "regardless of what people think about the process, PA is a fixture in U.S. management practice." By using the suggestions outlined above, and via this text, it is hoped PA becomes a more efficient and effective and less "painful" process in your institution.

REFERENCES

Belcastro, Patricia. 1998. *Evaluating Library Staff: A Performance Appraisal System*. Chicago: American Library Association.

Bernardin, H. John. 1986. "Subordinate Appraisal: A Valuable Source of Information About Managers," *Human Resource Management* 25(3): 421–439.

Coens, Tom, and Mary Jenkins. 2000. *Abolishing Performance Appraisals: Why They Backfire and What to Do Instead*. San Francisco: Berrett-Koehler Publishers.

Dorfman, Peter W., Walter G. Stephan, and John Loveland. 1986. "Performance Appraisal Behaviors: Supervisor Perceptions and Subordinate Reactions," *Personnel Psychology* 39(3): 579–597.

Greenberg, Jerald. 1986. "Determinants of Perceived Fairness of Performance Evaluations," *Journal of Applied Psychology* 71(2): 340–342.

Gross, Steven E. 1995. *Compensation for Teams: How to Design and Implement Team-Based Reward Programs*. New York: AMACOM.

Hauenstein, Neil M. A. 1998. "Training Raters to Increase the Accuracy of Appraisals and the Usefulness of Feedback," in *Performance Appraisal: State of the Art in Practice*, edited by James W. Smither. San Francisco: Jossey-Bass.

Heneman, Robert L., and Maria T. Gresham. 1998. "Performance-Based Pay Plans," in *Performance Appraisal: State of the Art in Practice*, edited by James W. Smither. San Francisco: Jossey-Bass.

Ilgen, Daniel R. 1993. "Performance Appraisal Accuracy: An Elusive and Sometimes Misguided Goal," in *Personnel Selection and Assessment: Individual and Organizational Perspectives*, edited by Heinz Schuler, James L. Farr, and Mike Smith. Hillsdale, NJ: Lawrence Erlbaum Associates.

Longenecker, Clinton O., Henry P. Sims, Jr., and Dennis A. Gioia. 1987. "Behind the Mask: The Politics of Employee Appraisal."

Academy of Management Executives 1(3): 183–193.

Rowe, Anita. 1993. "Understanding Diversity Blind Spots in the Performance Review," *CUPA Journal* 44(4): 9–10.

Simonsen, Peggy. 1998. "Give Positive Feedback," *The CPA Journal* 68(5): 74, 76.

Swinburne, Penny. 2001. "How to Use Feedback to Improve Performance," *People Management* 7(11): 46–48.

Wilson, Thomas B. 1995. *Innovative Reward Systems for the Changing Workplace.* New York: McGraw Hill.

FURTHER READINGS ABOUT PERFORMANCE APPRAISAL

The following are some fairly recent articles and a book or two that can provide additional information and ideas for making the PA process more effective and useful. None of the items are cited elsewhere in the book and represent only a sampling of the literature that is available on the topic.

GENERAL

Boswell, Wendy R., and John W. Boudreau. 2002. "Separating the Developmental and Evaluative Performance Appraisal Uses," *Journal of Business and Psychology* 16(3): 391–412.

Deblieux, Michael. 2003. *Performance Appraisal Sourcebook.* Alexandria, VA: Society for Human Resource Management.

Lindo, David K. 2003. "Can You Answer Their Questions?" *Supervision* 64(1): 20–22.

Moore, David R., Mei-I Chang, and Andrew R. Dainty. 2002. "Competence, Competency and Competencies: Performance Assessment in Organizations," *Work Study* 51(6): 314–319.

Painter, Charles N. 2003. "Ten Steps for Improved Appraisals," *Supervision* 64(10): 12–14.

Waugh, Skip. 2002. "Delivering Solid Performance Reviews," *Supervision* 63(8): 16–17.

COACHING, MENTORING, LEARNING

Bard, Mary, and Elaine Moore. 2000. "Mentoring and Self-Managed Learning," *International Journal of Market Research* 42(3): 255–275.

Billet, Stephen. 2001. "Learning Through Work." *Journal of Workplace Learning* 13(516): 209–214.

Burrow, Jim, and Paula Berardinelli. 2003. "Systematic Performance Improvement—Refining the Space Between Learning and Results." *Journal of Workplace Learning* 15(1): 6–14.

Dutton, Gail. 2001. "Making Reviews More Efficient and Fair," *Workforce* 80(4): 76–81.

Feeley, Thomas H. 2002. "Comments on Halo Effects in Rating and Evaluation Research," *Human Communication Research* 28(4): 578–586.

LEGAL ISSUES

Doyle, Tanya, and Brian Kleiner. 2002. "Issues in Employment Litigation," *Managerial Law* 44(1/2): 151–155.

Martin, David C., Kathryn Bartol, and Patrick Kehoe. 2000. "Legal Ramifications of Performance Appraisal," *Public Personnel Management* 29(3): 379–406.

Posthuma, Richard. 2003. "Procedural Due Process and Procedural Justice in the Workplace," *Public Personnel Management* 32(2): 181–196.

Williams, Scott David, William Slonaker, and Ann Wendt. 2003. "An Analysis of Employment Discrimination Claims Associated with Layoffs," *S.A.M. Advanced Management Journal* 68(1): 49–56.

TEAMS

Cox, James H., and Donald D. Tippett. 2003. "An Analysis of Team Rewards of the U.S. Army Corps of Engineers Huntsville Center," *Engineering Management Journal* 15(4): 11–20.

Kozial, Mark J. 2000. "Giving and Receiving Performance Evaluations: The Power of Teamwork," *CPA Journal* 70(12): 23–28.

Miles, Sandy J., and Glynn Mangold. 2002. "Impact of Team Leader Performance on Team Member Satisfaction: The Subordinate Perspective," *Team Performance Management* 8(5, 6): 113–121.

O'Connell, Matthew, Dennis Doverspike, and Alana Cober. 2002. "Leadership and Semiautonomous Work Team Performance," *Group & Organization Management* 27(1): 50–65.

Sivasubramaniam, Nagaraj, William D. Murry, Bruce J. Avolio, and Dong I. Jung. 2002. "A Longitudinal Model of the Effects of Team Leadership and Group Potency on Group Performance," *Group & Organization Management* 27(1): 66–97.

360°/CEO ASSESSMENT

Anderson, Brooke, and Brian Kleiner. 2003. "How to Evaluate the Performance of Chief Executive Officers Effectively," *Management Research News* 26(2–4): 3–12.

Beehr, Terry A., et al. "Evaluation of 360 Degree Feedback Ratings." *Journal of Organizational Behavior* 22(7): 775–784.

Jackson, John H., and Martin M. Greller. 1998. "Decision Elements for Using 360° Feedback," *Human Resource Planning* 21(4): 18–28.

Penny, James A. 2003. "Exploring Differential Item Functioning in a 360 Degree Assessment," *Organizational Research Methods* 6(1): 61–80.

Smither, James W., et al. 2003. "Can Working with an Executive Coach Improve Multisource Feedback Ratings Over Time?" *Personnel Psychology* 56(1): 23–45.

Whiddett, Steve, and Martin Galpin. 2002. "Better by Design" 360-Degree Feedback Systems," *Training and Management Development Methods* 16(3): 209–212.

LIBRARY-SPECIFIC AND MEDIA CENTERS

Avery, Elizabeth F., Terry Dahlin, and Deborah A. Carver. 2001. *Staff Development: A Practical Guide*, 3rd ed. Chicago: American Library Association.

Bradshaw, Lynn K. 2002. "Local District Implementation of State Mandated Teacher Evaluation Policies and Procedures: The North Carolina Case," *Journal of Personnel Evaluation in Education* 16(2): 113–127.

Bryant, Miles. 2002. "The Role of the Principal in the Evaluation of the School's Library Media Specialist," *School Libraries Worldwide* 8(1): 85–91.

Cihak, Herbert E. 1999. "Coaching Library Support Staff," *Library Mosaics* 10(2): 10–12.

Holloway, Karen L. 2003. "Developing Core and Mastery-Level Competencies for Librarians," *Library Administration & Management* 17(2): 94–98.

Kumrow, David, and Becky Dahlen. 2002. "Is Peer Review an Effective Approach for Evaluating Teachers?" *The Clearing House* 75(5): 238–242.

Martey, A. K. 2002. "Appraising the Performance of Library Staff in a Ghanaian Academic Library," *Library Management* 23(2/3): 403–416.

Osif, Bonnie A. 2002. "Evaluation and Assessment, Part 1: Evaluation of Individuals." *Library Administration & Management* 16(1): 44–48.

Russell, Carrie. 1998. "Using Performance Measurement to Evaluate Teams and Organizational Effectiveness," *Library Administration & Management* 12(3): 159–165.

Todaro, Julie. 1999. "The Beast Within." *Library Administration & Management* 13(4): 192–195.

Young, E. Mae. 1995. "Evaluating School Library Media Specialists: From Performance Expectations to Appraisal Conference." *Journal of Personnel Evaluation in Education* 9(2): 171–189.

PUBLIC EMPLOYEES

Cederblom, Doug, and Dan E. Pemerl. 2002. "From Performance Appraisal to Performance Management," *Public Personnel Management* 31(2): 131–140.

Ellickson, Mark C. 2002. "Determinants of Job Satisfaction of Municipal Government Employees," *Public Personnel Management* 31(3): 343–358.

Heinrich, Carolyn J. 2002. "Outcome-Based Performance Management in the Public Sector," *Public Administration Review* 62(6): 712–726.

Heneman, Robert L. 2003. "Job and Work Evaluation: A Literature Review," *Public Personnel Management* 32(1): 47–72.

Kikoski, John F. 1999. "Effective Communication in the Performance Appraisal Interview: Face-to-Face Communication for Public Managers in the Culturally Diverse Workplace," *Public Personnel Management* 28(2): 301–322.

Meier, Kenneth J., and Laurence J. O'Toole. 2002. "Public Management and Organizational Performance," *Journal of Policy Analysis and Management* 21(4): 629–637.

Rector, Perry, and Brian H. Kleiner. 2002. "Creating Productivity in Public Institutions," *Management Research News* 25(3): 43–50.

Roberts, Gary E. 2003. "Employee Performance Appraisal System Participation: A Technique That Works," *Public Personnel Management* 32(1): 89–98.

RATING THE RATERS

Becker, Geraldine A., and Charles E. Miller. 2002. "Examining Contrast Effects in Performance Appraisals: Using Appropriate Controls and Checking Accuracy," *Journal of Psychology* 136(6): 667–684.

Murphy, Kevin R., and Richard De Shon. 2000. "Interrater Correlations Do Not Estimate the Reliability of Job Performance Ratings," *Personnel Psychology* 53(4): 873–900.

Prien, Kristin O., Erich P. Prien, and William Wooten. 2003. "Interrater Reliability in Job Analysis," *Public Personnel Management* 32(1): 125–142.

THE PROCESS

Brannick, Michael T., and Edward Levine. 2002. *Job Analysis.* Thousand Oaks, CA: Sage Publications.

Chang, I-Wei, and Brian H. Kleiner. 2002. "How to Conduct Job Analysis Effectively," *Management Research News* 25(3): 73–81.

Chenhall, Robert H., and Kim Langfield-Smith. 2003. "Performance Measurement and Reward Systems, Trust, and Strategic Change," *Journal of Management Accounting Research* 15:117–131.

De Cremer, David, and Robert C. Ruiter. 2003. "Emotional Reactions Toward Procedural Fairness as a Function of Negative Information," *Journal of Social Psychology* 143(6): 793–795.

Flynn, Peter. 2001. "You Are Simply Average," *Across the Board* 38(2): 51–55.

Groeschl, Stefan. 2003. "Cultural Implications for the Appraisal Process," *Cross Cultural Management* 10(1): 67–80.

Grote, Dick. 2000. "Performance Appraisal: Solving Tough Challenges," *HR Magazine* 45(7): 145–150.

—. 2000. "Secrets of Performance Appraisal," *Across the Board* 37(5): 14–20.

Kerssens-van Drongelen, Inge, and Olaf A. M. Fisscher. 2003. "Ethical Dilemmas in Performance Measurement," *Journal of Business Ethics* 45(1): 51–59.

Losyk, Bob. 2002. "How to Conduct a Performance Appraisal," *Public Management* 84(3): 8–11.

Smith, Wanda J., K. Vernard Harrington, and Jeffery D. Houghton. 2000. "Predictors of Performance Appraisal Discomfort: A Preliminary Examination," *Public Personnel Management* 29(1): 21–32.

III. PERFORMANCE APPRAISAL FORMS YOU CAN ADAPT

CERRITOS COMMUNITY COLLEGE DISTRICT

DECISION SHEET: FACULTY EVALUATION

TENURED FACULTY

At the conclusion of the review process, this Decision Sheet shall be separated from the Faculty Evaluation Criteria form which shall be forwarded to the evaluatee. At the option of the evaluatee, the completed Faculty Evaluation forms may be forwarded with the Decision Sheet to the Personnel Services Office for placement in the evaluatee's personnel file.

This Decision Sheet shall be forwarded by the evaluation team chair through the appropriate division dean/division chair or area administrator to the Personnel Services Office for placement in the evaluatee's personnel file.

Name of Evaluatee (print): _____

Division/Area: _____ Semester/Year: _____

_____ Review process satisfactorily completed _____
                                                   (date)
_____ Review in Progress: report expected by _____
                                                (date)
_____ Review Team recommends Administrative follow-up
_____ Review Team recommends Administrative review
_____ Review Team cannot reach a unanimous decision. (Note: if this item is checked, one of the two immediately preceding decisions must also be checked; the appropriate division dean/division chair or area administrator, in consultation with the appropriate Vice President, shall initiate an administrative follow-up of the evaluatee's performance.)

Peer Review Team: _____   _____
                          (signature)   (date)

                  _____   _____
                          (signature)   (date)

                  _____   _____
                          (signature)   (date)

Note: The evaluatee may respond in writing in respect to the accuracy, relevance, and completeness of the evaluation by submitting such written response to the Personnel Services Office within 20 workdays following the date he/she receives the evaluation. Such response (if any) shall become a part of the evaluation report and be placed in the evaluatee's personnel file.

Received by:_____   _____
                    Evaluatee's Signature   (date)

            _____   _____
            Division Dean/Division Chair/Area Administrator   (date)

            _____   _____
                  Personnel Services Office   (date)

                                                           IN-48 1/96

Form 1. Faculty Evaluation, Tenured Faculty

CERRITOS COMMUNITY COLLEGE DISTRICT

DECISION SHEET: FACULTY EVALUATION

PROBATIONARY FACULTY

To be completed by Evaluation Team at conclusion of evaluation process. This Decision Sheet will be attached to the Faculty Evaluation forms utilized in the evaluation procedure. The Faculty Evaluation forms and Decision Sheet shall be forwarded by the evaluation team chair through the division dean/division chair or area administrator, to the Personnel Services Office for placement in evaluatee's personnel file.

Evaluatee: _____
        (print name)

Division/Area: _____   Semester/Year: _____

Probationary Status: ☐ First Contract (year one)   ☐ Third Contract (year three)
                        ☐ Second Contract (year two)   ☐ Third Contract (year four)

_____ Review Completed: _____
                (date)

The Evaluation Team makes the following recommendation(s) (mark all that apply):

_____ Offer Second Contract for the following academic year (applies only to employee working under first contract)

_____ Offer Third Contract for the following two academic years (applies only to employee working under second contract)

_____ Third-Year Review completed (applies only to employee working under third contract and completing third year)

_____ Award Tenure (applies only to employee working under third contract and completing fourth year)

_____ Further Evaluation to be conducted prior to _____
       (if further evaluation is to be conducted, a   (date)
       remediation plan must be developed)

_____ Remediation Plan Developed

_____ Do not enter into a contract for the following year (does not apply to employee working under third contract and completing third year)

_____ Review team cannot reach a unanimous decision. (Note: if this item is checked, the appropriate division dean/division chair or area administrator in consultation with the appropriate Vice President, shall initiate an administrative follow-up of the evaluatee's performance.)

Evaluation Team: _____   _____
                        (signature)   (date)

                _____   _____
                        (signature)   (date)

                _____   _____
                        (signature)   (date)

Form 2. Faculty Evaluation, Probationary Faculty

Note: The evaluatee may respond in writing in respect to the accuracy, relevance, and completeness of the evaluation by submitting such written response to the Personnel Services Office within 20 workdays following the date he/she receives the evaluation. Such response (if any) shall become a part of the evaluation report and be placed in the evaluatee's personnel file.

Received by:_____   _____
                Evaluatee's Signature   (date)

_____   _____
Division Dean/Division Chair/Area Administrator   (date)

_____   _____
           Personnel Services Office   (date)

IN-49 4/01

Form 2 *continued*

CERRITOS COMMUNITY COLLEGE DISTRICT

DECISION SHEET: FACULTY EVALUATION

PART-TIME FACULTY

Evaluatee: _____
(print name)

Division Area: _____   Semester/Year: _____

Review Completed: _____
(date)

Areas of Evaluation:
- Knowledge in subject matter or in field of service
- Techniques of instruction and/or performance
- Effectiveness of communication
- Acceptance of responsibility

Evaluation:

_____   Satisfactory

_____   Recommended for further evaluation**

**   If recommendation for further evaluation is given, please list the areas and/or specific sub-areas in which evaluation should take place.

Evaluation Team:_____   _____
(signature)   (date)

_____   _____
(signature)   (date)

_____   _____
(signature)   (date)

Note: The evaluatee may respond in writing in respect to the accuracy, relevance, and completeness of the evaluation by submitting such written response to the Personnel Services Office within 20 workdays following the date he/she receives the evaluation. Such response (if any) shall become a part of the evaluation report and be placed in the evaluatee's personnel file.

Received by:_____   _____
Evaluatee's Signature   (date)

_____   _____
Division Dean/Division Chair/Area Administrator   (date)

_____   _____
Personnel Services Office   (date)

IN-50 1/96

Form 3. Faculty Evaluation, Part-Time Faculty

CERRITOS COMMUNITY COLLEGE DISTRICT

FACULTY PEER-REVIEW CHECKOFF SHEET

Evaluatee: _____ Division/Area: _____ Semester/Year: _____
      (print name)

Tenured: ☐Probationary: ☐First Contract (year one) ☐Third Contract (year three)
        ☐Second Contract (year two) ☐Third Contract (year four)

Overview: The procedure for faculty peer review requires the establishment of a review team. In most cases the evaluation team will be composed of a minimum of two or more members. It is necessary that the team and the evaluatee meet and establish a schedule for evaluation and review. Shown below is a suggested time line to be followed as well as a task checklist.

Spring	Fall Semester		Spring Semester	
14th/15th week of Spring Semester preceding evaluation	4th/6th week of Fall Semester evaluation year	12th/15th week	Prior to the 4th/6th week Spring Semester Second Review	Decision Sheet required by March 1
Establish the review committee	First meeting to set schedule and procedures	Class visitations Review conference	Final conference (if necessary)	

CHECKLIST Peer Review Faculty Evaluations

_____ 1. Select evaluation team and team chairperson. Notify division dean, division chair or area administrator of selections.

_____ 2. Review evaluation procedure and requirements. Establish schedule for meetings, class visitations, and review conferences.

_____ 3. Team members review class visitations, portfolios, course materials, techniques, evaluatees' performance and student evaluations.

_____ 4. Conference with evaluatee, review findings. If satisfactory sign Decision Sheet and forward to division dean, division chair or area administrator. If further evaluation or review is necessary, establish schedule and process.

Form 4. Faculty Peer-Review Checkoff Sheet

If further evaluation is necessary:

_____ 5. Follow-up conference with evaluatee. Must be accomplished by the 6th week of the Spring semester.

_____ 6. Decision Sheet signed and filed (prior to March 1).

SIGNATURES OF EVALUATION TEAM:

Chairperson _____ Members _____

IN-52 8/2000

Form 4 *continued*

CERRITOS COMMUNITY COLLEGE DISTRICT

FACULTY EVALUATION CRITERIA FORM

Evaluatee: _____   Area of Responsibility: _____
      (print name)

Division/Area: _____   Semester/Year: _____

Tenured: ☐
Probationary: ☐ First Contract (year one)   ☐Third Contract (year three)
             ☐ Second Contract (year two)   ☐Third Contract (year four)
Part-Time: ☐

If the evaluatee is either a contract (probationary) or a part-time faculty member, this completed form must be forwarded with the appropriate Decision Sheet to the Personnel Services Office for placement in the evaluatee's personnel file.

I. KNOWLEDGE OF SUBJECT MATTER

a) Has a comprehensive knowledge of the subject/area of responsibility (degrees and experience)
      ☐ Satisfactory   ☐ Needs Improvement   ☐ Not Applicable
b) Maintains currency in the discipline/area of responsibility
      ☐ Satisfactory   ☐ Needs Improvement   ☐ Not Applicable
c) Is well informed on available materials
      ☐ Satisfactory ☐ Needs Improvement   ☐ Not Applicable
d) Knows basic methods of testing, evaluating, test interpretation and assessment of students' skills, issues and concerns
      ☐ Satisfactory   ☐ Needs Improvement   ☐ Not Applicable
Comments:

II. TECHNIQUES OF INSTRUCTION AND/OR PERFORMANCE: PRESENTATION/INTERACTION WITH STUDENTS/STUDENT EVALUATIONS

a) Adheres to content and objectives of course outline of record
      ☐ Satisfactory   ☐ Needs Improvement   ☐ Not Applicable
b) Follows objectives appropriate to area of responsibility
      ☐ Satisfactory   ☐ Needs Improvement   ☐ Not Applicable
c) Organizes lessons/activities to meet student needs
      ☐ Satisfactory   ☐ Needs Improvement   ☐ Not Applicable

Form 5. Faculty Evaluation Criteria Form

d) Presents the material and information with clarity
    ☐ Satisfactory   ☐ Needs Improvement   ☐ Not Applicable

e) Shows interest in subject/area of responsibility
    ☐ Satisfactory   ☐ Needs Improvement   ☐ Not Applicable

f) Makes effective use of time
    ☐ Satisfactory   ☐ Needs Improvement   ☐ Not Applicable

Comments:

TECHNIQUES

a) Maintains an environment conducive to student learning/participation and development
    ☐ Satisfactory   ☐ Needs Improvement   ☐ Not Applicable

b) Uses appropriate methods, materials and techniques responsive to needs of students and consistent with department/area practices
    ☐ Satisfactory   ☐ Needs Improvement   ☐ Not Applicable

c) Uses appropriate methods of evaluation
    ☐ Satisfactory   ☐ Needs Improvement   ☐ Not Applicable

Comments:

III. EFFECTIVENESS OF COMMUNICATION

a) Demonstrates proficiency in written and oral English enabling clear, effective communication
    ☐ Satisfactory   ☐ Needs Improvement   ☐ Not Applicable

b) Explains fully objectives, procedures and methods of evaluation
    ☐ Satisfactory   ☐ Needs Improvement   ☐ Not Applicable

c) Explains fully alternatives, approaches, responsibilities and methods for success
    ☐ Satisfactory   ☐ Needs Improvement   ☐ Not Applicable

d) Communicates interest in the subject matter/area of responsibility
    ☐ Satisfactory   ☐ Needs Improvement   ☐ Not Applicable

e) Shows pose, confidence and occasional humor
    ☐ Satisfactory   ☐ Needs Improvement   ☐ Not Applicable

f) Maintains appropriate role in students/faculty relationship
    ☐ Satisfactory   ☐ Needs Improvement   ☐ Not Applicable

g) Manifests good rapport with students/staff
    ☐ Satisfactory   ☐ Needs Improvement   ☐ Not Applicable

Comments:

Form 5 *continued*

IV. ACCEPTANCE OF RESPONSIBILITY

a) Is punctual and meets scheduled obligations
      ☐ Satisfactory   ☐ Needs Improvement   ☐ Not Applicable
b) Follows up on responsibilities to students and staff
      ☐ Satisfactory   ☐ Needs Improvement   ☐ Not Applicable
c) Maintains records satisfactorily
      ☐ Satisfactory   ☐ Needs Improvement   ☐ Not Applicable
d) Attends assigned meetings
      ☐ Satisfactory   ☐ Needs Improvement   ☐ Not Applicable
e) Is cooperative and willing to accept constructive criticism, when it is given in an appropriate manner
      ☐ Satisfactory   ☐ Needs Improvement   ☐ Not Applicable

Comments:

ADDITIONAL COMMENTS

Signatures of Evaluation Team Members:

_____	_____	_____
Signature	Signature	Signature
_____	_____	_____
Date	Date	Date

NOTE: The evaluatee may respond in writing in respect to the accuracy, relevance, and completeness of the evaluation by submitting such written response to the Personnel Services office within 20 workdays following the date he/she receives the evaluation. Such response (if any) shall become a part of the evaluation report and be placed in the evaluatee's personnel file.

Acknowledgment of review/receipt by evaluatee (Evaluatee's signature does not necessarily imply agreement)

_____	_____
Evaluatee's Signature	Date

Form 5 *continued*

COLORADO STATE UNIVERSITY

PERFORMANCE PAY PROGRAM

Planning Confirmation and Overall Evaluation Form

General Information

Planning Period: From_____ To_____

Employee _____	Social Security Number	_____
Job Title _____	Position Number	_____
Department & _____	Supervisor	_____
4-digit mail code		

Performance Planning Management

The PDQ for this position was reviewed and is current and accurate.
Supervisor Initials:_____ Date:_____
This Program has been reviewed and understood.
Supervisor Signature _____ Date: _____
Employee Signature _____ Date: _____

Mid-Year Progress Review Meeting

At least one coaching, or progress review, meeting is required for each evaluation period; more are recommended. Indicate the date the meeting was held and the issues that were discussed.
Issues Discussed:

Supervisor Signature _____ Date: _____
Employee Signature _____ Date: _____

Overall Evaluation Rating

The overall rating for the Evaluation period:
Level 1 _____ Level 2_____ Level 3_____ Level 4 _____
Supervisor Signature _____ Date: _____
Reviewer Signature _____ Date: _____
Employee Signature _____ Date: _____
I agree with this evaluation: _____ I disagree with this evaluation: _____

Please make department/employee copies and then forward the original copy to Human Resource Services no later than May 30th. Overall Evaluation Rating section MUST have signature of employee, supervisor and reviewer to be accepted.

Form 6. Planning Confirmation and Overall Evaluation Form

PLANNING AND EVALUATION FORM

STANDARDS/GOALS/OBJECTIVES ASSOCIATED WITH SUCCESS IN THIS POSITION

"Standards/Goals/Objectives" are specific statements or requirements and agreed upon by the supervisor and the employee. "Measurement Method" reflects the evaluation basis for the expected results. "Results achieved" are the accomplishments of the employee during the evaluation period.

	Standard/Goal/Objective:	Results Achieved:
		_____ Level 4
1	Measurement Method:	
		_____ Level 3
		_____ Level 2
		_____ Level 1

	Standard/Goal/Objective:	Results Achieved:
		_____ Level 4
2	Measurement Method:	
		_____ Level 3
		_____ Level 2
		_____ Level 1

Form 7. Planning and Evaluation Form, Standards/Goals/Objectives Associated with Success in This Position

	Standard/Goal/Objective:	Results Achieved:
		_____ Level 4
3	Measurement Method:	
		_____ Level 3
		_____ Level 2
		_____ Level 1

	Standard/Goal/Objective:	Results Achieved:
		_____ Level 4
4	Measurement Method:	
		_____ Level 3
		_____ Level 2
		_____ Level 1

	Standard/Goal/Objective:	Results Achieved:
		_____ Level 4
5	Measurement Method:	
		_____ Level 3
		_____ Level 2
		_____ Level 1

S.M.A.R.T. GOALS

Specific—they precisely define the work involved.
Measurable—quantitative, qualitative, and timely.
Agreed—both supervisor and employee are committed.
Realistic—an acceptable but stretching challenge.
Timed—specify completion and review dates.

There are five types of standards/goals/objectives:
- To achieve routine work assignments.
- To resolve identified problems.
- To support innovation.
- For professional development.
- To support institutional or departmental goals.

Form 7 *continued*

Behaviors Associated with Success in This Position

Check behaviors that will be evaluated. As with standards/goals/objectives, careful discussion of expectations should occur. Use the blank spaces to weigh job-specific behavior:

> E = Essential   I = Important   N = Not Applicable

Then, Please rate according to the following levels for performance:

_____ **Job Knowledge/Potential**: Possesses knowledge of established policies and procedures. Possesses sufficient skills and knowledge to perform all parts of the job effectively and efficiently. Provides technical assistance to others and is consulted by others on technical matters. Pursues professional development. Displays innovation.
Level 1 _____ Level 2 _____ Level 3 _____ Level 4 _____

_____ **Accountability**: Meets changing conditions and situations in work responsibilities. Accepts constructive criticism and suggestions and makes appropriate changes. Handles conflict in a constructive manner. Seeks solutions acceptable to all. Willingness to accept supervision. Can consistently be relied on to perform job. Seldom needs to be reminded. Is fully ready to work at beginning of work schedule and continues until workday is done. Does not abuse leave practices.
Level 1 _____ Level 2 _____ Level 3 _____ Level 4 _____

_____ **Interpersonal Relations**: Maintains smooth working relations, support and respect of others. Demonstrates tact and diplomacy in negotiations or confrontations with others. Contributes to employee morale and motivations. Is accessible to others and responsive to their questions, needs and concerns. Supports and appreciates the diversity of co-workers, students, customers, and visitors. Shares information, credit and opportunities. Displays an appropriate balance between personal effort and team effort.
Level 1 _____ Level 2 _____ Level 3 _____ Level 4 _____

_____ **Communications**: Demonstrates effective listening skills. Uses appropriate language and terminology. Speaks in a manner that is understood, courteous and effective. Seeks and considers ideas from others on issues that affect them. Keeps supervisor and co-workers informed. Prepares written documents that are complete, clear and understandable. Is considerate of the communication skills of others.
Level 1 _____ Level 2 _____ Level 3 _____ Level 4 _____

_____ **Customer Service**: Provides prompt and friendly service to internal and external customers. Helps identify customer needs through courteous questioning and a sincere desire to be helpful. Follows up with customers, as appropriate, to insure satisfaction. Considers and recommends alternatives to costumers when needed.
Level 1 _____ Level 2 _____ Level 3 _____ Level 4 _____

_____ **Competence/Responsibility**: Maintains quality/quantity standards. Accepts responsibility for all areas of job. Uses time effectively with minimal errors. Completes work thoroughly in a reasonable amount of time. Meets or surpasses established goals. Works accurately, neatly, and attends to detail.
Level 1 _____ Level 2 _____ Level 3 _____ Level 4 _____

_____ **Motivation/Commitment**: Displays drive and energy in accomplishing tasks. Handles several responsibilities concurrently. Conveys positive and professional image of work unit to others. Puts forth extra

---

Form 8. Behaviors Associated with Success in This Position

effort when needed. Agrees to modify schedule or adapt Programs when necessary. Self-starter. Displays positive attitude in work assignments and interactions with others.

Level 1 _____ Level 2 _____ Level 3 _____ Level 4 _____

_____ **Problem Solving/Reasoning**: Recognizes and analyzes work related problems. Uses available resources to evaluate and recommend potential solutions. Ability to use good judgment to arrive at sound conclusions. Ability to take timely action.

Level 1 _____ Level 2 _____ Level 3 _____ Level 4 _____

_____ **Safety**: Aware of job safety procedures. Keeps abreast of changes in safety procedures. Practices safety work habits. Reports possible safety hazards to supervisor. Attends safety-training programs, as appropriate.

Level 1 _____ Level 2 _____ Level 3 _____ Level 4 _____

_____ **Supervision/Performance Management**: Employees supervised demonstrate productivity, competence and high morale. Provides supervision, feedback and training for employees. Utilizes employee's skills and abilities. Conducts performance Planning and evaluations for employees in a timely manner. Develops goals, objectives and deadlines and communicates them to employees. Resolves routine personnel issues or problems.

Level 1 _____ Level 2 _____ Level 3 _____ Level 4 _____

Additional benchmarked behaviors/competencies available on the web at: http:www .colostate.edu/Depts/HRS/cpp/index.html

Level 1 _____ Level 2 _____ Level 3 _____ Level 4 _____

Level 1 _____ Level 2 _____ Level 3 _____ Level 4 _____

Level 1 _____ Level 2 _____ Level 3 _____ Level 4 _____

Form 8 *continued*

Training and Development Programs

_____

_____

_____

_____

_____

_____

Narrative Section

(For use by Supervisor to amplify the evaluation or Employee to explain disagreement with the evaluation; attach additional sheets if necessary).

_____

_____

_____

_____

_____

_____

_____

Form 8 *continued*

PERFORMANCE PAY DISPUTE RESOLUTION FORM

Date _____

Employee's Name _____ Job Title _____

Department & 4-digit mail code _____ Supervisor _____

I wish to have the following reviewed:

_____ 1. My performance plan or lack of a plan. The error or problem is:

_____ 2. My performance rating. The error or problem is:

_____ 3. The application of the CSU Performance Pay Program, process, or policies to my plan or evaluation. The error or problem is:

_____ 4. Full payment of my award. The error or problem is:

To resolve this issue, I have taken the following actions:

_____

_____

_____

_____

_____

RESOLUTION BEING REQUESTED: _____

_____

_____

_____

_____

Employee's Signature: _____ Date: _____

For additional information on the dispute resolution process including the form to use in proceeding to the external process consult the User Guide, Section VII available on the web at: http://www.colostate.edu/Depts/HRS/cpp/user_guide/toc.html, or by contacting the CSU Employee Relations Manager at 970-491-3548.

Submit copies to your supervisor, reviewer and to Human Resource Services.

Form 9. Performance Pay Dispute Resolution Form

HAYWARD PUBLIC LIBRARY

LIBRARY PAGE PERFORMANCE EVALUATION

Name: Date of Hire:

Date of Last Evaluation: Supervisor:

O = Outstanding G = Good A = Average N = Needs Improvement U = Unsatisfactory

TASK PERFORMANCE		O	G	A	N	U
Following Directions:	Demonstrates ability to learn new tasks, and retains instruction.					
Efficiency:	Speed and accuracy. Uses time wisely.					
Dependability:	Rarely needs reminding. Follows through with tasks.					
Initiative:	Seeks work assignments. Wants to learn.					
WORK HABITS						
Attendance:	Always at work or advises library of absence.					
Punctuality:	Always on time. Works to end of shift.					
Attitude:	Cooperation and courtesy toward public and staff.					
Conduct:	Keeps idle conversation to a minimum and does not disrupt the work of others.					

Special Assignments or Skills:	Outstanding	Good	Average	Needs Improvement	Unsatisfactory
1.					
2.					
3.					

Employer Comments:

Overall Evaluation:	Outstanding	Good	Average	Needs Improvement	Unsatisfactory

OVERALL PERFORMANCE SUMMARY

_____

HIGH ACHIEVEMENT AREAS   GOALS FOR NEXT APPRAISAL

_____

Form 10. Library Page Performance Evaluation

Supervisor/Rater's Signature

Title: Date:

(Signature certifies that evaluation was completed by supervisor of employee during period of evaluation, that it was shown to and discussed with the employee, that employment standards have been clearly defined for the employee, and that it is an accurate statement of the employee's work performance).

EMPLOYEE COMMENTS

(Reaction, Assistance Required, Personal Goals, etc.)

Employee Statement Attached? ☐

Employee's Signature: Date:

(Signature certifies that evaluation has been read and discussed with supervisor and that the criteria used are understood. It does not necessarily indicate agreement or disagreement with ratings/comments).

Reviewed by:

Comments:

Reviewed by:

Original: Human Resources (Employee's File)
            Copy 1. Employee.
            Copy 2. Department Personnel File.
            Copy 3. Supervisor's File.

Form 10 *continued*

CITY OF HAYWARD

PERFORMANCE APPRAISAL FORM

Concerning

Employee Name	Classification Title
Department/Division Name	Reason for Appraisal	Appraisal Date (Sent) (Returned)
Date of Hire	Period of Report From:	To:

Describe present assignment:

0—Not Observed/Not Applicable
1—Inadequate
2—Marginal-Needs to Improve
3—Competent
4—Highly Competent
5—Superior

POINTS OF EVALUATION

1. **Expected Output**
   Does the quantity and quality of work performed by the employee
   meet the requirements of the job as you have explained them to the
   employee? Is the work performed accurately?

   0 1 2 3 4 5
   ☐ ☐ ☐ ☐ ☐ ☐

2. **Deadlines/Commitments**
   Does the employee meet deadlines and keep commitments;plan and
   schedule work to get expected results within allocated time, and
   anticipate problems in meeting deadlines?

   0 1 2 3 4 5
   ☐ ☐ ☐ ☐ ☐ ☐

POINTS OF EVALUATION

3. **Technical Knowledge**
   Does the employee have adequate knowledge of the technical aspects
   of the job and job responsibilities, including knowledge of the City's
   policies and procedures, and their application?

   0 1 2 3 4 5
   ☐ ☐ ☐ ☐ ☐ ☐

Form 11. Performance Appraisal Form

4. **Safety Procedures**

0	1	2	3	4	5
☐	☐	☐	☐	☐	☐

Is the employee committed to the enforcement of the City's safety/ loss control program? Does the employee routinely observe all safety practices, recognizing and correcting hazards?

5. **Orderly and Organized**

0	1	2	3	4	5
☐	☐	☐	☐	☐	☐

Are the employee's work methods and work area orderly and organized in order that work is performed in an efficient and safe manner?

6. **Uses Time Effectively**

0	1	2	3	4	5
☐	☐	☐	☐	☐	☐

Does the employee recognize the relative urgency of assignment and personally accommodate the workload, in order to get the job done on time?

7. **Works with the Public**

0	1	2	3	4	5
☐	☐	☐	☐	☐	☐

Does the employee establish and maintain good rapport with the public; persist diplomatically in order to obtain information or cooperation and overcome personality differences when they arise?

8. **Works with Fellows**

0	1	2	3	4	5
☐	☐	☐	☐	☐	☐

Is the employee friendly, personable and considerate? Does the employee adapt; give and accept criticism well and ignore personal differences in the interest of furthering the goals of the group project?

POINTS OF EVALUATION

9. **Ability to Adjust**

0	1	2	3	4	5
☐	☐	☐	☐	☐	☐

Does the employee accept changing practices, policies, procedures, priorities and people; and adjust and respond to changing conditions appropriately?

10. **Self-Improvement Activity**

0	1	2	3	4	5
☐	☐	☐	☐	☐	☐

How has the employee reacted to the counseling and suggestions which wereprompted by the last formal appraisal? What was accomplished toward the goals and objectives established in the previous appraisal interview? If the employee has failed to follow through, indicate reason(s) why.

11. **Attendance and Punctuality**

0	1	2	3	4	5
☐	☐	☐	☐	☐	☐

Indicate time off the job during the past year, due to:
Sick Leave   (2002 City Average: 67 hours)
Comments—Attendance:
Comments—Punctuality:

Form 11 *continued*

OVERALL PERFORMANCE SUMMARY

HIGH ACHIEVEMENT AREAS   GOALS FOR NEXT APPRAISAL

Supervisor/Rater's Signature

Title: Date:

(Signature certifies that evaluation was completed by supervisor of employee during period of evaluation, that it was shown to and discussed with the employee, that employment standards have been clearly defined for the employee, and that it is an accurate statement of the employee's work performance).

EMPLOYEE COMMENTS

(Reaction, Assistance Required, Personal Goals, etc.)

Employee Statement Attached? ☐

Employee's Signature: Date:

(Signature certifies that evaluation has been read and discussed with supervisor and that the criteria used are understood. It does not necessarily indicate agreement or disagreement with ratings/comments).

Comments:

Reviewed by:

Original: Human Resources (Employee's File)
                 Copy 1. Employee.
                 Copy 2. Department Personnel File.
                 Copy 3. Supervisor's File.

Form 11 *continued*

Management Unit Supplement

Name: _____

0—Not Observed/Not Applicable
1—Inadequate
2—Marginal-Needs to Improve
3—Competent
4—Highly Competent
5—Superior

POINTS OF EVALUATION

12. Measures/Evaluates Work

0	1	2	3	4	5
☐	☐	☐	☐	☐	☐

Does the supervisor use acceptable workload efficiency and effectiveness measures to gauge the performance of work and its organization?

13. Plan/Assign/Direct Work

0	1	2	3	4	5
☐	☐	☐	☐	☐	☐

Prior to beginning a project, does the supervisor effectively plan and assign work for the most efficient use of personnel resources and equipment? Are the supervisor's estimated times for completion of projects generally correct?

14. Organizes/Coordinates

0	1	2	3	4	5
☐	☐	☐	☐	☐	☐

During a project, does the supervisor effectively organize and coordinate people and resources to meet or exceed performance objectives; and execute plans and activities within the budget appropriation?

15. Decisions/Judgment

0	1	2	3	4	5
☐	☐	☐	☐	☐	☐

Does the supervisor effectively apply logic and decision making principles; select the most appropriate decision from among options, share the decision with others as appropriate, and follow through with decisions?

POINTS OF EVALUATION

16. Training/Development

0	1	2	3	4	5
☐	☐	☐	☐	☐	☐

Does the supervisor maintain high performance by initiating timely employee training, performance evaluations, and assisting employees with career planning?

17. Cost Reduction Activities

0	1	2	3	4	5
☐	☐	☐	☐	☐	☐

Does the supervisor aggressively work to find and implement effective methods to reduce the expense of achieving the City's goals?

Form 12. Management Unit Supplement

18. Delegation of Authority

    0 1 2 3 4 5

    ☐ ☐ ☐ ☐ ☐ ☐

Does the supervisor assign responsibility to others and "step away" from assignments yet still maintain control; using delegation as a means of time management? Does the supervisor accept the work responsibility for negative results of delegated work?

19. Technically Aware

    0 1 2 3 4 5

    ☐ ☐ ☐ ☐ ☐ ☐

Does the supervisor remain aware of current developments and writings related to the job? Does the supervisor have an ongoing program of self-improvement to expand job related knowledge and skills?

20. Negotiate/Settle Disputes

    0 1 2 3 4 5

    ☐ ☐ ☐ ☐ ☐ ☐

Does the supervisor effectively settle disputes without engendering employee hostility and grievance procedures?

21. Meets Budget Goals

    0 1 2 3 4 5

    ☐ ☐ ☐ ☐ ☐ ☐

Does the supervisor develop and achieve relevant objectives, translate goals and objectives into useful activities and effectively deal with barriers to meeting agreed upon goals and objectives?

Form 12 *continued*

Name: _____ Date: _____

EMPLOYEE INPUT SHEET

OPTIONAL

(For preparation by the employee)

To the Employee: Before meeting with your supervisor to discuss your performance review, write out answers to the following questions:

1. How would you summarize your achievements since the last Performance Planning discussion?

2. What are the most interesting parts of your job? The least?

3. What help would you like your supervisor to give you?

4. What specific job targets do you propose for the next Performance Planning period?

5. What changes, if any, would you like to see made with regard to your job, work procedures or organization that would help you to improve your performance?

6. What work would you like to do in the future? How can you prepare for it?

Form 13. Employee Input Sheet

HUNTINGTON LIBRARY

PERFORMANCE APPRAISAL

Name _____   Appraisal Date _____

Title _____   Date of Hire _____

Department _____   Supervisor _____

INSTRUCTIONS: Refer to *"Guidelines for Supervisors"* for information. Please type or print legibly using black or blue ink. Use the reverse of the page if necessary.

1. **GENERAL PERFORMANCE RESULTS:** Evaluate the employee's work performance and accomplishments over the review period. If appropriate, include a discussion of specific goals and objectives established during the year and the extent to which these goals and objectives were met or not met. SAFETY ISSUES: Comment on the employee's safety record (e.g., attendance at training sessions, safe work habits, use of personal protective equipment, etc.). Was the employee involved in any work-related accidents? Were they avoidable? For a supervisory staff member being appraised, also comment on the safety record of his/her staff.

2. **GENERAL PERFORMANCE CHARACTERISTICS:** Consider characteristics and attitudes of the employee which are relevant to job performance, such as interpersonal skills, attitudes, initiative, judgment, teamwork, adherence to deadlines, meeting commitments, following instructions and willingness to learn. Comment only on how such characteristics have affected the employee's job performance and give examples.

3. **PLANS FOR IMPROVEMENT:** Comment on specific ways in which the employee's performance might be improved. Consider both what the employee may need to do to improve and what the supervisor could do to help the employee improve performance. Include agreed-upon actions, target dates

Form 14. Performance Appraisal

and expected results. SAFETY IMPROVEMENTS: Comment on specific ways the employee's safety behavior might be improved (Additional training? Use of personal protective equipment?). For a supervisory staff member, what must he/she do to keep his/her staff free of future injuries? (Conduct "tail-gate" or "just-in-time" training? Monitor safety behavior of staff?).

4. CHOOSE OPTION (A) OR (B) TO COMPLETE:
A. Overall performance rating:

Superior__   Good__   Satisfactory__   Needs Improvement__   Unacceptable__

B. Narrative summary of performance:

5. ADDITIONAL COMMENTS:

_____   _____
Supervisor   Date   Personnel   Date

_____   _____
Next Level of Management   Date   Employee   Date

*Employee's signature does not necessarily indicate agreement with this performance appraisal, but rather that the appraisal has been received and understood. Written comments by the employee may be made on a separate sheet.

Form 14 *continued*

SUPPLEMENTAL PERFORMANCE APPRAISAL (FORM A) FOR MANAGERIAL STAFF

Name: _____   Date: _____

In addition to the standard Performance Appraisal, this supplement should be completed for all staff members with supervisorial responsibility. Please comment on the staff member in terms of:

* <u>Leadership</u>: Effectiveness in gaining commitment and inspiring teamwork and accomplishment among subordinates; communication of departmental and institutional goals.

* <u>Development of Staff</u>: Effectiveness in training and coaching staff; giving performance feedback and encouraging improvement; supporting professional development; conducting effective performance reviews.

* <u>Administration</u>: Effectiveness in planning, organizing and executing departmental work; delegation and follow-up skills.

* <u>Budget Management</u>: Effectiveness in planning and managing the department, program and/or project budget.

* <u>Interpersonal Relationships and Professional Conduct</u>: Effectiveness in interacting with staff throughout the institution; extent to which the employee's conduct meets the institution's standards of professionalism.

APPRAISAL COMMENTS:

Form 15. Supplemental Performance Appraisal (Form A) for Managerial Staff

PERFORMANCE RATING DEFINITIONS

Superior

Performance of this caliber is rare. This rating describes performance that consistently exceeds the highest standards and requirements, especially in the principal areas of responsibility.

Good

Indicates performance that routinely meets high performance standards in all areas of responsibility and may occasionally exceed requirements of the position in terms of quality and quantity of work produced.

Satisfactory

Indicates performance which meets expectations. Also may be a few occasions where standards were not met, but on balance, performance was acceptable over the course of the review period.

Needs Improvement

This performance does not fully meet job requirements in areas of major responsibility. The individual may demonstrate the ability to complete some assignments; however, the need for further development and improvement is clearly recognized.

Unacceptable

Indicates that the person's performance is below minimum job requirements, even when close supervision has been provided.

Form 16. Performance Ratings Definitions

LOYOLA MARYMOUNT UNIVERSITY

ADMINISTRATIVE & PROFESSIONAL STAFF

2001 STAFF DEVELOPMENT REVIEW

I.   GENERAL INFORMATION

Name	Title
Division	Dept/Office
Service Date	Time in Present Position
This Development Review Cycle—From:	To:
Date Prepared	Reviewer

II.   POSITION FUNCTION (Supervisor and employee review the job description at the time of this review).

Have you reviewed the job description with this employee?   ___ Yes   ___ No
Are there any responsibilities to be changed?   ___ Yes   ___ No

III.   DEVELOPMENT REVIEW INSTRUCTIONS

The following are instructions for completing the Staff Development Review form.

- Prior to conducting the review, survey the employee's job description to determine if duties have changed since last year.
- Prior to conducting the review, refer to the attachment titled "How to Give a Development Review Tips for Supervisors" and "How to Receive a Development Review Tips for Staff Members." These are helpful tips for giving and receiving reviews.
- Evaluate the staff member's performance and development for a 12-month period through the date of review.
- Under subsection A, evaluate the employee's performance of the duties and responsibilities in his/her job description and on the projects in his/her goals and objectives. Included in this attachment are the Performance Factors Guidelines that are common to most Administrative and Professional staff positions. Please review the attached guidelines document prior to completing the form.
- Evaluate the employee's performance on each performance factor by checking the appropriate rating for each item.
- Each rating (outstanding, highly effective, effective, needs improvement and unacceptable), corresponds to each performance factor. For example, the first performance factor represents (outstanding), the second (highly effective), the third (effective), the fourth (needs improvement) and the fifth (unacceptable).
- Provide written justification of the ratings as well as staff development plans and goals. For the extremes, (outstanding and unacceptable), a written justification must be provided.

Form 17. Administrative and Professional Staff Development Review

- Under subsection B and C, describe the employee's accomplishments and development and make recommendations for any needed improvements in performance.
- If you need to attach a separate sheet for comments, please do so.

A. PERFORMANCE FACTORS: Review the attachment on Performance Factors (outstanding, highly effective, effective, needs improvement and unacceptable). Evaluate the employee's performance on each factor by checking the appropriate rating for each item.

	OUTSTANDING	HIGHLY EFFECTIVE	EFFECTIVE	NEEDS IMPROVEMENT	UNACCEPTABLE
1. QUALITY OF WORK					
2. LMU SERVICE STANDARDS					
3. PRODUCTIVITY					
4. PUNCTUALITY					
5. WRITTEN COMMUNICATION					
6. ORAL COMMUNICATION					
7. KNOWLEDGE OF JOB					
8. INITIATIVE AND RESOURCEFULNESS					
9. JUDGMENT					
10. WORKING RELATIONSHIPS					
11. SENSITIVITY TO DIVERSITY					
12. TIME MANAGEMENT AND PLANNING					

	ACCEPTABLE	NEEDS IMPROVEMENT	UNACCEPTABLE
13. ATTENDANCE			

THE FOLLOWING ITEMS ARE TO BE COMPLETED FOR **SUPERVISORY** A&P STAFF:

	OUTSTANDING	HIGHLY EFFECTIVE	EFFECTIVE	NEEDS IMPROVEMENT	UNACCEPTABLE
1. SUPERVISION OF OTHERS					
2. DEVELOPMENT OF STAFF					
3. FISCAL MANAGEMENT					

Form 17 *continued*

Use the space below for comments related to the above performance factors. If more space is needed, please attach a comment sheet.

B. EXCEPTIONAL ACCOMPLISHMENTS: Describe any exceptional accomplishments which go beyond the employee's job description (e.g., committee work, special projects, service to the LMU community, job-related education and training). If more space is needed, please attach a comment sheet.

C. AREAS FOR IMPROVEMENT: Describe any areas for improvement. If more space is needed, please attach a comment sheet.

IV. **STAFF DEVELOPMENT PLAN/GOALS AND OBJECTIVES**: Describe any plans including goals and objectives for this employee's professional development. Specify whether these plans are for improvement in the employee's present position, development of new skills, and/or career advancement. Include the steps to be taken by both the employee and the employee's supervisor. If more space is needed, please attach a comment sheet.

V.   SIGNATURES

A. To be completed by the **Supervisor** at the end of the development review cycle:

I have discussed this review with the employee and explained the procedure for filing a rebuttal if s/he disagrees.

Signature _____   Date _____

B. To be completed by the **Employee** at the end of the development review cycle:

_____ I have read and discussed my development review with my supervisor and have received a copy.

_____ I disagree with portions of this development review and have a right to file a rebuttal in my personnel file. (See below)

Steps:
- Prepare a written rebuttal to your supervisor and send a copy to Human Resources.
- The rebuttal will be attached with your review in your personnel file.

Signature _____   Date _____

C. To be completed by the **Supervisor's Supervisor** at the end of the development review cycle:

Signature _____   Date _____

DISTRIBUTION:
Original: Human Resources
Copies: Supervisor and Employee

LOYOLA MARYMOUNT UNIVERSITY

ADMINISTRATIVE & PROFESSIONAL STAFF

PERFORMANCE FACTORS GUIDELINES

The following represents the performance factors guidelines. Please refer to these guidelines when you are evaluating the employee's performance.

1. QUALITY OF WORK

Thoroughness, accuracy and neatness of work produced

- **(Outstanding)** Work is consistently error free, thorough, neat, correct, logically organized and statistically accurate.
- **(Highly Effective)** Work is nearly always error free (with a few very minor errors), thorough, neat, correct, logically organized and statistically accurate.
- **(Effective)** Work contains some acceptable errors that may require some review and editing by supervisor.
- **(Needs Improvement)** Work reflects errors that require careful review and correction by supervisor or partial reworking/revision.
- **(Unacceptable)** Work is frequently not acceptable or useable.

2. LMU SERVICE STANDARDS

Effectiveness of demonstrating the LMU Service Standards to the LMU community, including students, parents, faculty, staff and outside guests.

- **(Outstanding)** Exceptional service orientation; exceptionally friendly and helpful toward others.
- **(Highly Effective)** Good service orientation; friendly and helpful toward others.
- **(Effective)** Regularly meets service expectations.
- **(Needs Improvement)** Sometimes forgets service orientation and serves at a substandard level.
- **(Unacceptable)** Rarely demonstrates LMU's service standards. Often rude and offensive toward others.

3. PRODUCTIVITY

Meets established deadlines; sets new goals upon task completion.

- **(Outstanding)** Exceeds expectations with regard to volume and deadlines; sets new goals upon completion of task; is cooperative, energetic and resourceful; develops new ideas or approaches to problems.
- **(Highly Effective)** Meets deadlines and volume expectations; does more than is required; sets new goals, is constructive, energetic and develops new ideas and approaches to problems.

- **(Effective)** Meets performance expectations of a reasonable proportion of deadlines; does what is required; sets new goals and develops new ideas or approaches to problems.
- **(Needs Improvement)** Performs below expectations, frequently misses deadlines and is not goal oriented.
- **(Unacceptable)** Amount of work produced is unacceptable. Does not meet deadlines or set goals.

4. PUNCTUALITY

Reporting to work or appointments on time; frequency of leaving work before end of shift.

- **(Outstanding)** Always on time for work and/or appointments and remains at work as needed.
- **(Highly Effective)** Rarely tardy in reporting for work and for appointments; very rarely leaves work early.
- **(Effective)** Seldom tardy for work or for appointments; seldom leaves work early.
- **(Needs Improvement)** Sometimes tardy for work or for appointments; sometimes leaves work early without a valid reason.

Form 18. Administrative and Professional Staff Performance Factors Guidelines

- **(Unacceptable)** Often tardy for work or for appointments; often leaves work early.

5. WRITTEN COMMUNICATION

Clarity of communication; organization and consistency of ideas.

- **(Outstanding)** Written communication is exceptional because it is logically organized, accurate, stylistically consistent, and persuasive; spelling, grammar and composition are correct.
- **(Highly Effective)** Written communication is well organized, accurate, consistent and persuasive; review of spelling, grammar and composition is sometimes warranted.
- **(Effective)** Meets expectations of clarity and consistency in written communication, which contains some errors and may require editing by supervisor.
- **(Needs Improvement)** Written communication contains significant errors, which require correction by supervisor, heavy editing or partial redrafting.
- **(Unacceptable)** Written communication is unacceptable in terms of clarity, organization and content.

6. ORAL COMMUNICATION

Clarity of communication; organization and consistency of ideas.

- **(Outstanding)** Oral communication is exceptional; engages the recipient; concise, logical and clearly understandable.
- **(Highly Effective)** Oral communication is consistently concise and understandable.
- **(Effective)** Meets expectations of oral communication in a concise and logical manner.
- **(Needs Improvement)** Oral communication is sometimes confusing and misunderstood by others.
- **(Unacceptable)** Oral communication is not acceptable. Expressed ideas must be passed onto other personnel for presentation and understanding.

7. KNOWLEDGE OF JOB

Mastery of all phases of job; adapts information and procedures to new tasks.

- **(Outstanding)** Has an exceptionally thorough grasp of all facets of the job; understands nuances of the university, the office and the job.
- **(Highly Effective)** Has a good grasp of the job; rarely requires assistance.
- **(Effective)** Has grasp of the job; requires, minimal supervision; some opportunities for additional knowledge, experience or training do exist.
- **(Needs Improvement)** Needs improvement to perform the job; requires supervision and additional training.
- **(Unacceptable)** Lacks knowledge and skills to effectively perform duties and responsibilities of the job. Training required may be excessive.

8. INITIATIVE AND RESOURCEFULNESS

Thinks constructively and originates action.

- **(Outstanding)** Completely self-reliant, handles novel or problem situations creatively; consistently formulates solutions to problems; stays on top of situations and originates action (pro-active).
- **(Highly Effective)** Sometimes needs assistance, but generally finds a solution to novel or problem situation; stays ahead of situations and originates action.
- **(Effective)** Meets expectations for finding solutions to problems and sometimes originates action.
- **(Needs Improvement)** Seldom finds solutions to novel or problem situations without assistance, usually depends on others for direction; seldom originates action and is usually reactive.
- **(Unacceptable)** Overwhelmed by problems; shows no initiative; cannot seem to formulate acceptable solutions; always reactive.

9. JUDGMENT

Analyzes facts, considers related impact, and arrives at sound conclusions.

- **(Outstanding)** Exceptional ability to analyze the facts, consider related impacts, and arrive at sound conclusions; consistently reflects discretion and good taste; always demonstrates discernment.

- **(Highly Effective)** Most often analyzes facts, considers impacts and reaches sound conclusions; frequently reflects discretion, good taste and discernment.
- **(Effective)** Exhibits reasonable ability to analyze, draw inferences, reach judgments and demonstrate discernment and good taste.
- **(Needs Improvement)** Seldom reflects the ability to analyze, draw inferences, reach judgments and exercise discretion seldom demonstrates discernment.
- **(Unacceptable)** Demonstrates almost no ability to analyze, draw inferences, reach judgments, and reflect discretion and good taste.

10. WORKING RELATIONSHIPS

Effectiveness of interpersonal relations with faculty and other staff employees as well as attitude toward job and LMU.

- **(Outstanding)** consistently displays exceptional enthusiasm toward working with others and toward their work; excellent team worker who actively creates good will.
- **(Highly Effective)** Displays enthusiasm toward working with others and toward their work; exercises tact and discretion; a good team worker; courteous.

- **(Effective)** Displays genuine interest in working with others and their work; cooperative and pleasant; creates a favorable impression.
- **(Needs Improvement)** Displays marginal interest in working with others and in their work; occasionally uncooperative, unfriendly, curt or irritable; sometimes has negative effect on others.
- **(Unacceptable)** Indifferent exhibits no interest in working with others and their work. Defensive and argumentative. Cooperates only when forced to and has negative effect on others.

11. SENSITIVITY TO DIVERSITY

Degree to which the employee's actions indicate that s/he values the uniqueness of each individual, and respects human differences wherever s/he encounters them.

- **(Outstanding)** consistently demonstrates his/her respect for diversity. Sets an example for others; displays behavior that clearly shows an appreciation of the uniqueness of the individual and attempts to utilize, positively, human differences.
- **(Highly Effective)** Shows, by example, that s/he appreciates human differences and values diversity. Educates him/herself concerning diversity and actively seeks to share his/her knowledge and experience with

others, as well as gaining from experience.

- **(Effective)** Shows, by example, that s/he values diversity and respect.
- **(Needs Improvement)** Needs improvement and training to achieve a better understanding of human differences.
- **(Unacceptable)** Often makes statements or displays body language or behavior that indicates insensitivity.

12. TIME MANAGMENT AND PLANNING

Flexibility in planning and coordinating work; adherence to schedules.

- **(Outstanding)** Exceptional ability to balance priorities effectively; consistently grasps what takes precedence and works on what is most urgently needed; meets schedules and deadlines.
- **(Highly Effective)** Has a good grasp of priorities and what should take precedence; responds to most urgent priorities first; usually meets deadlines and schedules.
- **(Effective)** Meets expectations of setting priorities with some consultation; and may need assistance in coordinating work plans, scheduling and deadlines.
- **(Needs Improvement)** Cannot seem to meet deadlines without supervision; does not seem to grasp how to prioritize.

Form 18 *continued*

- **(Unacceptable)** Fails to meet deadlines or schedules; cannot manage time.

13. ATTENDANCE

The dependability of the individual in adhering to availability and attendance standards. Is at work at times other than approved vacation and holidays

- **(Acceptable)** The supervisor finds that the employee's attendance is acceptable.
- **(Needs Improvement)** The supervisor finds that the employee's attendance needs improvement.
- **(Unacceptable)** The supervisor finds that the employee's attendance is unacceptable.

Form 18 *continued*

The following items apply to SUPERVISORY Administrative & Professional staff.

1. SUPERVISION OF OTHERS

Degree to which the supervisor obtains optimum productivity and respect from subordinates, models appropriate behavior, and effectively deals with adversity and challenge.

- **(Outstanding)** Exceptional skill in directing, guiding, motivating and inspiring top performance of work team; consistently models appropriate behavior; deals positively with adversity and challenge; causes productivity of work group to be exceptionally high.
- **(Highly Effective)** Models appropriate behavior and obtains cooperation of work team; gets the job done on time with quality results; deals with adversity and challenge in a positive manner.
- **(Effective)** Demonstrates an acceptable ability to lead effectively; obtains adequate cooperation and gets the job done on time; seldom fails to model appropriate behavior or deal effectively with adversity and challenge; productivity of work team meets requirements.
- **(Needs Improvement)** Generally displays a lack of ability to direct, guide and motivate; has trouble getting the job done and frequently deals inappropriately with difficult or challenging situations; productivity of work team is lower than expectations.

- **(Unacceptable)** Frequently exhibits a lack of the qualities necessary to lead others; is not effective in dealing with adversity and challenge; productivity of work team supervised is considerably lower than requirements; morale is low as indicated by the numbers of grievances, tardies, absences and accidents.

2. DEVELOPMENT OF STAFF

Plans assignments and delegates responsibilities to maximize employees' performance and potential; encourages and practices two-way communication; recognizes accomplishments; suggests and provides training and development opportunities.

- **(Outstanding)** Consistently plans assignments and delegates responsibilities to maximize employee performance and potential; always encourages and practices two-way communication, listens well and suggests and provides training.
- **(Highly Effective)** Plans assignments and delegates responsibilities to maximize employee performance and potential; often encourages and practices two-way communication, listens well, and recognizes accomplishments; often suggests and provides some training.

- **(Effective)** Displays acceptable ability to plan assignments and delegate responsibilities; sometimes encourages and practices two-way communication, listens, and recognizes accomplishments; sometimes suggests and provides training.
- **(Needs Improvement)** Seldom plans assignments and delegates responsibilities well; seldom encourages and practices two-way communication or listens; seldom recognizes accomplishments or suggests and provides training.
- **(Unacceptable)** Ability to plan assignments, delegate responsibilities, give encouragement and listen to maximize employee performance and potential is not acceptable.

3. FISCAL MANAGEMENT (IF APPLICABLE)

Anticipates spending needs; keeps expenditures within budget.

- **(Outstanding)** Exceptionally skilled in planning expenditures to stay within the budget; always evaluates and adjusts spending plans to meet changing circumstances or unexpected problems.
- **(Highly Effective)** Keeps most accounts within budget; demonstrates a high ability to evaluate and adjust spending plans to meet changing circumstances or unexpected problems.

Form 18 *continued*

- **(Effective)** Keeps an acceptable portion of accounts within budget; demonstrates some ability to evaluate and adjust spending to meet changing circumstances or unexpected problems.

- **(Needs Improvement)** Few accounts stay within budget; demonstrates little ability to evaluate and adjust spending plans to meet changing circumstances or unexpected problems.

- **(Unacceptable)** Cannot keep accounts within budget; demonstrates no ability to adjust spending plan.

Form 18 *continued*

LOYOLA MARYMOUNT UNIVERSITY

OFFICE & TECHNICAL STAFF AND SERVICE STAFF

2001 STAFF DEVELOPMENT REVIEW

I.   GENERAL INFORMATION

Name   Title

Division   Dept/Office

Service Date   Time in Present Position

This Development Review Cycle—From: To:

Date Prepared   Reviewer

II.   POSITION FUNCTION (Supervisor and employee review the job description at the time of this review).

Have you reviewed the job description with this employee?   ___ Yes   ___ No

Are there any responsibilities to be changed?   ___ Yes   ___ No

III.   DEVELOPMENT REVIEW INSTRUCTIONS

The following are instructions for completing the Staff Development Review form.

- Prior to conducting the review, review the employee's job description to determine if duties have changed since last year.
- Prior to conducting the review, refer to the attachment titled "How to Give a Development Review Tips for Supervisors" and "How to Receive a Development Review Tips for Staff Members." These are helpful tips for giving and receiving reviews.
- Evaluate the staff member's performance and development for a 12-month period through the date of review.
- Under subsection A, evaluate the employee's performance of the duties and responsibilities in his/her job description and on the projects in his/her goals and objectives. Included in this attachment are the Performance Factors Guidelines that are common to most Office & Technical/Service staff positions. Please review the attached guidelines document prior to completing the form.
- Evaluate the employee's performance on each performance factor by checking the appropriate rating for each item.
- Each rating (outstanding, highly effective, effective, needs improvement and unacceptable) corresponds to each performance factor. For example, the first performance factor represents (outstanding), the second (highly effective), the third (effective), the fourth (needs improvement) and the fifth (unacceptable).

Form 19. Office, Technical, and Service Staff Development Review

- Provide written justification of the ratings as well as staff development plans and goals. For the extremes, (outstanding and unacceptable), a written justification must be provided.
- Under subsection B and C, describe the employee's accomplishments and development and make recommendations for any needed improvements in performance.
- If you need to attach a separate sheet for comments, please do so.

A.   PERFORMANCE FACTORS: Review the attachment on Performance Factors (outstanding, highly effective, effective, needs improvement and unacceptable). Evaluate the employee's performance on each factor by checking the appropriate rating for each item.

	OUTSTANDING	HIGHLY EFFECTIVE	EFFECTIVE	NEEDS IMPROVEMENT	UNACCEPTABLE
1. QUALITY OF WORK					
2. LMU SERVICE STANDARDS					
3. PRODUCTIVITY					
4. PUNCTUALITY					
5. DEPENDABLITY					
6. KNOWLEDGE OF JOB					
7. INITIATIVE AND RESOURCEFULNESS					
8. UTILIZATION OF TIME					
9. WORKING RELATIONSHIPS					
10. SENSITIVITY TO DIVERSITY					

	ACCEPTABLE	NEEDS IMPROVEMENT	UNACCEPTABLE
11. ATTENDANCE			

THE FOLLOWING ITEMS ARE TO BE COMPLETED FOR THOSE WHO SUPERVISE O&T STAFF OR SERVICE STAFF:

	OUTSTANDING	HIGHLY EFFECTIVE	EFFECTIVE	NEEDS IMPROVEMENT	UNACCEPTABLE
1. SUPERVISION OF OTHERS					
2. DEVELOPMENT OF STAFF					

Form 19 *continued*

Use the space below for comments related to the above performance factors. If more space is needed, please attach a comment sheet.

B.   EXCEPTIONAL ACCOMPLISHMENTS: Describe any exceptional accomplishments which go beyond the employee's job description (e.g., committee work, special projects, service to the LMU community, job-related education and training). If more space is needed, please attach a comment sheet.

C.   AREAS FOR IMPROVEMENT: Describe any areas for improvement. If more space is needed, please attach a comment sheet.

IV.   STAFF DEVELOPMENT PLAN/GOALS AND OBJECTIVES: Describe any plans including goals and objectives for this employee's professional development. Specify whether these plans are for improvement in the employee's present position, development of new skills, and/or career advancement. Include the steps to be taken by both the employee and the employee's supervisor. If more space is needed, please attach a comment sheet.

Form 19 *continued*

V.   SIGNATURES

A. To be completed by the **Supervisor** at the end of the development review cycle:

I have discussed this review with the employee and explained the procedure for filing a rebuttal if s/he disagrees.

Signature _____   Date _____

B. To be completed by the **Employee** at the end of the development review cycle:

_____ I have read and discussed my development review with my supervisor and have received a copy.

_____ I disagree with portions of this development review and have a right to file a rebuttal in my personnel file. (See below)

Steps:
*   Prepare a written rebuttal to your supervisor and send a copy to Human Resources.
*   The rebuttal will be attached with your review in your personnel file.

Signature _____   Date _____

C. To be completed by the **Supervisor's Supervisor** at the end of the development review cycle:

Signature _____   Date _____

DISTRIBUTION:
Original: Human Resources
Copies: Supervisor and Employee

LOYOLA MARYMOUNT UNIVERSITY

OFFICE & TECHNICAL STAFF AND SERVICE STAFF

PERFORMANCE FACTORS GUIDELINES

The following represents the performance factors guidelines. Please refer to these guidelines when you are evaluating the staff member's performance.

1. QUALITY OF WORK
Thoroughness, accuracy and neatness of work produced
- **(Outstanding)** Work is consistently error free, thorough, neat, correct, logically organized and statistically accurate.
- **(Highly Effective)** Work is nearly always error free (with a few very minor errors), thorough, neat, correct, logically organized and statistically accurate.
- **(Effective)** Work contains some acceptable errors that may require some review and editing by supervisor.
- **(Needs Improvement)** Work reflects errors that require careful review and correction by supervisor or partial reworking/revision.
- **(Unacceptable)** Work is frequently not acceptable or useable.

2. LMU SERVICE STANDARDS
Effectiveness of demonstrating the LMU Service Standards to the LMU community, including students, parents, faculty, staff and outside guests.

- **(Outstanding)** Exceptional service orientation; exceptionally friendly and helpful toward others.
- **(Highly Effective)** Good service orientation; friendly and helpful toward others.
- **(Effective)** Regularly meets service expectations.
- **(Needs Improvement)** Sometimes forgets service orientation and serves at a substandard level.
- **(Unacceptable)** Rarely demonstrates LMU's service standards. Often rude and offensive toward others.

3. PRODUCTIVITY
OFFICE & TECHNICAL
Volume of work produced.
- **(Outstanding)** Amount of work produced is exceptional and exceeds expectations.
- **(Highly Effective)** Output is frequently more than required and regularly exceeds expectations.
- **(Effective)** Volume of work produced meets expectations and sometimes exceeds expectations.
- **(Needs Improvement)** Productivity and volume of work produced occasionally falls below expectations.
- **(Unacceptable)** Unacceptable level of productivity; often below expectations.

4. PUNCTUALITY
Reporting to work or appointments on time; frequency of leaving work before end of shift.
- **(Outstanding)** Always on time for work and/or appointments and remains at work as needed.
- **(Highly Effective)** Rarely tardy in reporting for work and for appointments; very rarely leaves work early.
- **(Effective)** Seldom tardy for work or for appointments; seldom leaves work early.
- **(Needs Improvement)** Sometimes tardy for work or for appointments; sometimes leaves work early without a valid reason.
- **(Unacceptable)** Often tardy for work or for appointments; often leaves work early.

5. DEPENDABILITY
Degree and amount of supervision required and reliability exhibited in following established procedures and completing assigned work.

Form 20. Office, Technical, and Service Staff Performance Factors Guidelines

- **(Outstanding)** Exceptional degree of independence and reliability; continuously follows established procedures in completing assigned work without much follow up.
- **(Highly Effective)** Exhibits a high degree of independence; follows established procedures; rarely requires follow up.
- **(Effective)** Meets expectations of following established procedures and completes regular assignments with minimum supervision. May need supervision on critical projects.
- **(Needs Improvement)** High degree of direction needed. Occasionally fails to establish procedures or requires checking on routine work assignments. Marginal reliability.
- **(Unacceptable)** Fails to follow established procedures and requires supervision on all assignments and procedures. Totally unreliable.

6. KNOWLEDGE OF JOB
Mastery of all phases of job; adapts information and procedures to new tasks.
- **(Outstanding)** Has an exceptionally thorough grasp of all facets of the job; understands nuances of the university, the office and the job.
- **(Highly Effective)** Has a good grasp of the job; rarely requires assistance.
- **(Effective)** Has grasp of the job; requires, minimal supervision; some opportunities for additional knowledge, experience or training do exist.
- **(Needs Improvement)** Needs improvement to perform the job; requires supervision and additional training.

- **(Unacceptable)** Lacks knowledge and skills to effectively perform duties and responsibilities of the job. Training required may be excessive.

7. INITIATIVE AND RESOURCEFULNESS
Employee's resourcefulness in anticipating and performing needed tasks, and in initiating efforts to improve his/her job knowledge and performance.
- **(Outstanding)** Completely self-reliant. Continuously thinks constructively and exercises an exceptional degree of independent action in solving problems. Regularly deals with ambiguous situations effectively.
- **(Highly Effective)** Frequently able to anticipate needs, initiate action, cope with irregularities and problem solve, with little or no supervision.
- **(Effective)** Meets expectations for solving problems with some supervision or with some assistance from others. Can be depended upon to initiate efforts to improve job knowledge and performance.
- **(Needs Improvement)** Able to act independently on occasion in finding solutions to problems. Generally depends on supervisor or others for direction.
- **(Unacceptable)** Occasionally initiates efforts to improve job knowledge and performance.

8. UTILIZATION OF TIME
Effectiveness with which time is used in attending to and completing assignments.
- **(Outstanding)** Continuously balances priorities and utilizes time to the fullest. Exceeds

expectations. Regularly on time in completing assignments.
- **(Highly Effective)** Frequently balances priorities and efficiently utilizes time during or between assignments and in completing assignments.
- **(Effective)** Use of time during or between assignments meets expectations. Ordinarily balances priorities and completes assignments on time.
- **(Needs Improvement)** Occasionally wastes time during or between assignments. Sometimes fails to balance priorities or complete assignments on time.
- **(Unacceptable)** Constantly wastes time during and between assignments. Does not balance priorities to complete assignments on time.

9. WORKING RELATION-SHIPS
Effectiveness of interpersonal relations with faculty and other staff employees as well as attitude toward job and LMU.
- **(Outstanding)** Consistently displays exceptional enthusiasm toward working with others and toward their work; excellent team worker who actively creates good will.
- **(Highly Effective)** Displays enthusiasm toward working with others and toward their work; exercises tact and discretion; a good team worker; courteous.
- **(Effective)** Displays genuine interest in working with others and their work; cooperative and pleasant; creates a favorable impression.

Form 20 *continued*

- **(Needs Improvement)** Displays marginal interest in working with others and in their work; occasionally uncooperative, unfriendly, curt or irritable; sometimes has negative effect on others.
- **(Unacceptable)** Indifferent exhibits no interest in working with others and their work. Defensive and argumentative. Cooperates only when forced to and has negative effect on others.

10. SENSITIVITY TO DIVERSITY

Degree to which the employee's actions indicate that s/he values the uniqueness of each individual, and respects human differences wherever s/he encounters them.

- **(Outstanding)** Consistently demonstrates his/her respect for diversity. Sets an example for others; displays behavior that clearly shows an appreciation of the uniqueness of the individual and attempts to utilize, positively, human differences.
- **(Highly Effective)** Shows, by example, that s/he appreciates human differences and values diversity. Educates him/herself concerning diversity and actively seeks to share his/her knowledge and experience with others, as well as gaining from experience.
- **(Effective)** Shows, by example, that s/he values diversity and respect.
- **(Needs Improvement)** Needs improvement and training to achieve a better understanding of human differences.
- **(Unacceptable)** Often makes statements or displays body language or behavior that indicates insensitivity.

11. ATTENDANCE

The dependability of the individual in adhering to availability and attendance standards. Is at work at times other than approved vacation and holidays

- **(Acceptable)** The supervisor finds that the employee's attendance is acceptable.
- **(Needs Improvement)** The supervisor finds that the employee's attendance needs improvement.
- **(Unacceptable)** The supervisor finds that the employee's attendance is unacceptable.

Form 20 *continued*

MAINE ASSOCIATION OF SCHOOL LIBRARIES

SLMS EVALUATION—EVALUATION FORM

Focus Area:

Performance Criteria:

•

•

•

•

•

•

• **Commendations**:

Recommendations for improvement:

Strategies for improvement:

Date

_____   _____
Library Media Specialist Signature   Administrator's Signature

Form 21. SLMS Evaluation—Evaluation Form

MAINE ASSOCIATION OF SCHOOL LIBRARIES

SLMS EVALUATION—ACTION PLAN

Sample of one of several focus areas developed during initial supervisor and Library Media Specialist conference. See also related Sample Action Plan for magazine use, designed by Library Media Specialist to assist goal).

Focus Area: Curriculum development and implementation—the use of magazines within the information literacy framework.

Performance Criteria:
- Demonstrates depth of knowledge of the research process.
- Integrates specific research skills and strategies within social studies discipline.
- Demonstrates collaborative skills with teachers.
- Maintains good interpersonal relationships with students.
- Employs appropriate teaching practices, including.
    a. Sets high, measurable expectations, communicated clearly to students.
    b. Use a variety of tools to measure individual student performance.
    c. Incorporates relevant elements of Maine Learning Results.
    d. Involves students in goal setting and assessment design.

Commendations:

Recommendations for Improvement:

Strategies for Improvement:

Date

_____   _____
Library Media Specialist Signature   Administrator's Signature

Form 22. SLMS Evaluation—Action Plan

MAINE ASSOCIATION OF SCHOOL LIBRARIES

LIBRARY MEDIA SPECIALIST'S PREPARATION FOR EVALUATION

Step 1. Complete before initial conference with supervisor.
Step 2. Include in notebook with documentation

PART I. LEADER, PLANNER, AND MANAGER

As a leader, planner and manager, the Library Media Specialist provides leadership in the planning, management and evaluation of school library media programs. Examples focus on the element most relevant to the indicator.

S = Enter score from rubric   **D = Enter D if you can document this**

| 5 = Exceeds district expectations | 3 = Meets district expectations | 0 = Fails to meet expectations | N = Not yet possible |

Indicator	Examples Applying Specifically to Leadership	Examples Applying Specifically to Planning	Examples Applying Specifically to Management
1. Directs, organizes, and supervises the personnel and services essential to a unified library media program centered on students' needs and the instructional goals of the school. S D ___ ___			a. Uses an evaluation tool to assess volunteer and support staff performance. b. Provides materials, equipment, and support in a well-organized, formal yet flexible, manner. (Reference books circulate within the building; the library maintains a web site.)
2. Initiates and maintains formal contacts with	a. Previews and evaluates demos, computer programs,		

Form 23. Library Media Specialist's Preparation for Evaluation, Part I: Leader, Planner, and Manager

principal & teachers to evaluate library media programs, facilities, materials,equipment, and personnel. S D ____ ____	books and other media for possible purchase or other use. b. Designs and administers surveys to teachers, students and administrators regarding library use, programs, and materials.		
3. Prepares financial plans for the Library Media Center, including an annual budget. S D ____ ____		a. Analyzes curriculum changes, collects library statistics, and reflects this in short-range budget. b. Includes elements of long-range goals in budget.	a. Exhibits good record-keeping of LMC usage, circulation, Interlibrary-Loans, class visits, teacher contacts, and wise use of software reports from LMC vendors such as EBSCO or automation provider. b. Ties budget to program development, state collection guidelines, school policies, and justifies with a narrative backup.
4. Develops and maintains a written long-range plan for library media services, and integrates the		a. Participates formally in sustained local technology planning and implementation.	

activities designated in the plan into the total school curriculum. S D ____ ____		b. Provides input to professional development committee.	
5. Establishes and maintains an environment in the Library Media Center in which students and staff can work at productive levels. S D ____ ____			a. Models behavior to demonstrate expectations of students and to demonstrate Library Media Center philosophy. b. Reinforces expectations via consistent, equitable application.
6. Communicates the philosophy and goals of the school library media program to the students, faculty, administration, and community. S D ____ ____	a. Includes philosophy and goals within a library-maintained website. b. Models the philosophy and goals. "Walks the talk."		
7. Translates curriculum needs into library media program goals and objectives.		a. Uses a proactive approach to develop collaborative projects, planning material support and team programs with teachers using curriculum calendars.	

Form 23 *continued*

S D ____ ____		b. Sends "what are you doing" questionnaires to all teachers. c. Requests copies of all research assignments in advance.	
8. Works with administrators and other appropriate personnel to develop long-range goals and objectives for school or district. S D ____ ____	a. Membership in leadership teams, district technology teams, literacy committee, curriculum committees. b. Involves administration, students, and teachers in development of long-range collection development policies.	a. Assists in grant writing that involves district initiative. b. Actively works to implement Learning Results.	
9. Establishes relationships with colleagues, students, parents, and community which reflect recognition of and respect for every individual. S D ____ ____	a. Personal credibility of LMS has been established through confidentiality regarding library usage. b. Promotes and works toward equity of access to resources in and beyond the Library Media Center.		

Form 23 *continued*

10. Participates in the recruiting, hiring and training of other professional, paraprofessional, clerical, student and volunteer staff in the Library Media Center. S D ___ ___			a. Sets the criteria for hiring. b. Develops and administers orientation programs and written evaluation procedures for volunteers.
11. Develops and continually updates the professional expertise necessary to function effectively in the Library Media Specialist role. S D ___ ___		a. Maintains currency in the profession via relevant journals, active membership in professional organizations, selective workshop and conference attendance. b. Plans sharing of new expertise with colleagues and/or school faculty.	
12. Networks with other professionals through participation in local, state and national organizations. S D ___ ___	a. Contributes to and participates in local and regional resource-sharing (Includes MaineCat, ILL, local library, Maine State Library video collection.		

Form 23 *continued*

MAINE ASSOCIATION OF SCHOOL LIBRARIES

LIBRARY MEDIA SPECIALIST'S PREPARATION FOR EVALUATION

Step 1. Complete before initial conference with supervisor.
Step 2. Include in notebook with documentation

PART II. TEACHER

As a teacher, the Library Media Specialist instructs learners on a formal and informal basis in skills related to reading, research, production of materials and the use of information and instructional technologies. Examples focus on the element most important to the indicator.

S = Enter score from rubric D = Enter D if you can document this

5 = Exceeds district expectations	3 = Meets district expectations	0 = Fails to meet expectations	N = Not yet possible

Indicator	Examples Applying Specifically to Students	Examples Applying Specifically to Teachers
1. Works to ensure the integration of information skills throughout the school's instructional program. S D ___ ___	a. Information literacy skills are present in all subject area curricula. b. Log of focus lessons on information literacy in each content area.	
2. Plans, teaches, evaluates and reinforces instruction designed to make students and staff effective users of information.	a. Log of staff development workshops. b. Evidence of regularly scheduled student classes. c. Evidence of student products and presentations.	

Form 24. Library Media Specialist's Preparation for Evaluation, Part II: Teacher

S D _____ _____	d. Visual evidence of directions posted for use of various resources.	
3. Prepares financial plans for the Library Media Center, including the annual budget. S D _____ _____		a. Directions are posted for each production process. b. Log of staff workshops held for each new piece of equipment.
4. Assists teachers in promoting reading and provides reading experiences for students in groups and as individuals. S D _____ _____		a. One or more teachers are involved in the Maine Student Book Awards program. b. Provides book talks in the classroom.
5. Promotes life-long learning by fostering positive attitudes toward libraries and by working to develop students' viewing, listening and critical listening skills. S D _____ _____	a. Evidence that students are using other libraries effectively. b. Evidence that students are independent users of the library.	
6. Monitors rights and responsibilities of users relating to the generation and flow of information and ideas (e.g., copyright, confidentiality/privacy, intellectual freedom).	a. Copyright rules are posted on all copiers and computers. b. Students have access to all resources regardless of age.	

Form 24 *continued*

S D _____ _____	c. Records are not being kept on who reads what.	
7. Provides sfaf development opportunities for school personnel in the selection, use, evaluation and production of media and new and emerging technologies. S D _____ _____		a. Surveys staff for retention, deletion, addition of new software. b. Models the use of a technology with students.
8. Participates in district, building, department and grade-level curriculum design and assessment projects on a regular basis. S D _____ _____		a. Head of the Language Arts committee. b. Participates in the technology committee.
9. Contributes to the development of complete instructional units with teachers, using a systematic instructional design process. S D _____ _____		a. Works as a partner in an I-Search unit with the Language Arts teacher. b. Joins with teaching staff in planning and preparing for fairs (e.g., science, history, environment).
10. Performs clearinghouse function for professional material and opportunities available from education agencies outside the school.		a. Provides staff development opportunities using resources beyond the school.

Form 24 *continued*

S D ____ ____		b. Includes teacher resource links on library web site.
11. Assesses information skills and the research process on a regular planned basis for student, teacher and staff use. S D ____ ____		a. Maintains currency in the profession via relevant journals, active membership in professional organizations, selective workshop and conference attendance. b. Plans sharing of new expertise with colleagues and/or school faculty.

MAINE ASSOCIATION OF SCHOOL LIBRARIES

LIBRARY MEDIA SPECIALIST'S PREPARATION FOR EVALUATION

Step 1. Complete before initial conference with supervisor.
Step 2. Include in notebook with documentation.

PART III INFORMATION SPECIALIST

As an information specialist, the Library Media Specialist provides access to information and ideas by assisting students and staff in identifying information resources and in interpreting and communicating intellectual content.

S = Enter score from rubric   D = Enter D if you can document this

5 = Exceeds district expectations	3 = Meets district expectations	0 = Fails to meet expectations	N = Not yet possible

Indicator	Examples Applying Specifically to Students	Examples Applying Specifically to Teachers
1. Makes resources available to students and teachers through a systematically developed and organized collection of library media material available outside the school. S D ____ ____	a. Provides a "new books" shelf" or display of new materials. b. Posts clear and appropriate signage throughout the library.	a. Maintains online catalog. b. Use of Library district traveling books. c. Maintains a professional collection area.
2. Keeps abreast of current literature by reading reviewing journals and other selection sources. S D ____ ____	a. Able to recommend a title on a new controversial topic. b. Able to recommend an award-winning new work of fiction.	a. Circulates articles, catalogs, journals, etc. to appropriate teachers on topics that impact curriculum and instruction. b. Solicits and includes ideas for titles of new fiction.

Form 25. Library Media Specialist's Preparation for Evaluation, Part III: Information Specialist

3. Develops flexible circulation, loan policies that ensure equity of access to users. S D ____ ____	a. Effectively communicates to students all procedures and expectations in the process of using the library and borrowing materials. b. Provides library services to home-school students.	a. Provides book carts in the classroom on request. b. Provides special reserve on request.
4. Assures access to information resources by providing an accurate and efficient retrieval system. S D ____ ____	a. Orientation to use of library catalog. b. Use of MaineCat online. c. Provides intra-net CD-ROM resources.	a. Maintains an up-to-date automated card catalog system in good working order. b. Provides access to materials outside of the district.
5. Implements policies that respect the rights of users to confidentiality and unrestricted access to information resources. S D ____ ____	a. Provides assistance in research using the Internet when filters block a legitimate search. b. Maintains confidential student records via password or other means.	a. Provides unfiltered Internet access. b. Maintains confidentiality in the loan and request of materials.
6. Assists all users in identifying, locating and interpreting information. S D ____ ____	a. Conducts reference interviews. b. Works with students to find suitable resources or to interpret them.	a. Preselects, along with teachers, materials for specific assignments. b. Works collaboratively with classroom teacher during library class time.

Form 25 *continued*

7. Arranges for flexible scheduling of facilities, staff time and collections to meet the needs of individuals, small groups and large groups for research, browsing, recreational reading, viewing, or listening at the point of need. S D _____ _____	a. Provides for small group discussion and collaborative work. b. Communicates "open door" policy to students as well as clearly defined student responsibilities.	a. Teaches a course for teachers after school or during staff development. b. Identifies staff training needs in the area of technology and reports findings to appropriate people.
8. Assesses and promotes effective use of instructional technology. S D _____ _____	a. Maintains student Internet access in the library. b. Trains student assistants.	a. Head of the Language Arts committee. b. Participates in the technology committee.

Step 2 Meet with the Supervisor. Develop a plan of action based on several shared priorities. Include an observation schedule and an assessment strategy.

Form 25 *continued*

MAINE ASSOCIATION OF SCHOOL LIBRARIES

SUPERVISOR'S PREPARATION FOR LMS EVALUATION

Step 1. Complete before initial conference with Library Media Specialist

PART I. LEADER, PLANNER, AND MANAGER

As a leader, planner and manager, the Library Media Specialist provides leadership in the planning, management and evaluation of school library media programs.

S = Enter score from rubric   M = More information needed before scoring

S	M		
		1.	Directs, organizes, and supervises the personnel and services essential to a unified library media program centered on students' needs and the instructional goals of the school.
		2.	Initiates and maintains formal contacts with principal and teachers to evaluate library media programs, facilities, materials, equipment and personnel.
		3.	Prepares financial plans for the Library Media Center, including an annual budget.
		4.	Develops and maintains a written long-range plan for library media services, and integrates the activities designated in the plan into the total school curriculum.
		5.	Establishes and maintains an environment in the Library Media Center in which students and staff can work at productive levels.
		6.	Communicates the philosophy and goals of the school library media program to the students, faculty, administration and community.
		7.	Translates curriculum needs into library media program goals and objectives.
		8.	Works with administrators and other appropriate personnel to develop long range goals and objectives for the school or district.
		9.	Establishes relationships with colleagues, students, parents and community which reflect recognition of and respect for every individual.
		10.	Participates in the recruiting, hiring and training of other professional, paraprofessional, clerical, student and volunteer staff in the Library Media Center.
		11.	Develops and continually updates the professional expertise necessary to function effectively in the Library Media Specialist role.
		12.	Networks with other professionals through participation in local, state and national organizations.

Form 26. Supervisor's Preparation for LMS Evaluation, Part I: Leader, Planner, and Manager

MAINE ASSOCIATION OF SCHOOL LIBRARIES

SUPERVISOR'S PREPARATION FOR LMS EVALUATION

Step 1. Complete before initial conference with Library Media Specialist

PART II TEACHER

As a teacher, the Library Media Specialist instructs students on a formal and informal basis in skills related to reading, research, production of materials and the use of information and instructional technologies

S = Enter score from rubric   M = More information needed before scoring

S	M		
		1.	Works to ensure the integration of information skills throughout the school's instructional program.
		2.	Plans, teachers, evaluates and reinforces instruction designed to make students and staff effective users of information.
		3.	Assists staff members in producing instructional audiovisual aids.
		4.	Assists teachers in promoting reading and provides reading experiences for students in groups and as individuals.
		5.	Promotes lifelong learning by fostering positive attitudes toward libraries and by working to develop students' viewing, listening and critical thinking skills.
		6.	Monitors rights and responsibilities of users relating to the generation and flow of information and ideas (e.g., copyright, confidentiality/privacy, intellectual freedom.
		7.	Provides staff development opportunities for school personnel in the selection, use, evaluation, and production of media and new and emerging technologies.
		8.	Participates in district, building, department and grade level curriculum design and assessment projects on a regular basis.
		9.	Contributes to the development of complete instructional units with teachers, using a systematic instructional design process.
		10.	Performs clearinghouse function for professional materials and opportunities available from education agencies outside the school.
		11.	Assess information skills and the research process on a regular planned basis for student, teacher and staff use.

Form 27. Supervisor's Preparation for LMS Evaluation, Part II: Teacher

MAINE ASSOCIATION OF SCHOOL LIBRARIES

SUPERVISOR'S PREPARATION FOR LMS EVALUATION

Step 1. Complete before initial conference with Library Media Specialist

PART III INFORMATION SPECIALIST

As a leader, planner and manager, the Library Media Specialist provides leadership in the planning, management and evaluation of school library media programs.

S = Enter score from rubric   M = More information needed before scoring

S	M	
		1. Makes resources available to students and teachers through a systematically developed and organized collection of library media materials, supplemented with resources available outside the school.
		2. Keeps abreast of current literature by reading review journals and other selection resources.
		3. Develops flexible circulation, loan and use policies that ensure equity of access to users.
		4. Assures access to information resources by providing an accurate and efficient retrieval system.
		5. Implements policies that respect the rights of users to confidentiality and unrestricted access to information resources.
		6. Assists all users in identifying, locating and interpreting information.
		7. Arranges for flexible scheduling of facilities, staff time and collections to meet the needs of individuals, small groups and large groups for research, browsing, recreational reading, reviewing or listening at the point of need.
		8. Assess and promotes effective use of instructional technology.

Form 28. Supervisor's Preparation for LMS Evaluation, Part III: Information Specialist

CONFIDENTIAL
CITY OF MOUNTAIN VIEW
PERFORMANCE EVALUATION

MANAGEMENT AND PROFESSIONAL EMPLOYEES

Employee: _____   Evaluation Period: _____
Position/Dept.: _____   Date: _____

I.   Evaluation of Employee's Standards: *(See description of ratings.)*

	Exceptional	Very Good	Good	Needs Improvement
1. Customer Contact and Service Skills				
2. Interpersonal Effectiveness (Internal)				
3. Job Knowledge, Skills and Abilities				
4. Decision Making, Problem Solving				
5. Organizing and Planning				
6. Personal Responsibility and Initiative				
7. Communication Skills				
8. Flexibility and Adaptability				
9. Supervisory Skills (*If Applicable*)				
Job-Specific Standards (Defined by Employee and Supervisor as part of annual goal setting)				
Comment:				

II. Comments on Overall Performance: *(Include evaluation of employee's achievement of objectives and other accomplishments.)*

III. To ensure that all City employees are reminded of and are familiar with various policies, as part of the annual evaluation process, the following policies were provided to and reviewed with _____, who demonstrated an understanding of the policies and required reporting procedures. _____ has agreed to follow the reporting procedures when he/she has knowledge of possible violations. (Employee and supervisor to initial in the blank.)

Form 29. Performance Evaluation, Management and Professional Employees

_____   City of Mountain View Harassment/Discrimination Policy and Complaint Procedure

_____   City of Mountain View Workplace Violence Prevention Policy

IV.   Needs Improvement: *(Explanation of ratings, if applicable.)*

V.   Objectives for Next Year (Listing):

VI.   Management/Professional Development Plan:

VII. Reviewing Manager Comments *(Optional)*:

VIII. Employee Comments *(Optional)*:

Evaluated by: _____   _____
                       Supervisor   *Date*

Received by: _____   _____
                       Employee   Date

Approved for Content by: _____   _____
                       Department Head   *Date*

Approved by: _____   _____
                       Employee Services Director   *Date*

PerfEval
Mgmt Eval^

Form 29 *continued*

Media Coordinator Name _____   Date _____
Period/Time _____   Observer/Evaluator _____

Media Coordinator Formative Observation Instrument

Instructions: Use this form to observe functions and practices that occur during the school year. Be sure to code each instance of a MC PAl practice as follows:
appropriate use of practice; strong or positive use of practice (+); weak or negative use of practice (-).

Function/Practice I. Planning and Faciliating Teaching and Learning	Date of Conference/ Observation	Data Source if applicable	Comments
1.1 Assesses learning and information needs			
1.2 Plans and works collaboratively with teachers			
1.3 Works to provide flexible access to services			
1.4 Instructs in the effective use of media center and resources (for lesson observation see Media Coordinator FODI)			

Media Coordinator Name _____ Date _____
Period/Time _____ Observer/Evaluator _____

Media Coordinator Formative Observation Data Instrument

Instructions: Use this form to observe an instructional activity conducted by the media coordinator. NOTE: the following practices are based on the TPAI-R and are provided to assist evaluators in recording. Be sure to code each instance of a MCPAI practice as follows: appropriate use of practice; strong or positive use of practice (+); weak or negative use of practice (-).

Function/Practice I. Planning and Facilitating Teaching and Learning (continued)	Date of Conference/ Observation	Data Source if applicable	Comments
I. Instructional Time 1.1 Materials Ready			
1.2 Class started quickly			
1.3 Time-on-task for learning			
II. Student Behavior 2.1 Rules—Administrative matters			
2.2 Rules—Verbal participation			
2.3 Rules—Movement			
2.4 Frequently monitors behavior			
2.5 Stops inappropriate behavior			
2.6 Reflective practice—Student behavior			
III. Instructional Presentation 3.1 Links to prior learning			
3.2 Understands content; makes it meaningful			
3.3 Speaks fluently			

Form 31. Media Coordinator Formative Observation Data Instrument

Function/Practice I. Planning and Facilitating Teaching and Learning (continued)	Date of Conference/ Observation	Data Source if applicable	Comments
3.4 Relevant examples			
3.5 High rate of success on tasks			
3.6 Brisk pace			
3.7 Effective, smooth transitions			
3.8 Assignment clear			
3.9 Adapts instruction to diverse learners			
3.10 Develops critical thinking, problem solving, and performance skills			
3.11 Uses technology to support instruction			
3.12 Students engaged, responsible for learning			
IV. Instructional Monitoring 4.1 Maintains deadlines, standards			
4.2 Circulates to check students' performance			
4.3 Uses varied work products to check progress			
4.4 Questions clear, one at a time			
4.5 Uses responses to adjust teaching			
V. Instructional Feedback 5.1 Feedback on in-class work			
5.2 Prompt feedback on out-of-class work			

Form 31 *continued*

Function/Practice I. Planning and Facilitating Teaching and Learning (continued)	Date of Conference/ Observation	Data Source if applicable	Comments
5.3 Affirms correct response quickly			
5.4 Sustaining feedback after incorrect response			
5.5 Fosters active inquiry supportive interaction			
VI. Facilitating Instruction 6.1 Aligned instructional plans			
6.3 Maintains accurate records			
6.4 Appropriate instructional activities			
6.5 Available resources support program			
1.5 Incorporates information literacy			
1.6 Advocates and promotes reading and life-long learning			
1.7 Collaborates with the Instructional Technology Facilitator to provide leadership in the use of instructional technology resources			
1.8 Plans for personal professional development			

Summary Comments:

Above Standard _____   At Standard _____
Below Standard _____   Unsatisfactory _____

Function/Practice II. Planning and Facilitating Information Access and Delivery, Evaluation, and Use	Date of Conference/ Observation	Data Source if applicable	Comments
2.1 Creates and maintains a learning environment			
2.2 Works to provide flexible access to resources			
2.3 Organizes school library media facilities and resources			
2.4 Encourages use of print and electronic resources and services			
2.5 Works cooperatively with other libraries and agencies to share resources			
2.6 Adheres to and communicates copyright and ethical use of all resources			
2.7 Advocates for intellectual freedom			

Summary Comments:

Above Standard _____   At Standard _____
Below Standard _____   Unsatisfactory _____

Form 31 *continued*

Function/Practice III. Planning and Facilitating Program Administration	Date of Conference/ Observation	Data Source if applicable	Comments
3.1 Works with school staff to design and implement short- and long-range plans			
3.2 Develops and implements an ongoing collection development and evaluation planning process			
3.3 Evaluates and selects resources			
3.4 Maintains a collection addressing curricular needs and learning goals			
3.5 Evaluates the school library media program			
3.6 Plays a leading role in the school's budgetary process			
3.7 Leads, in partnership with the Instructional Technology Facilitator, the Media and Technology Advisory Committee			
3.8 Interacts effectively with students, staff, administration, parents, and the community			
3.9 Prepares and submits accurate reports			
3.10 Adheres to laws, policies, rules, and regulations			
3.11 Carries out non-instructional duties			

Summary Comments:

Above Standard _____   At Standard _____
Below Standard _____   Unsatisfactory _____

Form 31 *continued*

Strengths:

Areas for Improvement (Prioritize):

MEDIA COORDINATOR PERFORMANCE APPRAISAL INSTRUMENT—REVISED

Media Coordinator's Name   School

INSTRUCTIONS

- Based on the evidence from observation, documentation, and discussion, the evaluator will rate the media coordinator's performance on the 3 major functions listed below.
- The evaluator must add pertinent comments at the end of each major function.
- The media coordinator must be provided an opportunity to react to the evaluator's ratings and comments.
- The evaluator and media coordinator must review and discuss the results of the appraisal and any recommended actions pertinent to it.
- The evaluator and media coordinator must sign the instrument in the assigned spaces.
- The instrument must be filed in the media coordinator's personnel folder.
- The rating scale's four Levels of Performance are described below.

RATING SCALE

Above Standard

Performance is consistently above defined job expectations. The media coordinator demonstrates outstanding teaching practice and program management skills. The media coordinator seeks to provide leadership; take initiative; expand scope of competencies; and undertakes additional, appropriate responsibilities.

At Standard

Performance is consistently adequate/acceptable. Teaching practices fully meet all performance expectations at an acceptable level. The media coordinator maintains an adequate scope of competencies and performs additional responsibilities as assigned.

Below Standard

Performance within this function is sometimes inadequate/unacceptable and needs improvement. The media coordinator requires supervision and assistance to maintain an adequate scope of competencies and sometimes fails to perform additional responsibilities as assigned.

Unsatisfactory

Performance is consistently inadequate/unacceptable and most practices require considerable improvement to meet minimum performance expectations. The media coordinator requires close and frequent supervision in the performance of all responsibilities.

Form 32. Media Coordinator Performance Appraisal Instrument—Revised

MAJOR FUNCTION: Planning and Facilitating Teaching and Learning	Above Standard	At Standard	Below Standard	Unsatisfactory

1.1 Assesses learning and information needs of students and staff
1.2 Plans and works collaboratively with teachers to use appropriate resources that address curricular needs and learning goals
1.3 Works with the principal and school leadership team to provide flexible access to the instructional services of the school library media coordinator
1.4 Instructs students and staff in the effective use of the media center and its resources
1.5 Incorporates information literacy into day-to-day instruction
1.6 Advocates and promotes reading and life-long learning through motivational activities
1.7 Collaborates with the Instructional Technology Facilitator to provide leadership in the school's use of instructional technology resources to enhance learning
1.8 Follows a plan for personal professional development and actively seeks out opportunities to grow professionally

Comments:

MAJOR FUNCTION: Planning and Facilitating Information Access and Delivery, Evaluation, and Use	Above Standard	At Standard	Below Standard	Unsatisfactory

2.1 Creates and maintains an environment conducive to learning
2.2 Works with the principal and school leadership team to provide flexible access to school library media center resources to accommodate individuals and groups simultaneously
2.3 Organizes school library media facilities and resources in a manner that supports the mission, goals, and objectives of the school and maximizes intellectual and physical access to resources
2.4 Encourages the widest possible use of print and electronic resources and services—within the school library media center, throughout the school, and through remote access
2.5 Works cooperatively with other libraries and agencies to share resources that enhance teaching and learning
2.6 Adheres to and communicates copyright as well as other laws and guidelines pertaining to the distribution and ethical use of all resources
2.7 Advocates the principles of intellectual freedom

Form 32 *continued*

Comments:

MAJOR FUNCTION: Planning and Facilitating Program Administration	Above Standard	At Standard	Below Standard	Unsatisfactory

3.1 Works with school staff to design and implement short- and long-range plans that ensure balance among all aspects of the school library media coordinator's role and responsibilities

3.2 Develops and implements an ongoing collection development and evaluation planning process, in collaboration with the Media and Technology Advisory Committee, that focuses on a variety of formats and resources to meet diverse learning needs

3.3 Evaluate and select resources that build a collection addressing curricular needs and learning goals in collaboration with teachers, technology staff, and students

3.4 Maintains a collection addressing curricular needs and learning goals

3.5 Evaluates the school library media program on a continual basis according to accepted standards of quality

3.6 Plays a leading role in the school's budgetary process to ensure funding for the school library media program to support school-wide goals

3.7 Leads, in partnership with the Instruction Technology Facilitator, the Media and Technology Advisory Committee in effective decision making to promote the media and technology program

3.8 Interacts effectively with students, staff, administration, parents, and the community to promote and expand the school library media program

3.9 Prepares and submits accurate reports as required

3.10 Adheres to established laws, policies, rules, and regulations

3.11 Carries out non-instructional duties as assigned and/or as need is perceived

Comments:

Form 32 *continued*

Evaluator's Summary Comments

Media Coordinator's Reaction to Evaluation:

_____   _____
Evaluator's Signature and Date   Media Coordinator's Signature and Date

Signature indicates the evaluation was reviewed and discussed

Form 32 *continued*

MEDIA COORDINATOR PERFORMANCE APPRAISAL INSTRUMENT—REVISED

MATRIX OF DATA SOURCES

Strategies for interpreting observation data, reviewing additional documents, and obtaining additional information during a conference.

North Carolina Department of Public Instruction
Instructional Technology Division
August 2002

Form 33. Media Coordinator Performance Appraisal Instrument—Revised: Matrix of Data Sources

Matrix of Data Sources

Media Coordinator Performance Appraisal—Revised

MCPAI-R	Observation Issues	Documentation Sources	Typical Questions for Conferences
MAJOR FUNCTION: Planning and Facilitating Teaching and Learning			
1.1 Assesses learning and information needs of students and staff.	"Although the ultimate responsibility for the integration of information skills into the instructional program rests with media professionals, an effective instructional program relies on collaboration with teachers, administrators, students, support staff, and parents, all working together to support desired outcomes for students. This collaboration impacts teaching and learning by supporting the instructional process through planning, implementation, and evaluation. Instructional units developed through collaboration expand classroom walls to encompass the media center and resources beyond the school. In this way, students become self-directed lifelong learners, complex thinkers, quality producers, collaborative workers, and community contributors." (*IMPACT for Administrators: A Resource for Evaluating Media and Technology Programs and Personnel, p. 7*)	**Look For**: Collaboration with teachers and other staff to use diagnostic information obtained from tests and other assessment procedures to develop and revise objectives. **Examples**: planning notes or forms, lesson plans that incorporate diagnostic information; rubrics for collaboratively evaluating research activities and projects with teachers and/or tasks **Look For**: Collaboration with teachers to assess information needs of students. **Examples**: planning notes or forms, lesson plans that incorporate information resources that support classroom objectives **Look for**: Collaboration with teachers to assess their staff development needs in the areas of technology and curriculum. **Examples**: surveys to determine staff development needs **Look for**: Collaboration with teachers to assess their information needs. **Examples**: e-mail correspondence; planning notes or forms; reports of informal conversations	**Interview Question:** What methods do you use to evaluate student learning in collaboration with classroom teachers? **Interview Question:** What methods do you use to determine the information needs of students? **Interview Question:** What methods do you use to determine the learning needs of faculty and staff? **Interview Question:** What methods do you use to determine the information needs of faculty and staff?

Form 33 *continued*

MCPAI-R	Observation Issues	Documentation Sources	Typical Questions for Conferences
1.2 Plans and works collaboratively with teachers to use appropriate resources that address curricular needs and learning goals.	"The quality and effectiveness of a media program depends on the ability of media professionals to provide equal access to resources and to deliver information in a variety of formats in order to support the diverse needs of students and teachers. For example, the most current information on a topic may be located through dynamically updated and authoritative electronic subscription information sources or on the Internet. Print resources, however, can offer information that has been researched and aggregated into a readily accessible format. Media professionals have a responsibility to assist teachers in identifying and using the most appropriate format for a given learning activity." (*IMPACT for Administrators: A Resource for Evaluating Media and Technology Programs and Personnel, p. 10*)	**Look for**: Evidence of collaborative planning with teachers to align resources with instructional objectives. **Examples**: lesson plans; reports of informal and formal contacts with colleagues; teacher request forms for provision of resources for classrooms timelines; E-mail; grade-level and departmental meeting participation	**Interview Question:** What strategies do you use to encourage teachers to inform and plan with you, so that the lessons you teach are integrated into the classroom instructional units and use a variety of appropriate resources to meet school and system-wide curricular goals?
1.3 Works with the principal and school leadership team to provide flexible access to the instructional services of the school library media coordinator.	"Flexible access allows any student, teacher, or staff member to access the services of the school library media coordinator when needed to support and enhance teaching and learning, thus impacting student achievement. Flexible access enables the school library media coordinator to plan with teachers and staff for instructional purposes." (IMPACT for Administrators:	**Look For**: Presentations and memos providing input to the school leadership team and principal in planning the school-wide schedule; documents such as media coordinator's schedule, plan book that shows opportunities for every student to use the media center; teacher request forms for provision of instructional services.	**Interview Question:** How do you provide media skills instruction that is integrated with classroom objectives?

Form 33 *continued*

MCPAI-R	Observation Issues	Documentation Sources	Typical Questions for Conferences
1.3 Works with the principal and school leadership team to provide flexible access to the instructional services of the school library media coordinator (*continued*).	A Resource for Evaluating Media and Technology Programs and Personnel, p. 8) Please note that 1.3 refers to the instructional services of the school library media coordinator rather than the media center facility which is covered in 2.2.		
1.4 Instructs students and staff in the effective use of the media center and its resources.	"A learner-centered approach to instruction focuses attention on media programs as vital instructional forces that expand, support, and complement classroom learning with appropriate resources." (IMPACT: Guidelines for Media and Technology Programs, p. 4)	**Look For:** Lesson plans and instructional materials that demonstrate media skills instruction integrated with classroom objectives. Orientation process developed for students and teachers; media center handbook; treasure hunts; floor maps; introduction and modeling the use of new materials; promotion of the use of the most appropriate resources to accomplish specific tasks (e.g., using a book versus the Internet). **Interview Question:** How do you ensure/advocate for flexible access to your instructional services?	**Interview Question:** How do you orient students and teachers to the media center?

Form 33 *continued*

MCPAI-R	Observation Issues	Documentation Sources	Typical Questions for Conferences
1.5 Incorporates information literacy into day-to-day instruction.	Information literacy is the ability of an individual to find, evaluate, comprehend, use, and present information. It involves a variety of skills and abilities: • The ability to read and/or create visual depictions of information such as charts, diagrams, graphs, and multimedia presentations. • The ability to solve problems and present those solutions in a coherent, usable manner for others to understand and implement. • The ability to think critically, detect biases and misinformation, and comprehend the "gray areas" of information and decisions. • The ability to use information ethically, giving attribution to others when appropriate. • The ability to use technology effectively, efficiently, and appropriately. • The ability to understand when to choose various formats for both information gathering and presentation. Teaching information literacy should be a major focus of the school library media coordinator's job, but it is not the SLMC 's sole responsibility to see that students are information literate. Information literacy is best taught in a collaborative environment in which media and technology	**Look For**: Formal training process for assistance and volunteers; schedule of training sessions; training manuals. **Examples**: plan book, meeting minutes, media center schedule and notes showing collaborative planning sessions with teachers; working copy of the NC Standard Course of Study and LEA scope and sequence; memos and email **Examples**: lesson or unit plans, samples of student work, bibliographies, pathfinders, WebQuests **Look For**: Evidence of teaching strategies that address multiple learning styles. **Examples**: differentiated lesson plans; sites; pathfinders	**Interview Question:** What, if any, methods do you use for training student assistants, media assistants, and volunteers? (Where applicable) **Interview Question:** How do you collaborate with teachers to integrate the Information Skills curriculum into other content areas and student experiences? **Interview Question:** How do you collaborate with teachers to provide activities that enable students to apply information literacy skills (i.e., locate, analyze, evaluate, and synthesize information) to complete classroom assignments? **Interview Question:** How do you incorporate effective teaching strategies in day-to-day instruction?

Form 33 *continued*

MCPAI-R	Observation Issues	Documentation Sources	Typical Questions for Conferences
1.5 Incorporates information literacy into day-to-day instruction (*continued*).	professionals work with classroom teachers to design and implement projects and lessons that are relevant to classroom content and centered around a child's real-life information needs. (NCDPI)		
1.6 Advocates and promotes reading and life-long learning through motivational activities.	"Books and computer hardware alone do not create information-literate citizens. Print and electronic resources provide the foundation for an information-rich, technology-rich learning environment. Media programs must provide not only print and electronic resources, but they must also create an environment that promotes reading and life-long learning." (IMPACT for Administrators: A Resource for Evaluating Media and Technology Programs and Personnel, p. 6)	**Look For:** Motivational activities that foster reading enjoyment and lifelong learning. **Examples:** book talks, storytelling, visiting author (on site or online); book fairs, media fairs, and contests; literature festivals; sustained silent reading times for all, incentive programs; special events during Children's Book Week (November), School Library Media Month (April); National Library Week (April); posters; displays; Battle of the Books; NC Book Awards; student book reviews and artwork; Family Reading Night; School or Media Center Web page.	**Interview Question:** What strategies do you use to motivate students to read and to encourage life-long learning?
1.7 Collaborates with the Instructional Technology Facilitator to provide leadership in the school's use of instructional technology resources to enhance learning.	Collaboration should be evident in all areas of the school environment. The school library media coordinator and the instructional technology facilitator work closely together to promote the integration of a variety of technology resources into classroom instruction to meet the needs of all learners. They should encourage the use of Internet-based resources, online courses,	**Look For**: Evidence of efforts to investigate the value of emerging technologies for education; staff development opportunities identified or provided such as Web site design; non-print and Internet resources cataloged as part of the collection. **Examples**: newsletters, emails, presentations at staff meetings, Web pages, posters; modeling new technologies for staff	**Interview Question:** How do you collaborate with the Technology Facilitator to promote the use of current and emerging technologies to support the curriculum and enhance learning?

Form 33 *continued*

MCPAI-R	Observation Issues	Documentation Sources	Typical Questions for Conferences
1.7 Collaborates with the Instructional Technology Facilitator to provide leadership in the school's use of instructional technology resources to enhance learning (*continued*).	other distance-learning resources, and school television programming. (NCDPI)		
1.8 Follows a plan for personal professional development and actively seeks out opportunities to grow professionally.	The library media coordinator is an advocate for the appropriate use of media and technology within the school. Therefore, media professionals require constant updating of their professional skills and knowledge. They should continue to learn by attending regular system-level and state-level meetings and conferences and by reading current professional literature. (NCDPI)	**Look For**: Membership in professional organizations such as AASL, ALA, NCLA, MCASL, AECT, NCAECT, NCSLMA; attendance at professional meetings; review of professional journals on a regular basis for program and collection development information; subscription to one or more professional mail lists (e.g., LM_NET, AASL, SLMR, NCSLMA). **Look For**: Attendance at workshops, seminars, and/or credits earned from courses online or held at institutions of higher learning; report of newly-acquired skills; visits to other media centers.	**Interview Question:** How do you keep up-to-date in a rapidly changing profession such as yours? How is this addressed in your professional growth plan? **Interview Question:** How do you engage in reflective practice and address this in your professional growth plan?

Form 33 *continued*

MCPAI-R	Observation Issues	Documentation Sources	Typical Questions for Conferences
MAJOR FUNCTION: Planning and Facilitating Information Access and Delivery, Evaluation, and Use			
2.1 Creates and maintains an environment conducive to learning.	"The effective school library media program begins in an inviting, attractive school library media center that extends this welcoming climate to all the programs, services, and activities throughout the school. This warm and friendly atmosphere invites students and others to learn. The school library media specialist holds the key to creating a climate that is conducive to learning. Active, authentic learning involves personal construction of meaning, and this learning occurs most readily in a motivating and inviting climate." (Information Power: Building Partnerships for Learning, 1998, p. 88)	**Look For:** An attractive and inviting atmosphere; an atmosphere of respect for property and others; frequent monitoring of student behavior during whole class, small group, and independent activities and during transitions between instructional activities; an established set of rules and procedures aligned with school policies that govern the handling of routine administrative matters, student verbal participation, and movement; inappropriate behavior stopped promptly and consistently while maintaining the dignity of the student. **Examples:** signs stated in positive terms; posted rules; displays of student work and new materials; plants/pictures/ posters; topical displays of materials; bulletin boards; cleanliness	**Interview Question:** How do you make the media center a welcoming place where people can work and learn? **Interview Question:** How do you handle discipline problems that occur in the media center?
2.2 Works with the principal and school leadership team to provide flexible access to school library media center resources to accommodate individuals and groups simultaneously.	"Flexible access is beneficial to the learner. Lessons taught and learned in the school library media center should not be separate from what is taught and learned in the classroom. Multiple activities can successfully co-exist, and more than one grade level or class can access resources simultaneously. Flexible access helps create an environment in which students can become excited about learning and are able and eager to	**Look For:** Presentations and memos providing input to the school leadership team and principal in planning the school-wide schedule; students and teachers moving in and out of the media center as needed throughout the day; accommodating more than one group or class as appropriate.	**Interview Question:** How do you advocate for flexible access to school library media center resources? **Interview Question:** If you have implemented flexible access, how do you ensure that students and teachers have access to resources at the point of need?

Form 33 *continued*

MCPAI-R	Observation Issues	Documentation Sources	Typical Questions for Conferences
2.2 Works with the principal and school leadership team to provide flexible access to school library media center resources to accommodate individuals and groups simultaneously (*continued*).	complete assignments. It also gives full visibility to the creative capabilities of media professionals." (IMPACT for Administrators: A Resource for Evaluating Media and Technology Programs and Personnel, p. 8) Please note that 2.2 refers to the school media center facility rather than services of the school library media coordinator.	**Examples:** document such as media coordinator's schedule, circulation records, plan book that shows opportunities for every student to use the media center	**Interview Question:** How do you ensure that all students in the school have access even if teachers are reluctant?
2.3 Organizes school library media facilities and resources in a manner that supports the mission, goals, and objectives of the school and maximizes intellectual and physical access to resources.	"Physical access to information is prerequisite to intellectual access. The library media program's collection of resources, equipment, and facilities provides a central point of access for the learning community... The school library media specialist organizes and facilitates a physical environment designed specifically to meet the learning and information needs of students, teachers, and others, with an array of educational and informational resources that provide access to information both within the school and in the local, regional, and global communities." (Information Power: Building Partnerships for Learning, 1998, p. 86)	**Look For:** Main Use Area orderly arrangement of resources and equipment furniture; arrangement to accommodate large groups and small groups; clearly labeled shelves with standard Dewey classification; easy student access to nonprint resources; up-to-date online catalog • helpful user tools/finding aids • book lists • Internet bookmarks • computer user guides • pathfinders • facility organized for efficient circulation • circulation desk near entrance and situated for visual supervision • designated area for return of materials • accessible conference/small group activity area • professional collection for faculty use • parent collection.	**Interview Question:** How do you organize the media center's main use area so that it is well organized and resources are easily accessible?

Form 33 *continued*

MCPAI-R	Observation Issues	Documentation Sources	Typical Questions for Conferences
2.3 Organizes school library media facilities and resources in a manner that supports the mission, goals, and objectives of the school and maximizes intellectual and physical access to resources. (*continued*)		**Look For:** An organized media center that has identifiable areas. **Examples:** large signs and/or mobiles identifying general areas: • circulation • online catalog • large group instruction • independent work area • leisure reading • reference • listening/viewing/reading/computing • story sharing/storytelling • role playing or acting, puppetry • booktalking, literature discussion groups • professional collection • display/exhibit areas Support Areas (Note: Some media centers, have very little storage space and are often full of materials. The objective should be to have a neat, clean, well-organized space, even when full). **Examples:** administrative and planning area is evident production/workroom is organized to meet work needs equipment is stored in a place that is adequate, secure, and accessible (if available).	**Interview Question:** Are the various functional areas of the media center clearly identified? [Note: When the facility is too small, some areas will be combined with others.] **Interview Question:** How do you organize the media center's support areas so resources are easily accessible?

Form 33 *continued*

MCPAI-R	Observation Issues	Documentation Sources	Typical Questions for Conferences
2.3 Organizes school library media facilities and resources in a manner that supports the mission, goals, and objectives of the school and maximizes intellectual and physical access to resources. (continued)		**Look For:** • access to media facilities and resources for all students in compliance with ADA guidelines • free access to exits • properly stored flammable materials (e.g., spray paint, equipment cleaners) • safe production/workroom area (e.g., paper cutters and laminators inaccessible to young students) • adequately secured equipment to ensure student safety (e.g., safety straps on television carts) • appropriate use of extension cords in compliance with OSHA regulations.	**Interview Question:** To what extent are health and safety regulations considered in the arrangement of the facility?
2.4 Encourages the widest possible use of print and electronic resources and services—within the school library media center, throughout the school, and through remote access.	"The school library media program is grounded in the belief that access to information in all formats, at all levels, and to all members of the learning community is a crucial component of a culture of learning. The effective program offers a wide array of material sand services to help meet learning needs both within and beyond school walls. It can be the gateway to all the information resources the learning community needs for active, constructive learning. As the school's expert in information issues, the school library media specialist can play a central role in evaluating, acquiring, providing, and promoting information resources both within and	**Look For:** Publicity of resources through: • displays of new materials • communication to teachers when new materials arrive (e.g., notes, emails) • lists of new materials • booktalks • media center newsletters • contributions to school newsletter • media center and/or school Web site.	**Interview Question:** How do you encourage the use of the media center's resources and services?

Form 33 *continued*

MCPAI-R	Observation Issues	Documentation Sources	Typical Questions for Conferences
2.4 Encourages the widest possible use of print and electronic resources and services—within the school library media center, throughout the school, and through remote access (*continued*).	beyond the library media center." (Information Power: Building Partnerships for Learning, 1998, p. 65)	**Look For:** Promotion of services through: • thematic bibliographies • Web sites appropriate to classroom activities • list of staff development activities for teachers, administrators, and the community • planning forms, media reports, lesson plans • parent/community communication log • parent night/open house/special activities • regular hours including before and after school.	
2.5 Works cooperatively with other libraries and agencies to share resources that enhance teaching and learning of students and teachers.	"The school library media center can be the connection to other outside resources such as museums, businesses, community agencies and individuals, online services, and state agencies and resources." (IMPACT: Guidelines for Media and Technology Programs, p. 122)	**Look For:** • promotion of public library programs (e.g., storytelling, summer reading, reference services) • records of interlibrary loan • schedule of special speakers and events (e.g., authors, illustrators) • publicity for special community resources and programs (e.g., NC Zoo, Art Museum, History Museum, Natural History Museum, Discovery Place, college and university library services) • publicity for resources of community agencies (e.g., Boys' and Girls' Clubs, YMCA/YWCA, and other child service organizations) • collaboration with community learning centers and other organizations to share resources.	**Interview Question:** How do you work with community libraries and other agencies to make their resources and services available to the school community? **Interview Question:** How do you work in collaboration with public libraries in research activities, program planning, and special events?

Form 33 *continued*

MCPAI-R	Observation Issues	Documentation Sources	Typical Questions for Conferences
2.6 Adheres to and communicates copyright as well as other laws and guidelines pertaining to the distribution and ethical use of all resources.	"The school library media program is at the forefront of the complex and sensitive issues that surround information and its uses in today's society....the learning community looks to the school media program for guidance on these contemporary information concerns....Guided by the traditional standards of the progression as well as by evolving procedures and practices, the school library media specialist is an advocate for respecting intellectual property..." (Information Power: Building Partnerships for Learning, 1998, p. 93-94)	**Look For:** • presentation of copyright information at faculty meetings, in newsletters, and during staff development • copyright notices on appropriate equipment throughout the building • modeling and encouragement of appropriate ethical behavior among staff and students • copyright policies and procedures included in staff handbooks• AUP policies and procedures included in student and staff handbooks • provision of examples of bibliographic citations • up-to-date file of copyright permissions, purchase orders, software licenses or documentation, etc., to document legal compliance.	**Interview Question:** How do you inform the faculty and staff about laws and guidelines related to the ethical use of resources?
2.7 Advocates the principles of intellectual freedom.	"Intellectual freedom is 'prerequisite to effective and responsible citizenship in a democracy.' Throughout its history, the library media program has voiced its strong commitment to the right of intellectual freedom for the learning community. The school library media program continues to promote an atmosphere of free inquiry when faced with today's challenges to educational resources. Freedom of access to information and ideas is essential for students and others to become critical	**Look For:** • mission statement that promotes an atmosphere of free inquiry. • support of intellectual freedom for students and staff • presentation of the ALA/AASL Library Bill of Rights at faculty meetings. **Look For:** • an up-to-date file or notebook that includes a copy of the system- and building-level selection policy and procedures for handling challenges to materials in the school	**Interview Question:** How do you promote an atmosphere of free inquiry? **Interview Question:** How do you inform the faculty about the system- and building-level selection policies that ensure intellectual freedom for students and staff? **Interview Question:** How do you inform faculty about the procedures for handling challenges to materials?

Form 33 *continued*

MCPAI-R	Observation Issues	Documentation Sources	Typical Questions for Conferences
2.7 Advocates the principles of intellectual freedom. (continued)	thinkers, competent problem solvers, and life-long learners who contribute productively and ethically to society.... The school library media specialist is a leader in meeting the school's responsibility to provide resources and services that represent diverse points of view and that support and extend the curriculum with current, wide-ranging information. The school library media specialist provides ready access to resources, programs, and services that address the learning needs of students and others and that are free of constraints resulting from personal, partisan, or doctrinal disapproval." (Information Power: Building Partnerships for Learning, 1998, p. 91-92)	• presentation of information about selection policy and procedures at faculty meetings, in newsletters, and during staff development. **Look For:** • presentation of proper process and procedures for handling challenged materials for the Media and Technology Advisory Committee, staff, and administration • implementation of proper procedures when materials are challenged including the activities of the Media and Technology Advisory Committee • availability of relevant reconsideration form(s).	
MAJOR FUNCTION: Planning and Facilitating Program Administration			
3.1 Works with school staff to design and implement short- and long-range plans that ensure balance among all aspects of the school library media coordinator's role and responsibilities.	"Comprehensive, collaborative, and creative planning is essential to the library media program's long-term success. Plans are roadmaps for achieving program goals and objectives, and ongoing and dynamic planning is required to keep the library media program at the core of the school's learning community. Long-range, strategic plans must reflect the mission of the library media program, support the school's overall mission, and establish the program as critical to that	**Look For:** • plans for school-wide media program initiatives /resources/services (e.g., agenda and/or minutes of Media and Technology Advisory Committee meeting) • presentation of the plan to school leadership team • participation on building-level committees such as curriculum planning, school improvement, school schedule, budget, and governance • alignment of program with local, regional, state, and national guidelines.	**Interview Question:** How do you ensure that short- and long-term plans support the school's overall program goals and objectives? **Interview Question:** How do you work with the Media and Technology Committee to ensure that the needs of the whole school are being met?

Form 33 *continued*

MCPAI-R	Observation Issues	Documentation Sources	Typical Questions for Conferences
3.1 Works with school staff to design and implement short- and long-range plans that ensure balance among all aspects of the school library media coordinator's role and responsibilities (*continued*).	mission. The library media specialist has unique insights into current and potential uses of information and articulates the vision of an active, extended learning community that undergirds all phases of planning for the program." (Information Power: Building Partnerships for Learning, 1998, p. 107)	**Look For:** • a flexible schedule that provides optimal student/teacher access to media and technology resources and facilities • a daily/weekly/monthly schedule that shows teaching, instructional technology, collaboration, collection development, and program management as allowed within administrative guidelines.	**Interview Question:** What strategies to you use to make sure there is balance between meeting instructional needs and performing organizational/ management tasks?
3.2 Develops and implements an ongoing collection development and evaluation planning process, in collaboration with the Media and Technology Advisory Committee, that focuses on a variety of formats and resources to meet diverse learning needs.	"The school library media program offers a full range of instructional and information resources that all students need to meet their curriculum goals. Developed in close collaboration with teachers and others, the program's collections reflect the developmental, cultural, and learning needs of all the students. Evaluated and updated regularly, the collections also exhibit accepted and innovative learning theories, effective teaching practices and materials, and current scholarship in the subject areas." (Information Power: Building Partnerships for Learning, 1998, p. 90)	**Look For:** • a written collection development plan covering the next 3-5 years • annual evaluation and revision of the plan to reflect changes (e.g., curriculum, school goals, population changes) • system for gathering input from teachers (e.g., surveys, forms, suggestion box, formal and informal input) • agendas for Media and Technology Advisory Committee showing input into the planning process • evidence that the plan addresses diverse learning needs with a variety of resources.	**Interview Question:** Describe your collection development and evaluation planning process.

Form 33 continued

MCPAI-R	Observation Issues	Documentation Sources	Typical Questions for Conferences
3.3 Evaluates and selects resources that build a collection addressing curricular needs and learning goals in collaboration with teachers, technology staff, and students.	"Through collaborative collection development and evaluation, the program's collections promote active, authentic learning by providing a variety of formats and activities for linking information literacy with curricular objectives....Working collaboratively with teachers and others, the library media specialist is the catalyst for creating collections that promote curricular achievement and information literacy for all learners." (Information Power: Building Partnerships for Learning, 1998, p. 90-91)	**Look For:** • questionnaires and forms to solicit input from staff and students • lists of titles from Media and Technology Advisory Committee, staff, and students • input from teachers for professional materials—periodicals, books, online resources, and videos • preview of materials using Media and Technology Advisory Committee, faculty, and students. **Look For:** • InfoTech: The Advisory List • EvaluTech Web site • professional review journals • standard selection tools.	**Interview Question:** How do you involve others in the evaluation and selection of resources that address curriculum needs and learning goals? **Interview Question:** What selection tools do you regularly use?
3.4 Maintains a collection addressing curricular needs and learning goals.	"With a broad view of the curriculum, extensive knowledge of both traditional and electronic resources, and commitment to serve the full range of students and other members of the learning community, the school library media specialist can direct...the maintenance of current, comprehensive, high-quality collections." (Information Power: Building Partnerships for Learning, 1998, p. 90)	**Look For:** • collection mapping forms and other tools (e.g., average age of the collection report, standard selection tools such as InfoTech, EvaluTech, Elementary School Library Collection, Wilson catalogs, professional review periodicals) • ongoing weeding for wear, content, and timeliness using standard guidelines, (e.g., CREW, MUSTIE method) • circulation records (monthly reports of number of materials checked out to students and staff) showing patterns of use.	**Interview Question:** What strategies do you use to analyze and maintain an up-to-date media collection?

Form 33 *continued*

MCPAI-R	Observation Issues	Documentation Sources	Typical Questions for Conferences
3.4 Maintains a collection addressing curricular needs and learning goals.		**Look For:** • timely repair of resources (e.g., spine labels, torn pages, lamp replacement) • coordination of equipment repair (e.g., database of onsite/offsite repairs for individual equipment) and disposal according to system guidelines.	
3.5 Evaluates the school library media program on a continual basis according to accepted standards of quality.	"The evaluation of building-level programs is one of the most important, yet one of the most difficult, responsibilities of media and technology professionals. In this age of accountability, it is no longer enough to say that good school library media and instructional technology programs are important for good schools." (IMPACT: Guidelines for Media and Technology Programs, p. 168) One standard of quality that can be applied is the rubrics found in IMPACT: Guidelines for Media and Technology Programs and in IMPACT for Administrators: A Resource for Evaluating Media and Technology Programs and Personnel. The rubrics included in IMPACT provide a global perspective of school library media programs at minimum, developing, and outstanding levels. (NCDPI)	**Look For:** • written plans, goals, and objectives aligned with the school's mission statement • input from others (e.g., Media and Technology Advisory Committee, staff, and students) regarding the Media Program (e.g., surveys, suggestion box, questionnaires) • alignment with local, regional, state, and national guidelines (e.g., *IMPACT: Guidelines for Media and Technology Programs*, in *IMPACT for Administrators: A Resource for Evaluating Media and Technology Programs and Personnel*, State Technology Plan, *Information Power: Building Partnerships for Learning*, and SACs standards) • reflective analysis through an annual report that summarizes successes, challenges, and program highlights.	**Interview Question:** How do you assess the quality of the school library media program?

Form 33 *continued*

MCPAI-R	Observation Issues	Documentation Sources	Typical Questions for Conferences
3.6 Plays a leading role in the school's budgetary process to ensure funding for the school library media program to support school-wide goals.	"Budgeting is a collaborative effort. It needs the support of teachers, administrators, students, and the community. Resources purchased for school-wide use should be housed in the media center to ensure equity of access and the most effective use of limited funds. Acting in their leadership roles, the school library media coordinator and the Instructional Technology Facilitator (if applicable) seek the support of these groups and used school and community public relations strategies to: • ensure that budget requests are presented and considered within the appropriate context of program goals and objectives. • heighten awareness of the need for a wide variety of up-to-date resources and infrastructure to extend and enrich learning opportunities." (IMPACT for Administrators: A Resource for Evaluating Media and Technology Programs and Personnel, p. 15)	**Look For:** • a budget plan and procedure that involves the Media and Technology Advisory Committee(s) and focuses on the development and continuous evaluation of annual and long-range budget goals • participation in meetings of school-based budget committee to present recommendations of the Media and Technology Advisory Committee • budget expenditures that stay within allocations • up-to-date records in place for several years, clearly indicating allocations and balances • fund raising to supplement budget allocations, if appropriate • partnerships with the PTA and other organizations • pursuit of grant opportunities.	**Interview Question:** How do you develop and administer the Media Program budget?

Form 33 *continued*

MCPAI-R	Observation Issues	Documentation Sources	Typical Questions for Conferences
3.7 Leads, in partnership with the Instructional Technology Facilitator (ITF), the Media and Technology Advisory Committee (MTAC) in effective decision making to promote the media and technology program.	"Active involvement of the Media and Technology Committee in any project leads to better awareness, support, and commitment to the Media Program. In large schools, this committee may need to be two separate committees; one that is a Technology Advisory Committee and one that is a Media Advisory Committee. Whether the committees are combined or separate, they should include both the instructional technology facilitator and the school library media coordinator and be chaired by one or both of these professionals." (IMPACT for Administrators: A Resource for Evaluating Media and Technology Programs and Personnel, p. 14)	**Look For:** • collaboration with the ITF (if this position is available) to provide leadership for the Media and Technology Advisory Committee • interpretation of selection policy for members of the committee • collaboration with the committee to interpret the selection policy to the faculty and staff • partnership with the ITF to lead the MTAC in the reconsideration of challenged materials Examples: • scheduled meetings when appropriate agendas and minutes available • routing of appropriate information to committee members.	**Interview Question:** How do you provide leadership to the Media and Technology Advisory Committee? **Interview Question:** If there is an Instructional Technology Facilitator at your school, how do you work with him or her to collaborate in the leadership of the Media and Technology Advisory Committee?
3.8 Interacts effectively with students, staff, administration, parents, and the community to promote and expand the school library media program.	"It is important that the vision of Media and Technology programs reflect the instructional mission of the school. Because Media and Technology programs support the total instructional program of the school, it is especially important that media and technology staff assume leadership for communicating the vision for their programs within the school and in the community." (IMPACT for Administrators: A Resource for Evaluating Media and Technology Programs and Personnel, p. 17)	**Look For:** • voluntary participation in the total operation of the school • participation in the development of annual objectives of school • participation as an effective member in school-based committees • participation as an effective member of teacher teams • supervision of media assistants effectively (where applicable).	**Interview Question:** Describe strategies you use to create a positive working relationship with faculty and staff. **Interview Question:** How do you promote positive relationships between yourself and the students?

Form 33 *continued*

MCPAI-R	Observation Issues	Documentation Sources	Typical Questions for Conferences
3.8 Interacts effectively with students, staff, administration, parents, and the community to promote and expand the school library media program (*continued*).		**Look For:** • assistance provided in a helpful, professional manner • activities in the media center that engage students • supervision of student assistants (where applicable) club sponsorships, etc. **Look For:** • open house activities • special events such as family reading nights, book and technology fairs, etc. • participation in PTA/PTO activities • recruitment and effective management of volunteers • annual orientation process for volunteers • cooperation with the public library and community learning centers.	**Interview Question:** Describe methods you use to promote and maintain a good relationship between the school and the community.
3.9 Prepares and submits accurate reports as required	"Through regular administrative reporting,…the library media specialist conveys the program's leadership in fostering information literacy, and encouraging collaborative teaching and learning, and in developing sophisticated uses of information technology." (Information Power: Building Partnerships for Learning, 1998, p. 113) "The library media specialist develops and implements the policies and procedures necessary for the efficient and effective operation of the program. The library media	**Look For:** • annual report of media program activities • budget expenditures • accurate inventories of print, nonprint, and technology materials and equipment • catalog summary reflecting additions and deletions • timely submission of required reports (e.g., NCDPI Annual Media and Technology Report [AMTR]).	**Interview Question:** What kinds of reports to you prepare and submit? **Interview Question:** Have you met report deadlines consistently?

Form 33 *continued*

MCPAI-R	Observation Issues	Documentation Sources	Typical Questions for Conferences
3.9 Prepares and submits accurate reports as required (*continued*)	specialist…communicates the details of the program's day-to-day operation. Through careful and continuous attention to staffing, budgets, schedules, report writing, equipment maintenance, and other details, the library media specialist supervises and manages the program." (Information Power: Building Partnerships for Learning, 1998, p. 114)		
3.10 Adheres to established laws, policies, rules, and regulations.	"Laws, policies, rules, and regulations are required for schools to operate efficiently, effectively, and safely. While ignorance is no excuse for non-compliance, the school does have the responsibility of informing the library media coordinator of laws, policies, rules, and regulations. The library media coordinator is responsible for reading, interpreting and carrying out the laws, policies, rules, and regulations. The library media coordinator should ask for clarification when he/she has a question." (Based on TPAI Matrix of Data Sources, p. 17)	**Look For:** Adherence to laws, policies, rules, and regulations, including those that are specifically applicable to the media program. Examples: • materials and equipment selection • copyright • acceptable use policy (AUP) • Web site development • data privacy • accessibility • translation • school purchase requirements.	**Interview Question:** How have you gone about learning the laws, policies, rules, and regulations of your school? Why is it important to know and follow the laws, policies, rules, and regulations? Where do you go with questions?

Form 33 *continued*

MCPAI-R	Observation Issues	Documentation Sources	Typical Questions for Conferences
3.11 Carries out non-instructional duties as assigned and/or as need is perceived.	"When assigned non-instructional duties, the library media coordinator completes the assignments promptly and effectively. No organization, including schools, can anticipate every duty that must be covered. Library media coordinators take the initiative to act responsibly to perform duties that have not been assigned." (Based on TPAI Matrix of Data Sources, p. 17)	**Look For:** • committee assignments • club sponsorships (e.g., Battle of the Books, Quiz Bowl, Computer Club) • event participation (e.g., sports, social events, PTSA).	**Interview Question:** What non-instructional duties have you been assigned or volunteered for and how effective do you feel that you have been in carrying out those duties?

Form 33 *continued*

PERFORMANCE PLAN AND EVALUATION
(For Other Than Managers)

Name	Performance Period to

Department	Unit/Function

Title

OVERALL PERFORMANCE EVALUATION		PERFORMANCE RELATIVE TO EXPECTATIONS			
(Check appropriate rating)	Far Exceeds	Exceeds	Fully Meets	Marg. Meets	Does not Meet

AGREEMENT APPROVAL	DATE	FINAL PERFORMANCE EVALUATION	DATE
Rater:		Rater:	
Participant:		Approved By:	
Approved By:		Discussed with Participant on:	
Interim Review Dates:		Participant's Signature Affirming	
		Discussion Held:	

PART I: BASIC MANAGEMENT OBJECTIVES/JOB RELATED BEHAVIOR—List Objectives/Behaviors to be Rated

	PERFORMANCE RATING				
OBJECTIVE/BEHAVIOR	Far Exceeds	Exceeds	Fully Meets	Marg. Meets	Does not Meet
Job Knowledge					
Problem Analysis					
Planning and Organizing					
Initiative and Resourcefulness					
Responds to Department Goals/Public Need					
Decision Making					
Adaptability					
Interpersonal Effectiveness					
Personal Management					

Form 34. Performance Plan and Evaluation (For Other Than Managers)

PART II:

OVERALL JOB PERFORMANCE (Check appropriate rating)	Far Exceeds	Exceeds	Fully Meets	Marg. Meets	Does not Meet
Notable Unanticipated Events:					
Comments on Overall Performance:					
(List 3 greatest strengths and 3 greatest weaknesses)					

Part III: Areas of Focus

Name   Performance Period
                                              to

Level of Difficulty: Performance Rating

☐   ☐   ☐   ☐   ☐   ☐   ☐   ☐
Far Exceeds   Exceeds   Fully Meets   Far Exceeds   Exceeds   Fully Meets   Marg. Meets   Does not Meet

1 Expected Results/Timetable/Quality:

Achievement of Results:

Evaluation of Results/Comments:

Level of Difficulty: Performance Rating

☐   ☐   ☐   ☐   ☐   ☐   ☐   ☐
Far Exceeds   Exceeds   Fully Meets   Far Exceeds   Exceeds   Fully Meets   Marg. Meets   Does not Meet

2 Expected Results/Timetable/Quality:

Achievement of Results:

Evaluation of Results/Comments:

Level of Difficulty: Performance Rating

☐   ☐   ☐   ☐   ☐   ☐   ☐   ☐
Far Exceeds   Exceeds   Fully Meets   Far Exceeds   Exceeds   Fully Meets   Marg. Meets   Does not Meet

3 Expected Results/Timetable/Quality:

Achievement of Results:

Evaluation of Results/Comments:

Form 34 *continued*

Part III: Areas of Focus (cont'd)

Level of Difficulty: _____ Performance Rating

☐	☐	☐	☐	☐	☐	☐	☐
Far Exceeds	Exceeds	Fully Meets	Far Exceeds	Exceeds	Fully Meets	Marg. Meets	Does not Meet

4 Expected Results/Timetable/Quality:

Achievement of Results:

Evaluation of Results/Comments:

Level of Difficulty: _____ Performance Rating

☐	☐	☐	☐	☐	☐	☐	☐
Far Exceeds	Exceeds	Fully Meets	Far Exceeds	Exceeds	Fully Meets	Marg. Meets	Does not Meet

5 Expected Results/Timetable/Quality:

Achievement of Results:

Evaluation of Results/Comments:

Level of Difficulty: _____ Performance Rating

☐	☐	☐	☐	☐	☐	☐	☐
Far Exceeds	Exceeds	Fully Meets	Far Exceeds	Exceeds	Fully Meets	Marg. Meets	Does not Meet

6 Expected Results/Timetable/Quality:

Achievement of Results:

Evaluation of Results/Comments:

Form 34 *continued*

ANNUAL ACTIVITY REPORT AND SELF-ASSESSMENT

RAND LIBRARY

Name:

Unit:

Position:

Period Evaluated:

Overview of Job Responsibilities:

Major Accomplishments during this Period (relate to previous year's goals):

Professional Development Activities (classes, seminars, conference attendance):

Uncompleted Goals:

Goals for the coming Year (give metric for measuring progress):

Overall Self-Assessment:

_____   _____

Signature   Date

Form 35. Annual Activity Report and Self-Assessment

RAND

PERFORMANCE EVALUATION

Name

Review period

Summary of Responsibilities:

Accomplishments During Period Reviewed:

Professional Development Activities:

Strengths:

Areas for Development:

FY01 Goals:

Reviewed by:	Library Director/Designee
Employee Signature:	Discussion Date:

Form 36. Performance Evaluation

LIBRARY SPECIALIST NONEXEMPT PERFORMANCE REVIEW

Name:	RAND Start Date:
Job Classification:	Review Period:
Reviewed By:	Date Prepared:

Overview of Job Responsibilities:

The following are measurements to assist you in evaluating the employee's performance during the review period. On the following pages, write in the number that corresponds to your assessment of the skills demonstrated.

1	**Exceeds Requirements**	Performance is clearly excellent and consistently exceeds the requirements set for the assignment.
2	**Meets Requirements**	Performance is effective and fully meets the requirements for the assignment.
3	**Partially Meets Requirements**	Performance is usually satisfactory but there may be areas that need improvement.
4	**Does not Meet Requirements**	Performance does not meet the requirements for the assignment.

If a performance category is not relevant, write "N/A."

In the Comments Section for each category, provide examples or other details to explain why the reviewee received the rating in that category. If performance is below satisfactory, describe the problem or deficiency and indicate degree of improvement needed.

This performance review is intended to stimulate candid discussion between supervisor and employee, to evaluate the employee's performance, and to promote further improvement and development.

9/99

Form 37. Library Specialist Nonexempt Performance Review

Performance Categories	1	2	3	4
COMMITMENT AND SUPPORT:				
• Adheres to position and section objectives				
• Demonstrates ability to see impact of assignment on other sections as well as the overall mission of the Library				
• Follows instructions				
• Meets deadlines				
• Takes initiative				
• Displays flexibility/adaptability				
• Demonstrates service orientation				
• Takes responsibility for own development				
• Maintains good attendance				
• Is punctual				

COMMENTS:

TECHNICAL SKILLS/JOB KNOWLEDGE (as appropriate to the position):	1	2	3	4
• General library principles and procedures				
• Section operations and procedures				
• ROBIN system modules/Other systems				
• Library or industry standards & tools				
• General office automation skills				
• Other skills (please specify):				

COMMENTS:

PROBLEM-SOLVING AND DECISION-MAKING SKILLS:	1	2	3	4
• Identifies problem/Asks clarifying questions				
• Makes sound decisions at appropriate level				
• Follows through on resolving problems				

COMMENTS:

QUALITY/QUANTITY OF WORK:	1	2	3	4
• Establishes work priorities				
• Makes effective use of time and resources				
• Produces accurate and complete work				
• Organizes work area				

COMMENTS:

Form 37 *continued*

INTERPERSONAL/COMMUNICATION SKILLS:	1	2	3	4
• Interacts effectively with users				
• Interacts effectively with coworkers				
• Interacts effectively with managers				
• Maintains business-like demeanor				
• Accepts criticism and learns from mistakes				
• Communication skills (oral and written)				
• Leadership abilities/Ability to train and direct others in their work				
• Potential for advancement				

COMMENTS:

PROGRESS TOWARD LAST REVIEW'S GOALS:

GOALS FOR THE FUTURE:

OVERALL ASSESSMENT:

EMPLOYEE'S COMMENTS (optional):

_____   _____
Employee Signature*   Discussion Date

_____   _____
Supervisor   Library Director

 * Signature indicates acknowledgment of review but not necessarily agreement with supervisor's
   evaluation.

Form 37 *continued*

EMPLOYEE WORK PROFILE

WORK DESCRIPTION/PERFORMANCE PLAN

PART I—Position Identification Information

1. Position Number:	2. Agency Name & Code; Division/Department:
3. Work Location Code:	4. Occupational Family & Career Group:
5. Role Title & Code:	6. Pay Band:
7. Work Title:	8. SOC Title & Code:
9. Level Indicator: ☐ Employee ☐ Supervisor ☐ Manager Employees Supervised: Does employee supervise 2 or more employees (FTEs)? ☐ Yes ☐ No	10. FLSA Status: ☐ Exempt ☐ Non-Exempt Exemption/Partial Exemption Test (if applicable):
11. Supervisor's Position Number:	12. Supervisor's Role Title & Code:
13. EEO Code:	14. Effective Date:

PART II—Work Description & Performance Plan

15. Organizational Objective:

16. Purpose of Position:

17. KSA's and or Competencies required to successfully perform the work (attach Competency Model, if applicable):

18. Education, Experience, Licensure, Certification required for entry into position:

Form 38. Employee Work Profile, Work Description/Performance Plan

% Time	19. Core Responsibilities	20. Measures for Core Responsibilities
%	A. Performance Management (for employees who supervise others)	Examples of Measures for Performance Management: • Expectations are clear, well communicated, and relate to the goals and objectives of the department or unit; • Staff receive frequent, constructive feedback, including interim evaluations as appropriate; • Staff have the necessary knowledge, skills, and abilities to accomplish goals; • The requirements of the performance planning and evaluation system are met and evaluations are completed by established deadlines with proper documentation; • Performance issues are addressed and documented as they occur. • afety issues are reviewed and communicated to assure a safe and healthy workplace.
%	B.	
%	C.	
%	D.	
%	E.	
%	F.	
100%		

Form 38 *continued*

21. Special Assignments	22. Measures for Special Assignments
G.	
H.	

Optional

23. Agency/Departmental Objectives	24. Measures for Agency/Departmental Objectives
I.	
J.	
K.	
L.	

ADDENDUM—ORGANIZATIONAL CHART

This page is printed separate from the remainder of the Work Description/Performance Plan because it contains confidential employee information.

PART III—Employee Development Plan

25. Personal Learning Goals

26. Learning Steps/Resource Needs

Part IV—Review of Work Description/Performance Plan

27. Employee's Comments:	Signature:	Date:
	Print Name:	
28. Supervisor's Comments:	Signature:	Date:
	Print Name:	
29. Reviewer's Comments:	Signature:	Date:
	Print Name:	

Form 38 *continued*

EMPLOYEE WORK PROFILE

PERFORMANCE EVALUATION

The following pages are printed separate from the remainder of the EWP because they contain confidential employee information.

PART V—Employee/Position Identification Information

30. Position Number:

31. Agency Name & Code; Division/Department:

32. Employee Name:

33. Employee ID Number:

PART VI—Performance Evaluation

34. Core Responsibilities —Rating Earned	35. Core Responsibilities—Comments on Results Achieved
A. ☐ Extraordinary Contributor ☐ Contributor ☐ Below Contributor	
B. ☐ Extraordinary Contributor ☐ Contributor ☐ Below Contributor	
C. ☐ Extraordinary Contributor ☐ Contributor ☐ Below Contributor	
D. ☐ Extraordinary Contributor ☐ Contributor ☐ Below Contributor	
E. ☐ Extraordinary Contributor ☐ Contributor ☐ Below Contributor	
F. ☐ Extraordinary Contributor ☐ Contributor ☐ Below Contributor	

Form 39. Employee Work Profile, Performance Evaluation

36. Special Assignments —Rating Earned	37. Special Assignments—Comments on Results Achieved
G. ☐ Extraordinary Contributor ☐ Contributor ☐ Below Contributor	
H. ☐ Extraordinary Contributor ☐ Contributor ☐ Below Contributor	

38. Agency/Department Objectives —Rating Earned	39. Agency/Dept. Objectives–Comments on Results Achieved
I. ☐ Extraordinary Contributor ☐ Contributor ☐ Below Contributor	
J. ☐ Extraordinary Contributor ☐ Contributor ☐ Below Contributor	
K. ☐ Extraordinary Contributor ☐ Contributor ☐ Below Contributor	
L. ☐ Extraordinary Contributor ☐ Contributor ☐ Below Contributor	

40. Other significant results for the performance cycle:

Form 39 *continued*

Part VII - Employee Development Results

41. Year-end Learning Accomplishments:

Part VIII - Overall Results Assessment and Rating Earned

An employee receiving an overall rating of "Below Contributor" must have received at least one Notice of Improvement Needed/Substandard Performance form during the performance cycle.

An employee who earns an overall rating of "Below Contributor" must be reviewed again within three months.

An employee receiving an overall rating of "Extraordinary Contributor" must have received at least one Acknowledgment of Extraordinary Contribution form during the performance cycle. However, the receipt of an Acknowledgment of Extraordinary Contribution form does not guarantee an overall performance rating of "Extraordinary Contributor" for that performance cycle.

42. Overall Rating Earned
☐ Extraordinary Contributor
☐ Contributor
☐ Below Contributor

Part IX—Review of Performance Evaluation

43. Supervisor's Comments:	Signature:	Date:
	Print Name:	
44. Reviewer's Comments:	Signature:	Date:
	Print Name:	
45. Employee's Comments:	Signature:	Date:
	Print Name:	

Form 39 *continued*

EMPLOYEE WORK PROFILE
AGENCY OPTIONAL SECTIONS
Confidentiality Statement:

I acknowledge and understand that I may have access to confidential information regarding [employees, students, patients, inmates, the public]. In addition, I acknowledge and understand that I may have access to proprietary or other confidential information business information belonging to [Agency]. Therefore, except as required by law, I agree that I will not:
• Access data that is unrelated to my job duties at [Agency];
• Disclose to any other person, or allow any other person access to, any information related to [Agency] that is proprietary or confidential and/or pertains to [employees, students, patients, inmates, the public]. Disclosure of information includes, but is not limited to, verbal discussions, FAX transmissions, electronic mail messages, voice mail communication, written documentation, "loaning" computer access codes, and/or another transmission or sharing of data.

I understand that [Agency] and its [employees, students, patients, inmates, public], staff or others may suffer irreparable harm by disclosure of proprietary or confidential information and that [Agency] may seek legal remedies available to it should such disclosure occur. Further, I understand that violations of this agreement may result in disciplinary action, up to and including, my termination of employment.

_____   _____
Employee Signature   Date

Annual Requirements:

Activity	Current? If so, date completed?
Required In-Service or other training	☐ Yes _____ Date ☐ No ☐ N/A
Valid Licensure/Certification/Registration	☐ Yes _____ Date ☐ No ☐ N/A
Employee Health Update	☐ Yes _____ Date ☐ No ☐ N/A

Essential Job Requirements (Indicate by each E = Essential, M = marginal, or N/A)
Physical Demands and Activities:

__ Light lifting	<20 lbs.	Standing __	Sitting __	Bending __
__ Moderate lifting	20-50 lbs.	Lifting __	Walking __	Climbing __
__ Heavy lifting	>50 lbs.	Reaching __		Repetitive motion __
__ Pushing/pulling		Other _____		

Emotional Demands: Mental/Sensory Demands:
__ Fast pace   __ Avg. pace   Memory __   Reasoning __   Hearing __
__ Multiple priorities   Reading __   Analyzing __   Logic __
__ Intense customer interaction   Verbal communication __
__ Multiple stimuli   Written communication __
__ Frequent change   Other _____

Form 40. Employee Work Profile, Agency Optional Sections

INDEX

INDEX

ABOUT THE AUTHOR

Dr. G. Edward Evans is director of libraries at Loyola Marymount University. Prior to his current position, he was head of the anthropology library at Harvard University. He has been a full-time faculty member and administrator in library and information science programs at the University of California, Los Angeles, and the University of Denver. As a Fulbright scholar, he taught at the University of Iceland and has offered courses in management and collection development at library schools in Norway, Denmark, Sweden, and Finland. He has also served as an external examiner in management for the Department of Library Studies at the University of the West Indies. His publications include textbooks in the fields of public services, technical services, management, and collection development, in addition to numerous journal articles.